Genocide as Social Practice

Genocide, Political Violence, Human Rights Series

Edited by Alexander Laban Hinton, Stephen Eric Bronner, and Nela Navarro

Alan W. Clarke, *Rendition to Torture*

Lawrence Davidson, *Cultural Genocide*

Daniel Feierstein, *Genocide as Social Practice: Reorganizing Society under the Nazis and Argentina's Military Juntas*

Alexander Laban Hinton, ed., *Transitional Justice: Global Mechanisms and Local Realities after Genocide and Mass Violence*

Alexander Laban Hinton, Thomas La Pointe, and Douglas Irvin-Erickson, eds., *Hidden Genocides: Power, Knowledge, Memory*

Irina Silber, *Everyday Revolutionaries: Gender, Violence, and Disillusionment in Postwar El Salvador*

Samuel Totten and Rafiki Ubaldo, eds., *We Cannot Forget: Interviews with Survivors of the 1994 Genocide in Rwanda*

Ronnie Yimsut, *Facing the Khmer Rouge: A Cambodian Journey*

Genocide as Social Practice

Reorganizing Society under the Nazis and Argentina's Military Juntas

DANIEL FEIERSTEIN

Translated by Douglas Andrew Town

RUTGERS UNIVERSITY PRESS
NEW BRUNSWICK, NEW JERSEY, AND LONDON

LIBRARY OF CONGRESS CATALOGING-IN-PUBLICATION DATA

Feierstein, Daniel, 1967–
[Genocidio como práctica social. English]
Genocide as social practice : reorganizing society under the Nazis and Argentinás military juntas / Daniel Feierstein ; translated Douglas Andrew Town.
pages cm. — (Genocide, political violence, human rights series)
Includes bibliographical references.
ISBN 978–0–8135–6318–3 (hardcover : alk. paper) — ISBN 978–0–8135–6317–6 (pbk. : alk. paper) — ISBN 978–0–8135–6319–0 (e-book)
1. Genocide. 2. Holocaust, Jewish (1939–1945) 3. Genocide—Argentina.
I. Title.
HV6322.7.F4213 2014
304.6′630943—dc23

2013033862

A British Cataloging-in-Publication record for this book is available from the British Library.

First published in *Spanish as El genocidio como práctica social: Entre el nazismo y la experiencia argentina* (Buenos Aires: Fondo de Cultura Económica, 2007).

Visit our website: http://rutgerspress.rutgers.edu

Manufactured in the United States of America

CONTENTS

PART THREE
Toward a Historical Basis: Genocidal Social Practices in Argentina

FOREWORD

In recent years, the field of genocide studies has begun a critical reassessment. As this process has taken place, concepts and cases, old and new, have come into dialogue and important conversations and debates have begun. Several of these discussions emerge in Daniel Feierstein's *Genocide as Social Practice: Reorganizing Society under the Nazis and Argentina's Military Juntas*, which constitutes a key contribution to this turn in our understanding of genocide.

The title highlights the book's challenge. Genocide, it tells us, may centrally involve not just the mass destruction of a group of marginalized "others," as conventional understandings hold, but a profound internal reorganization of society amidst fear and terror. Viewing genocide as a social practice opens up an entirely different way of understanding such violence, one initially suggested by Raphael Lemkin, the person who coined the term. Not surprisingly, Professor Feierstein discusses Lemkin's work at length, even as he develops his own arguments about the nexus of genocide, power, and social life.

Professor Feierstein's book offers yet another provocation as it juxtaposes the Argentinian and Nazi cases. For many people, the destruction of European Jewry stands as the exemplar of genocide, a notion epitomized, through metonymy, by industrial mass murder at Auschwitz. *Genocide as Social Practice* argues that the 1976–1983 violence in Argentina, during which perhaps 20,000 people perished and many more suffered in fear and terror, was a case of genocide comparable—not in the numbers killed but in the social effects of the violence—to the Nazi reorganization of Germany and occupied Europe.

Professor Feierstein makes this argument through a detailed comparison of both cases. In doing so, he suggests that, like Auschwitz and other Nazi death camps, concentration camps in Argentina may also shed light on the genocidal process in general, and genocide as a social practice in particular.

His challenge to our understanding of genocide emerges in other ways as well. Written as a series of trials in Argentina were underway, *Genocide as Social Practice* asks us to take a closer look not just at our commonsense understandings of genocide, but also at the definition given in the 1948 United Nations Convention on the Prevention and Punishment of the Crime of Genocide.

This widely used legal definition specifies that genocide only takes place when a racial, ethnic, national, or religious group has been targeted for destruction. Political, economic, social, and other groups were excluded after much debate at the United Nations because they were said to be "mutable" categories. As a consequence, the events in Argentina—and other countries in Latin America and elsewhere—have often been described as political violence or, sometimes, "politicide."

Professor Feierstein's book asks us to reconsider such assumptions. Drawing inspiration, in part, from Lemkin, he argues in *Genocide as Social Practice* that the notion of "national groups" is much broader than conventionally understood and may encompass the destruction of political and other social groups heretofore excluded from the genocide studies canon. This claim significantly broadens the purview of genocide and is sure to generate debate.

First published in Spanish in 2007, *Genocide as Social Practice* has already had a major impact in parts of Latin America, particularly in Argentina, where Professor Feierstein is based. His ideas and arguments have informed legal debates there as lawyers, jurists, and members of civil society have debated whether or not the events that took place under the military junta can be considered genocide.

In a landmark decision in 2006 Judge Carlos Rozanski ruled that this violence constituted genocide—a decision that subsequently found support in other domestic courts before Judge Rozanski ruled in a second case in 2012 that the violence "unequivocally" qualified as genocide. The debate continues in Argentina. Now, with the publication of this translation of *Genocide as Social Practice,* it will commence in the English-speaking world as well.

While not everyone will agree with all of Professor Feierstein's arguments, readers will need to consider them seriously and, in so doing, reexamine their own preconceptions about genocide. Like the best of books, *Genocide as Social Practice* challenges its readers to engage in such critical thinking.

–Alexander Hinton, Center for the Study of Genocide
and Human Rights, Rutgers University

ACKNOWLEDGMENTS

I have the deep conviction that a theoretical book is a collective product. That is why, when one finishes such a book, somehow a feeling arises that one has appropriated the ideas, dreams, intuitions and labor of the many people with whom one has come in contact while writing the book. Perhaps the acknowledgments page is the space in which one tries—who knows if successfully—to ensure that such appropriation is not transformed into the vile practice of simple plagiarism.

Many people have collaborated with me in the task of constructing this text. Therefore, many can share in its merits but not, of course, in its defects, which are solely the result of my own thoughtlessness or inability to present ideas and concepts clearly. I must also now thank the many people who have made possible this newly revised edition, updated and prepared especially for an English-speaking audience.

I must acknowledge first the help of Guillermo Levy, a friend since adolescence who has thought with me about these issues for more than twenty years, always trying to be sure that theoretical analysis should inform political practice. It is difficult to identify in our writings what belongs to whom. We usually can't recall our original starting position once our discussions end. It does not seem that important, after all.

Survivors of the genocides both in Europe and Argentina have a relevant voice in this book, particularly in chapters 1, 6, 8, and 9. The conversations with Charles Papiernik—who lived for almost four years in the Auschwitz concentration camp—lasted through the year 2000. They gave rise to this book and to the many questions that guided my thinking in writing a large part of what I present here. Of equal importance are my conversations with Jack Fuchs (survivor of Auschwitz) and my interview with Marek Edelman (a major leader of the Jewish resistance in Warsaw). Also, the dialogue with survivors of the Argentinian repression was a central element in the overall purpose of this book, as were the interviews carried out as part of research projects that I have led at Tres de Febrero University (UNTREF) and the University of Buenos Aires. I recall, in particular, the many conversations, discussions, and coffees shared with Graciela Daleo and Adriana Calvo, who allowed me to cast original and lucid glances on well-reviewed processes. Also, the brief but profound talks with Mario Villani and Teresa Meschiatti, Jorge Paladino, Marga Cruz, Cachito Fukman, Carlos Loza, and Osvaldo Barros, among others, greatly illuminated this work.

I must also note the generosity of Graciela Daleo and Veronica Jeria, who graciously provided the recordings of the seminars delivered by the Asociación Ex-Detenidos Desaparecidos, as part of the Free Course on Human Rights at the School of Philosophy and Letters at the University of Buenos Aires, in 1996 and 1997. These recordings enabled me to design the comprehension axis for chapters 8 and 9. Without them these chapters would not exist; that is why I consider the survivors as virtual coauthors of those chapters.

I should mention particularly the friendship and constant dialogue with Eric Markusen (of the Danish Institute for International Studies, Denmark), who put me in contact with the International Association of Genocide Scholars in 2003. I also want to mention exchanges with Patricio Abalos Testoni, Gabriela Aguila, Joyce Apsel, Leonor Arfuch, Andrés Avellaneda, Matías Bailone, Rubén Chababo, Frank Chalk, Natalia Crocco, Vahakn Dadrian, Sarah Danielsson, Marcia Esparza, Patricia Funes, Beatriz Granda, Ted Gurr, Norma Fernández, Barbara Harff, Mario Heler, Henry Huttenbach, Inés Izaguirre, Verónica Jeria, Adam Jones, Goyo Kaminsky, Donna Lee Frieze, Daniel Lvovich, Juan Carlos Marín, Muhamed Mesic, Carlos Mundt, Hamurabi Noufouri, Enrique Oteiza, María Luz Roa, Luis Roniger, Carlos Rozanski, Steven Sadow, Héctor Schmucler, Martin Shaw, Lilia Sierra, Greg Stanton, Alejandra and Julieta Stupenengo, Adriana Taboada, Manuel Tenenbaum, Valeria Thus, Enzo Traverso, Jim Waller, Raúl Eugenio Zaffaroni, Mariela Zelenay, and Lior Zylberman.

In addition, I want to take the opportunity to acknowledge the institutional support provided by Aníbal Jozami and Martín Kaufmann (rector and vice rector of UNTREF), who always had confidence in my work.

Regarding the English edition, I must first thank the much-labored and engaged translation of Douglas Andrew Town; the commitment, friendship, and exchanges with Alex Hinton; the careful and profound editorial work of Nela Navarro; the manuscript preparation assistance of Noor Suleiman and Humberto Schettino; and the support of Marlie Wasserman for the publication of the book by Rutgers University Press. I also wish to offer my profound gratitude to the Auschwitz Institute for Peace and Reconciliation, UNTREF, Consejo Nacional de Investigaciones Cientificas y Técnicas (CONICET), and Ms. Edna Galo, all of whom so generously provided the funds for the translation of this new English version of this book. I also thank Gabriel Pèriés (friend, translator, and eminent scholar of the French counterinsurgency experience), and the Editorial Metispresses for the careful French version of this work, published in early 2013.

My partner, Fabiana Mon, has been an integral part of the objective and subjective aspects of this book. Without her companionship, her amiable reading of endless drafts, her warm way of questioning or commenting on each paragraph, her shrewdness on the ways of understanding mechanisms of normalization, and her exquisite common sense, I would not have been able to fully consider all the facets of the topic of this book.

My parents, Ricardo and Susana, gave me, perhaps without knowing it, the need to undo the knots of my subjectivity. They should not allow the blows, the deaths, or the deceptions to cloud the dreams they had. Those dreams have not abandoned them; they still subsist in a corner of their glances.

My sister, Liliana, who is today in Germany, has been a companion on these issues since childhood, both in Israel and Buenos Aires. These days, thousands of miles apart, we are sometimes still able to rebuild our parallel thinking. Her criticisms (lucid, incisive, impious) on the first version of this book were crucial to its clarity and revisions.

Thanks also go to my nephews, Tomás and Belén, for those long and profound talks on the dunes of Valeria del Mar.

Finally, I'd like to tell my children, Ezequiel and Tamara, that I hope to be able to collaborate in the fight to leave them a future that can dispense with the terror, allow them to keep smiling as they do today, or, at least, to let them know that their future is not something that I am willing to negotiate.

Genocide as Social Practice

Introduction

Bridging the Gap between Two Genocides

The starting point for this book arose from my intuition two decades ago that the policies pursued by the Argentine military dictatorship against political opponents and dissidents between 1976 and 1983 had important similarities to those pursued by the Third Reich, particularly before but even during World War II, despite the huge differences in the number of victims and historical contexts. The Nazis had resorted to ruthless methods not only to stifle dissent but—more importantly—to reorganize German society into a *Volksgemeinschaft*, or people's community, in which racial solidarity would supposedly replace class struggle. It was no coincidence that after seizing power in 1976, the Argentine military described its own program of forced disappearances, torture, and murder as a "Process of National Reorganization" aimed at remodeling society along "Western and Christian" lines.

This realization led me to explore an important but relatively neglected aspect of genocidal processes, namely, the ways in which annihilation has been used to destroy and reorganize social relations. In the pages that follow, I will encourage you to consider genocide not only as a latent potential of modernity but as a specific technology of power. A technology of power is a form of social engineering that creates, destroys, or reorganizes relationships within a given society. It influences the ways in which different social groups construct their identity, the identity of others, and the otherness of the Other, thus shaping the way that groups can relate to themselves and to one another. This does not mean that genocide's only function is to reorganize social relations or that societies can only be reorganized through genocide. It does mean, however, that genocide and social reorganization are closely connected. This connection is neither an obvious nor a necessary one, but it has been a constant of genocidal social practices in the second half of the twentieth century.

Does this mean that the Argentine repression should be considered an instance of "genocide" on the same level as the Nazi extermination? I do not intend to gloss over the fact that the magnitude and impact of these events as well as the political ends pursued by the perpetrators were very different. On the contrary, these differences will be explored in considerable detail in the chapters to follow. On the other hand, I have not chosen these two examples simply to create a convenient chronological narrative. The deeper purpose of this book is to analyze in detail the annihilation of human communities—an approach so far almost neglected in genocide studies. The reality of genocide as a social practice—a mechanism capable of destroying and reorganizing the fabric of entire societies—will become clearer as we trace the genesis of the Argentine repression through the counterinsurgency battles of the 1950s and 1960s in Indochina, Algeria, and Vietnam.

Of course, mass killings are an age-old phenomenon. However, the term "genocide" was first created by Raphael Lemkin in 1944 and enshrined as a legal term in the 1948 United Nations Convention on the Prevention and Punishment of the Crime of Genocide (CPPCG).[1] Since then, many attempts have been made to understand genocide, including studies in fields as diverse as law, history, sociology, psychology, anthropology, political science, communication theory, philosophy, theology, and ethics, to name just a few.[2] Most early studies of genocide focused on the annihilation of entire populations by the Nazis, including the murder of over six million European Jews, which had come as a profound moral and political shock to the West. Comparative studies of genocide did not appear until the late 1970s.[3] Most comparative studies have been attempts to understand Nazism against the background of earlier or later events and, through a process of comparison and contrast, to explain the meaning or meaninglessness—the rationality or irrationality—of genocidal social practices in the modern age.

Interpretations have varied according to historical periods and personal ideologies. Some authors have seen genocidal social practices as an isolated outbreak of savagery on the otherwise upward march of civilization. Daniel Goldhagen, for example, claims in *Hitler's Willing Executioners* (1996) that anti-Semitism was deeply embedded not only in the society of Nazi Germany but in German culture itself. Others, however, see genocide as a consequence of modernity. This idea was first put forward in the early 1930s by Walter Benjamin, a member of the Frankfurt School of social theory, who witnessed the rise to power of the Nazis. It is also to be found in the early work of Theodor Adorno, another member of the Frankfurt School and one of the few authors to write about genocide during and immediately after the Second World War. Similarly, scholars such as Zygmunt Bauman have seen genocide as a latent possibility within all modern civilized societies.

Nevertheless, these thinkers and their followers have all attempted in different ways to describe genocidal social processes within a historical narrative.

As the philosopher of history Hayden White has pointed out, historians are forced to use narrative and rhetorical strategies to represent the past. Indeed, what he calls the "poetics of history" includes not only the literary genres (romance, tragedy, comedy, satire) that historians use to weave their stories into a complete history, but also different types of argument (formist, mechanistic, organicist, contextualist) and ideology (anarchist, radical, conservative, liberal). According to Hayden White, these literary, argumentative, and ideological dimensions are all closely interrelated.[4]

Throughout this book we will examine various comparative studies of genocidal processes, most of which have been published at various moments in the field of genocide studies in English, French, or Spanish. For the time being, I will take just three studies in order to illustrate what Hayden White calls the "ideological implications" of discursive frames and the discursive consequences of selecting different historical examples. By looking briefly at narratives structured along different lines, the reader may also recognize what makes *Genocide as Social Practice* different from other accounts.

The first of these studies is by one of the best-known authors in comparative genocide studies, the U.S.-Armenian genocide scholar Vahakn Dadrian. Dadrian has argued in several works that it is both possible and desirable to compare the genocide of the Armenian and Jewish peoples. Even though he does not say so explicitly, his goals are as much political as academic. His work attempts to show that the genocide of the Armenian people—still denied by the Turkish state after nearly a century—was a social event comparable in its magnitude, severity, and consequences to the genocide of the Jewish people under Nazism.

Dadrian's interest in the Holocaust, however, is not only driven by his political agenda. His comparative work has traced lines of convergence and divergence between the Jewish and the Armenian genocides. Similarities include the minority status of both peoples and their history of persecution; their vulnerability in the territories where they lived; the presence of the necessary social conditions and structures for their annihilation; and the crucial roles played by political parties—the German National Socialist party and the Ittihad party of the Young Turks—among other factors.

Since the early 1970s, recognition for the Armenian genocide has grown, and Dadrian's views are now supported by a growing number of academics and politicians. By the late 1990s, his work had become accepted into the hegemonic academic "mainstream" of genocide studies, so much so that he decided to add another case to his comparative analysis, namely the 1994 Rwandan genocide.[5] In his article "Patterns of Twentieth-Century Genocides: The Armenian, Jewish, and Rwandan Cases" (2004), Dadrian traces a thread through three genocidal processes in which the victims were chosen because of their "ethnicity," even though this is a questionable concept in the case of Rwanda, where tensions between Hutus and Tutsis—groups that shared the same language, culture, and religion—were created by Belgian colonialism in the twentieth century.[6]

Dadrian himself was probably not aware that his choice of cases to exemplify the social practices of genocide in the twentieth century and his emphasis on ethnic and religious markers of "otherness" among the victims have narrative, ideological, and argumentative implications that—as suggested by Hayden White—are closely interconnected. Although Dadrian does not focus exclusively on ethnicity, the implicit argument is that of mainstream genocide studies, namely, that genocide is rooted in ethnic hatred. The ideological implication is that—with the exception of Germany—so-called first world countries where most mainstream genocide scholars live are blameless. The narrative dimension of Dadrian's 35-page article is perhaps more difficult to determine; but an emphasis on ethnic hatred implies a focus on horror and atrocities rather than rational planning for political ends.

The second of these studies is by Ben Kiernan, director of the Genocide Studies Program at Yale University. Kiernan is noted for his careful documentation of the genocide in Cambodia in the 1970s. Like Dadrian, Kiernan began by specializing in a particular instance of genocide before moving on to comparative studies. His aim has been to situate the Cambodian massacres within a historical sequence of mass killings, including of course the most emblematic case of the twentieth century: the Holocaust.[7]

Unlike Dadrian, however, Kiernan had to come to terms with the fact that the Cambodian genocide was carried out essentially for political reasons, while the Convention on the Prevention and Punishment of the Crime of Genocide adopted by the United Nations in 1948 expressly excludes crimes against political groups from its definition of genocide. Accordingly, Kiernan begins his study, "Twentieth-Century Genocide: Underlying Ideological Themes from Armenia to East Timor," published in 2003, with the Armenian genocide and the Nazi Holocaust, but—unlike Dadrian—he compares these not with Rwanda but with three cases where the political-ideological nature of genocide is obvious: Cambodia, where state-sponsored killing was carried out in the name of socialism; Indonesia, which suffered a vast anti-Communist purge in the mid-1960s; and East Timor, where a dispute over self-determination with the colonial power, Portugal, was followed by 25 years of brutal Indonesian military occupation.[8]

After analyzing the discourses surrounding these different genocides, Kiernan concludes that racism is always used to construct the "enemy." However, Kiernan argues that racism should be construed in a broad sense as focusing on ethnic, religious, or political affiliations. In fact, racist ideology gives meaning to the processes of stigmatization and subsequent annihilation, regardless of the actual concepts used to describe and identify the enemy in any specific case. Kiernan also claims that "territorial expansion" plays a fundamental role in genocidal states, as do various ways of "idealizing" a peasant population that is supposedly "less civilized" and, therefore, less exposed to the "evils of urban life," both material and moral.

In short, Kiernan and Dadrian make different assumptions about causation, and these assumptions are, to some extent, implicit in their choice of examples. Thus, Dadrian tends to emphasize ethnic hatred while Kiernan emphasizes ideological factors. This is true even when they are discussing the same genocides—the Armenian Massacres and the Nazi Holocaust. Although these are mostly differences in emphasis rather than of substance, they have the potential to create different and potentially contradictory explanations of genocidal social practices.

The third and last of these comparative studies is by Enzo Traverso, an Italian historian, who proposes an interesting and unorthodox historical sequence that takes the Holocaust as its endpoint rather than its starting point. In his book *The Origins of Nazi Violence* (2003), Traverso traces the legacy of European violence that created Nazism, especially genocides committed under European colonialism in the late nineteenth and early twentieth centuries. He thus examines the German annihilation of the Herero and Nama peoples of Namibia at the beginning of the twentieth century and Mussolini's use of poison gas against tribesmen during the Italian conquest of Abyssinia in 1935, which Henry Huttenbach has seen as a precursor of the Nazi gas chambers.[9]

On the other hand, Traverso rejects elsewhere the notion of common totalitarian threads between Nazism and Stalinism. This is in sharp contrast to the approach of conservative historian Ernst Nolte, who sees Nazism as a "European" response to the "Bolshevik terror" from Asia.[10] In Traverso's view, Nazi genocidal policy is linked to the legacy of colonialism through the concepts of "total war" and "conquest." Traverso shows that the Nazi atrocities that so shocked European public opinion after the Second World War had been committed without causing much moral concern among Nazis.

We could continue citing studies to show how comparisons of different historical events can give rise to different explanations of genocide—but I think the point is clear.[11] The problem in this book is to explain the connections between Nazism and the annihilation practices developed under the National Security Doctrine of the Cold War period and implemented in Argentina between 1974 and 1983. What sort of narrative is needed to link these two events via what Barbara Harff has called "post-colonial genocide" of the second half of the twentieth century?[12]

Dadrian, Kiernan, and Traverso have identified, respectively, the ethnic, ideological, and colonial roots of Nazi racism and genocide. It is my contention that the counterinsurgency wars of the 1950s and 1960s and, to a much larger extent, the development of the National Security Doctrine in many countries of Latin America may help to clarify the political idiosyncrasies of Nazism. These include the Nazis' construction of the prototypical victim—the Jewish Bolshevik—and their new diagram of power in which the annihilation of certain populations and the use of concentration camps were of fundamental importance.[13]

Historians who focus on the ethnic racism of Nazi Germany have tended to ignore the Nazi stereotype of the Jewish Bolshevik. The few historians that have tried to account for it have tended to subordinate the Nazis' ethnic racism to their ideological struggle against communism.[14] However, the figure of Jewish Bolshevik was an unusual concept which merged the political and ethnocultural into a unitary image. The Jewish Bolshevik was portrayed as the prototypical enemy of Western civilization. The need to defend the West—or more exactly "Western Christian" values—would be invoked again much more explicitly as a justification for genocide in Argentina.

There is another problem with attempts to understand the Nazis' goals in purely ethnic or ideological terms. They fail to explain why the ruling classes in Germany and much of Europe favored Hitler—at least until the outbreak of World War II. Nor do they explain how German society came to be so totally "reorganized" by the Nazis, particularly between 1933 and 1938 and again as the Third Reich collapsed in late 1944 and 1945. In focusing on the death camps in which Jewish and Roma communities were exterminated between 1942 and 1945, historians have tended to downplay the importance of the concentration camp system. And yet the first camps were opened almost as soon as the Nazis came to power in 1933 and remained a part of everyday life in Germany and Nazi-occupied Europe until the collapse of the regime in 1945. There has been no adequate account so far of the role played by concentration camps as stepping-stones to genocide or the range of victims imprisoned or murdered in them during the "reorganization" of German society and the Reich's military expansion eastward.[15]

This book is organized along two main lines. Its analytical framework seeks to understand the deliberate annihilation of human groups as a distinctive form of social engineering. In other words, processes of mass destruction in contemporary history are seen not as isolated occurrences, but as instances of a technology of power whose causes, effects, and specific consequences can be identified and described. At the same time, the book's historical or narrative framework aims to support this claim by exploring two annihilation processes in detail: the Nazi genocide, which began with different policies for different groups and evolved gradually between 1933 and 1945; and the state-sponsored repression in Argentina between 1974 and 1983.[16] The plan of the book is as follows.

Chapter 1 examines the legal, historical, sociological, and philosophical uses of the term "genocide" and asks to what extent the concept is applicable to the events in Argentina between 1974 and 1983. It also explains the concept of "genocide as a social practice" and the use of genocide as a technology of power.

Chapter 2 proposes a new classification of the social practices of genocide. This classification makes the destruction and reorganization of social relations more visible by establishing continuity between the "reorganizing genocide" first practiced by the Nazis and its more complex version—complex in terms of the symbolic and material closure of social relationships—later applied in Argentina.

Chapter 3 examines the effectiveness of genocidal social practices and technologies of power and their relationship with the unresolved contradictions of modernity. It also considers factors that facilitate the onset of genocide and that make it a meaningful choice for the perpetrators.

Chapters 4 to 8 place the Nazi and the Argentine genocides in their historical context and critically assess the different ways these events have been described in various disciplines. This earlier work is examined for possible clues to understanding genocide as a technology of power.

Chapter 9 uses testimonies of survivors to analyze the primary technological apparatus of the Nazi and the Argentine genocides—the concentration camp. I will contend that these camps were designed not only to punish individual prisoners but also to terrorize the wider population from which the inmates of the camps were drawn.

Finally, chapter 10 raises questions about the continuing relevance of genocidal social practices, about genocide's role in the development of modernity, and about how to construct a political culture capable of confronting and resisting these trends.

The objectives of any publication are shaped by where and when it is written. Dadrian, Kiernan, and Traverso write from the center of world politics and culture in Europe or the United States. On the other hand, I am writing from the periphery in Latin America.[17] I am aware as an Argentine Jewish historian and sociologist that my choice of narrative strategy is as subjective and politically motivated as any other. Indeed, my childhood in an Argentina crisscrossed by unmarked Ford Falcons transporting prisoners to concentration camps and my heritage as a descendant of a Jewish family who emigrated from Poland before the Nazi invasion haunt these pages and are never far below their surface. Having said that and without claiming that my approach is better or more comprehensive than any other, I do believe it produces a legitimate picture of the social practices of genocide during the second half of the twentieth century.

In any case, it is difficult in Argentina to speak about the Nazi genocide without referring at some point to our own recent history. This book grew out of an intuition about two historical events that have shaped my life. Of course, intuitive interpretations are of little value unless supported by evidence, and one of the main concerns of this book is to show that this path—this relationship of events—is valid.

It is for the reader to judge whether this intuition has been justified by the concepts it has generated—in particular, the notion of genocidal social practices as a technology of power and a means of reorganizing relationships within a given society.

PART ONE

Some Theoretical Questions

1

Defining the Concept of Genocide

> What I am is not important,
> whether I live or die—It is the same for me,
> the same for you.
> What we do is important.
> This is what I have learnt.
> It is not what we are
> but what we do.
>
> —James Fenton, "Children in Exile"[1]

The annihilation of population masses is an age-old phenomenon. The destruction of Troy by the Greeks, the razing of Carthage by the Romans, and the atrocities of the Mongols under Genghis Khan are just a few examples that can be found in any history book. Genocide, on the other hand, is a distinctly modern concept. The term "genocide" was first used by the Polish-Jewish legal scholar Raphael Lemkin at a conference in Madrid in 1933, but a legal definition of genocide was not incorporated into international law until 1948, following the programs of mass murder carried out by the Nazis during World War II. These programs included the extermination of such diverse groups as the Jewish and Gypsy populations of Europe, ethnic Poles and Russians, political opponents, children and adults with disabilities, homosexuals, and religious groups such as Jehovah's Witnesses, among others.

The first question we need to address, then, is whether genocide is simply a new name for an old practice or whether it refers to something qualitatively different from earlier mass annihilation processes. The model of genocide presented in this book suggests a distinctly modern phenomenon, first appearing in the nineteenth century although rooted in the early modern period (circa A.D. 1500 to 1800). The forced exodus of large numbers of Jews and Muslims from Spain in 1492 and the subsequent persecution of those who converted to Catholicism in order to escape expulsion is perhaps the earliest precursor of modern genocide, together with the European witch trials of the fifteenth and early sixteenth centuries. The distinguishing features of modern genocide are the ways in which it is legitimized as well as its consequences not only for the targeted groups but also for the perpetrators, the witnesses, and society as a whole.[2]

My contention is that modern genocides have been a deliberate attempt to change the identity of the survivors by modifying relationships within a given society. This is what sets modern genocide apart from earlier massacres of civilian populations, as well as from other processes of mass destruction. The fact that genocide has proved so effective in bringing about social changes—equaled only by revolutionary processes—suggests that it is not simply a spontaneous occurrence that reappears when historical circumstances are favorable. Rather, it is a process that starts long before and ends long after the actual physical annihilation of the victims, even though the exact moment at which any social practice commences or ceases to play a role in the "workings" of a society is always uncertain. It is important to bear this fact in mind if we are to develop effective early warning systems to prevent new instances of genocide.

Problems of Definition

More than half a century separates the drafting of the Convention on the Prevention and Punishment of the Crime of Genocide, adopted on December 9, 1948, and the complex sentences handed down by the international criminal tribunals for the former Yugoslavia and Rwanda in the second half of the 1990s. Before and during this time and afterward, debates have raged among sociologists and historians over definitions that would allow for empirical research. This suggests that the concept of genocide is essentially problematic.

The term "genocide", as coined by Lemkin, is a hybrid between the Greek root *genos* (family, tribe, or race) and the Latin suffix *-cide* (killing), but its exact meaning and translation into other languages remain controversial. Does *genos* refer to a common tribal origin, to genetic characteristics transmitted from generation to generation, or simply to certain features shared by a group? All these meanings are present in the Greek word *genos* and its Latin derivative *gens* denoting a family clan.

Reviewing the various legal, sociological, and historical definitions of genocide, M. Bjørnlund et al. found that the fundamental point of agreement was "the systematic annihilation of a population group as such," while the three main points of disagreement were the question of "intent," the nature of the groups included in these definitions, and the importance of actual physical annihilation, whether total or partial, as an essential element of genocide.[3]

Significantly, nearly all of these scholarly definitions take Article II of the 1948 Genocide Convention as their starting point:

> In the present Convention, genocide means any of the following acts committed with intent to destroy, in whole or in part, a national, ethnical, racial or religious group, as such:
>
> (a) Killing members of the group;
> (b) Causing serious bodily or mental harm to members of the group;
> (c) Deliberately inflicting on the group conditions of life calculated to bring about its physical destruction in whole or in part;
> (d) Imposing measures intended to prevent births within the group;
> (e) Forcibly transferring children of the group to another group

As Martin Shaw has pointed out, "The study of genocide has generally been framed by legal and historical, rather than sociological perspectives. Law provided the impetus to the definition of the crime, through the pioneering efforts of Raphael Lemkin and the drafters of the United Nations Convention; it has continued to provide much of the drive towards recognition of recent genocides, in the work of the international criminal tribunals for former Yugoslavia and Rwanda."[4]

However, this predominantly legal approach is unfortunate in that legal definitions tend to be narrowly focused, rooted in specific historical contexts, and difficult to modify. Law requires unambiguous categories as well as clear and convincing evidence in order to reach a judgment of guilty or not guilty. The categories established by the 1948 Genocide Convention, in particular its list of protected groups, were the result of political compromise but also a consequence of the jurisprudence of the Nuremberg Tribunal set up in 1945 to punish Nazi war criminals. The Nuremberg Tribunal held that the crimes against humanity required a connection with aggressive war, although it is now generally accepted that these crimes—like genocide itself—can be committed in peacetime.

In fact, any new legal definition of genocide will need to include the principle of equality before the law—a principle currently violated by the 1948 Genocide Convention, which protects some groups and not others—as well as incorporating the customary law that has emerged from the history of relations among human communities. In other words, any legal definition of genocide—beyond what has been achieved so far in international law—needs to be based on the concept of genocide in its unbiased sense, namely, the implementation of a massive and systematic plan intended to destroy all or part of a human group as such. In legal terms, modern genocide would be no different from the annihilation of population masses by the Ancient Greeks, Romans, or Mongols, and I will presume the legal definition to be inclusive in this way.

Genocide as a Social Practice

In contrast to the legal definition of genocide, the concept of genocide as a social practice allows historians and sociologists to adopt a broader and more flexible approach to the problems of causality and responsibility. It also helps to distinguish genocide from other social processes of mass destruction that have occurred at different periods of history, such as high death rates among certain segments of the population as the result of economic policies, or the more or less intentional destruction of the environment that has led to mass deaths.

Now, despite the obvious differences between law and the social sciences, we should point out that it is organization, training, practice, legitimation, and consensus that distinguish genocide as a social practice from other more spontaneous or less intentional acts of killing and mass destruction. Also, because a social practice is composed of shared beliefs and understandings as well as shared actions, a genocidal social practice may be one that *contributes* to genocide or attempted genocide, including symbolic representations and discourses promoting or justifying genocide.

In addition, it is clear from this definition that social practices are ongoing and under permanent construction. In many instances, the appropriateness of the term "genocide" has been questioned on the grounds that the process has not gone far enough to speak of full-blown genocide. But when does genocide actually begin? At what moment can we consider that the term is being correctly applied? Adopting the concept of genocidal social practices allows us to address a thorny methodological issue in history and the social sciences, namely, that of periodization. Moreover, because social practices are constructions that are open to deconstruction, academic studies should be able to contribute to policies to prevent and resist genocide.

Bearing all this in mind, I will define a genocidal social practice as a technology of power—a way of managing people as a group—that aims (1) to destroy social relationships based on autonomy and cooperation by annihilating a significant part of the population (significant in terms of either numbers or practices), and (2) to use the terror of annihilation to establish new models of identity and social relationships among the survivors. Unlike what happens in war, the disappearance of the victims forces the survivors to deny their own identity—an identity created out of a synthesis of being and doing—while a way of life that once defined a specific form of identity is suppressed. Accordingly, I will use the term "genocidal social practices" to distinguish these specific processes from the legal concept of genocide.[5]

The Legal Definition of Genocide: Law as a Producer of Truth

As mentioned earlier, the most widely accepted legal definition of genocide today is that approved by the United Nations in the 1948 Genocide Convention.

It is therefore important to understand the debates surrounding Article II of the Convention and, in particular, the question of protected groups.

In 1946 the United Nations had called upon member states to define a new criminal category stating that

> [g]enocide is a denial of the right of existence of entire human groups, as homicide is the denial of the right to live of individual human beings; such denial of the right of existence shocks the conscience of mankind, results in great losses to humanity in the form of cultural and other contributions represented by these groups, and is contrary to moral law and to the spirit and aims of the United Nations. Many instances of such crimes of genocide have occurred when racial, religious, political and other groups have been destroyed, entirely or in part. The punishment of the crime of genocide is a matter of international concern. (UN General Assembly Resolution 96 [I])

This resolution contained two significant elements. First, it contemplated the genocide of political groups; and second, it defined genocide through an analogy with homicide. The definition established the characteristics of the event through the type of crime committed (collective killing against individual killing) and not through the characteristics of the victims: "racial, religious and political" are simply examples, and the term "other" completes the categorization. For the same reason, the resolution did not define any criminal type, either.

At the drafting stage of the Convention, however, it was clear that the inclusion of social and political groups would jeopardize the acceptance of the Convention by a large number of states that did not want the international community to become involved in their internal political struggles.[6] The Soviet Union, Poland, Great Britain, and South Africa (among other states) were worried that enforcement of the Convention might violate principles of state sovereignty and nonintervention if such groups were to be included as targets of genocide.[7] As Ward Churchill notes, these countries sought to "narrow the Convention's definitional parameters of genocide in such ways as were necessary to exclude many of their own past, present and anticipated policies and practices from being formally codified as *crimen laesae humanitatis* (crimes against humanity) in international law."[8]

On the other hand, France, Yugoslavia, Bolivia, Haiti, and Cuba (among other states) insisted that the exclusion of political and social groups would allow most crimes of genocide to go unpunished. Donnedieu de Vabres, the primary French judge during the Nuremberg trials after World War II, argued that the express exclusion of political groups might be interpreted as legitimizing crimes against them.

At the drafting stage of the Convention, then, three key issues were raised: (1) whether the definition of genocide should be universal (like any other criminal categorization) or limited to certain groups; (2) whether the limitation was an aid to facilitate the approval of the Convention by the largest possible number of states; and (3) whether leaving certain groups explicitly out of the categorization might not represent a way of legitimating their annihilation.

Raphael Lemkin, who had played an important part in drafting the Convention, overcame the deadlock in the negotiations by arguing that political groups should be excluded because they lacked the cohesion or permanence of other groups. After arduous negotiations, it was finally decided that the protection of political and other excluded groups should be guaranteed by national legislations and by a Universal Declaration of Human Rights.

Thus, the United Nations defined genocide as a new legal typology, explicitly stated in Article II of the Convention. But by excluding political groups, the definition of genocide became arbitrarily restrictive. For example, religious belief systems were protected, whereas political belief systems were not. Worse still, the exclusion of political groups together with the "intent to destroy" requirement created an almost perfect catch-22.[9] In order to prove "intent," the prosecution had to demonstrate the existence of a coordinated plan. But coordinated plans are made by politicians or military commanders with political power. So, if the prosecution succeeded in proving "intent," the defense could argue that political leaders had targeted political opponents and so could not be tried under the Genocide Convention.

The question also arises how the intention to destroy a group *in part*—as opposed to *in whole*—can be anything but political. Lemkin himself recognized that genocide can pave the way for political domination: "Genocide has two phases: one, destruction of the national pattern of the oppressed group; the other, the imposition of the national pattern of the oppressor. This imposition, in turn, may be made upon the oppressed population which is allowed to remain or upon the territory alone, after removal of the population and the colonization by the oppressor's own nationals."[10]

As Donnedieu de Vabres predicted, it was political rivalries that would trigger most of the genocides committed during the Cold War period. But the wording of the Convention ensured that neither the hundreds of thousands murdered in Latin America by U.S.-backed military dictatorships between 1954 and 1990 nor the approximately two million people killed in Cambodia by the Khmer Rouge between 1975 and 1979 would count as victims of genocide. In fact, since the Genocide Convention came into effect in 1951 only two genocides have been recognized as such by international courts: the Rwandan Genocide of 1994 and the Srebrenica massacre of 1995.

The Principle of Equality before the Law: Inequality before Death?

The French philosopher and sociologist Michel Foucault has shown the circular relationship between power, legal discourse, and "truth," where law creates socially accepted "truths" that in turn perpetuate the status quo.[11]

It is unlikely that genocide would have become an everyday concept, much less a crime under international law, had it not been for the Holocaust. Europeans had always been less alarmed by mass atrocities in colonial Africa and in other parts of the world, that is, in places where victims were perceived as "others." After World War II, however, Europeans could not ignore the massacres that had taken place on European soil or treat them as mere accumulations of individual murders. The targeting of whole population groups was clearly different from repeated homicide or multiple murders. It was this understanding that drove the United Nations to codify a new type of international crime as "genocide."

Unfortunately, the form that this codification took shakes a body of individualistic criminal law to its very foundations. By focusing on the character of the victims, the 1948 Convention violates the principle of equality before the law, giving human life a relative rather than an absolute value. By restricting genocide to four groups (ethnic, national, racial, or religious), it creates a differentiated (that is, nonegalitarian) law. A planned and ruthless crime is only recognized for what it is if the victims share certain characteristics and not others.

In contrast, the laws of most countries define criminal acts in terms of behavior. Article 79 of the Argentine Criminal Code, for example, states that "whoever commits homicide will be condemned to prison for a period of 8 to 25 years." Aggravating circumstances, such as a family relationship between killer and victim, may increase the sentence, while mitigating circumstances, such as extreme provocation by the victim, may reduce it. But none of this alters the basic nature of the crime, and circumstances connected with the victim are established so that they do not alter the principle of equality before the law. In other words, a homicide is a homicide, regardless of who is killed. The same with any kind of crime in the Argentine Criminal Code.

On the other hand, by creating protected and unprotected groups of persons, the 1948 Convention actually legitimates the fundamental hypothesis underlying all acts of genocide, namely, that the lives of some are less significant than the lives of others. We might call this restrictive approach the dominant or "hegemonic" discourse since it has been incorporated by many states into their own legal codes. The political advantage of adopting this discourse is that once the perpetrators have been punished, events can be relegated to history without the need to confront uncomfortable questions such as which sectors of society benefited and continue to benefit from genocide.

Not surprisingly, not only historians and sociologists but also many leading jurists have challenged the definition of genocide enshrined in the Convention. Four cases are worth highlighting: the Whitaker Report, published by the United Nations Economic and Social Council Commission on Human Rights in 1985; the indictment of members of the Argentine military in 1999 by Spanish Judge Baltasar Garzón; the discussions and analyses of the International

Criminal Courts regarding events in the Balkans and Rwanda; and, finally, two Argentine sentences from 2006 and 2007 recognizing that genocide has been committed in Argentina.[12]

The Whitaker Report

Benjamin Whitaker became a member of the UN Sub-Commission on the Prevention of Discrimination and the Protection of Minorities in 1975. In 1983, he was appointed Special Rapporteur[13] and was asked to undertake a new study on genocide for the subcommission after disagreements occurred over a report drawn up by his predecessor, Nicodeme Ruhashyankiko.[14] Whitaker sent a questionnaire to UN members, organizations, and agencies; regional bodies; academics; and Non-Governmental Organisations (NGOs) in 1984, and in 1985 he published his *Revised and Updated Report on the Question of the Prevention and Punishment of the Crime of Genocide.*

The Whitaker Report, as it is usually known, analyzed genocidal processes that had occurred between 1948 and 1984. It proposed radical changes to the Convention by means of an additional optional protocol.[15] Proposals included the protection of groups based on political and sexual orientation as well as the prohibition of ethnocide and ecocide.[16] Similarly, it recommended that "advertent omission," calculated neglect, or negligence should become crimes and that the defense of "obeying superior orders" should be unacceptable. The report also recognized the difficulty of proving "intent" and advised that where documentary evidence was lacking, courts should be able to infer intent from the crimes committed. Finally, the report argued the need for an international criminal court, given the absurdity of expecting member states to put themselves on trial. "[I]n the case of 'domestic' genocides, these are generally committed by or with the complicity of Governments, with the bizarre consequence that the Governments would be required to prosecute themselves. In actual practice, mass murders are protected by their own Governments, save in exceptional cases, where these Governments have been overthrown" (Whitaker Report, paragraph 76). The Whitaker Report received a lukewarm response from the subcommission. International criminal courts were set up to deal with the Rwandan genocide and crimes in the former Yugoslavia, and Whitaker's suggestion that destruction of a group "in part" might refer to "a significant section of a group such as its leadership" (Whitaker Report, paragraph 29) has been endorsed in subsequent judicial decisions. However, the Convention continues to exclude political, economic, social, and sexual groups.

The Indictment of Baltasar Garzón

Under its domestic law, Spain has universal jurisdiction over serious crimes such as genocide even when these are committed outside Spain by foreign citizens. An action may be brought in the public interest by any Spanish citizen, and an investigating judge then gathers evidence and interviews witnesses to determine whether there is sufficient basis for the claims alleged in the complaint.[17] After studying depositions by several human rights organizations in Madrid in 1997, Judge Baltasar Garzón, as prosecuting magistrate, started proceedings against ninety-eight Argentine military members for crimes of "terrorism and genocide."

The legal arguments contained in his 156-page indictment of November 2, 1999, can be summarized as follows:

1. The requirement that victimized national groups be defined in terms of ethnicity in order to prove that genocide has taken place is unconstitutional under Spanish law (subsection one).
2. The extermination of "political groups" may be termed genocide (subsection two).
3. The term "national group" is appropriate to classify the victims in Argentina (subsection three).
4. The term "religious group" is also appropriate to classify the victims, bearing in mind the ideological nature of religious belief and also the Argentine military's explicit aim of establishing a "Western and Christian" order (subsections three and four).
5. Racist thinking is essentially political in nature. "Racial groups" are imaginary constructions that always refer in fact to "political groups" (subsection five).
6. The term "ethnic group" is also appropriate to classify the victims given the specific nature of the 'special treatment" given to the Judeo-Argentine population and its symbolic nature (subsection five).

We have already discussed the inconsistency in legal terms of excluding "political groups" from definitions of genocide. We will now examine Garzón's arguments (3), (4), and (5) in more detail.

Argument (3) is based on the fact that the perpetrators sought to destroy structures of social relationships within the state, in order to substantially alter the life of the whole. This is in line with Article 2 of the 1948 Convention (cited above), which defines genocide as "intent to destroy, in whole or in part, a national . . . group " The Argentine national group has been annihilated "in part," substantially altering social relationships across the nation. The 1990s have provided tragic examples in countries such as the former Yugoslavia or Rwanda of the extent to which destruction of part of a national group affects postgenocide economic, social, and political development.

The case of Yugoslavia is particularly relevant to this discussion since it involved a series of overlapping genocide processes, and the International Criminal Tribunal for the Former Yugoslavia (ICTY) was faced with the problem of determining which part of the population must be annihilated in order to qualify as genocide. Lemkin had already suggested that "in part" meant the destruction of a "substantial part" of the group; but how do we define "substantial"?

In a sentence published on 14 December 1999, ICTY stated that a "substantial part" could mean either (1) "a large majority of the group in question"; or (2) "political and administrative leaders, religious leaders, academics and intellectuals, business leaders and others . . . regardless of the actual numbers killed." The tribunal also advised that "[t]he character of the attack on the leadership must be viewed in the context of the fate or what happened to the rest of the group."[18] This clearly corroborates Garzón's argument (3) about the appropriateness of the term "national group" to classify the victims in Argentina.

Garzón's argument (4) highlights the "religious" and ideological purpose of the repression. As Garzón himself explains, the military government not only justified the repression as a defense of "Christian and Western" values, explicitly describing it as a "crusade," but also enlisted members of the Catholic Church to run detention centers. This religious worldview of "us" and "them" was clearly political and ideological, and makes the Convention's definition of genocide even more problematic by privileging religious beliefs over political ones.

Legal questions aside, Garzón's analysis of Argentina's state terrorism as an ideologically motivated genocide with religious characteristics provides a much more authentic and comprehensive account of events than the concepts of "politicide" or "political genocide" (see further discussion later in this chapter). This is because the aims of the repressors were not only political. Even the name the dictatorship gave to its campaign—Process of National Reorganization—clearly shows that it sought to radically transform morality, ideology, the family, and other institutions that regulate social relationships. To do so, the perpetrators eliminated anybody who embodied an alternative way of constructing social identity.

Garzón's argument (5) about the political nature of racism could be applied not only to events in Argentina but to Article II of the Convention itself. For modern anthropologists and biologists, race is not a scientifically meaningful term for describing human groupings.[19] The geneticist and evolutionary biologist Richard Lewontin, for example, found that just over 85 percent of human variation occurs *within* populations, not *between* them.[20] Moreover, racial groups blend into one another, forming a continuum. Therefore, a Human Rights Convention that claims to protect "racial groups" can only mean that it rejects racial discrimination, where race is really a metaphor for otherness—an otherness constructed as dangerous, deep-seated, and inassimilable. In this sense, race is clearly a political concept, used for political ends.

It is worth remembering that although Garzón uses the terms "race" and "ethnicity" more or less interchangeably, "race" refers to supposedly shared biological or genetic traits, while "ethnicity" is rooted more in cultural factors such as nationality, culture, ancestry, language, and beliefs. However, as S. Wallman has pointed out, English-speakers often confuse the two. "The term 'ethnic' popularly connotes '[race]' in Britain, only less precisely, and with a lighter value load. In North America, by contrast, '[race]' most commonly means color, and 'ethnics' are the descendents of relatively recent immigrants from non-English-speaking countries. '[Ethnic]' is not a noun in Britain. In effect there are no 'ethnics'; there are only 'ethnic relations.'" [21]

Finally, Garzón's argument (6) establishes an ideological continuity between the Nazi genocide and many later ones. Numerous eyewitness testimonies confirm that many of the Argentine officers involved in human rights abuses, torture, and murder in the 1970s identified with Nazi ideology and read or listened to speeches by Nazi leaders in their spare time. Detention centers and torture chambers were decorated with swastikas and pictures of Adolf Hitler. Jewish prisoners who happened to fall into this Latin American version of hell were treated with particular cruelty. However, it should be emphasized that most victims of Jewish origin were not selected because they were Jews but because of their political affiliations.

Even faced with the amount of evidence that Garzón gathered, which runs to thousands of pages, countries are often unwilling to recognize that genocide has taken place on their territory, and Argentina was no exception. Spain does not try individuals in absentia, and the Argentine government rejected all of Spain's requests for extradition. So, until Lieutenant Commander Adolfo Scilingo traveled to Spain voluntarily to testify, it seemed unlikely that the case would ever be heard.

Significantly, although its first ruling confirmed Garzón's charge of genocide, Madrid's Central Criminal Court finally sentenced Scilingo to 640 years for crimes against humanity. In its judgment of 19 April 2005, the court argued that under article 607 of the recently revised Spanish Penal Code, the crimes fitted the definition of crimes against humanity "better" than that of genocide.[22] We will return to this distinction in a moment. Nevertheless, if law is a creator of "truth," Garzón's great achievement in his indictment of the Argentine military was to include the voices of the victims alongside those of the perpetrators, including the victims' need for these events to be recognized as crimes of genocide.

The Rwandan Genocide

The subjective nature of race and ethnicity and the use of these concepts for political ends are particularly interesting in the Rwandan genocide, in which the International Criminal Tribunal for Rwanda (ICTR) noted that shared language, tradition, and legends made the Hutu and Tutsi groups almost objectively indistinguishable. Timothy Longman has shown how Christian missionaries in the early 1900s and later the Belgian colonial administration turned a flexible ethnic structure into a rigid one, excluding the Hutu from power and opportunities for advancement even though they made up more than 80 percent of the population: "To the missionaries, the Tutsi seemed tall and elegant, with refined features and light skin, in some ways closer in appearance to Europeans than to their short, stocky, dark Hutu compatriots. . . . The Tutsi, not surprisingly, failed to challenge the missionaries' assertions of their superiority and instead participated in the development of a mythico-history that portrayed them as natural rulers, with superior intelligence and morals."[23]

However, in the late 1950s, as ethnic tensions increased, the Belgian administration rapidly replaced Tutsi chiefs and officials with Hutu. When Rwanda achieved independence in 1962, the government was almost entirely Hutu. This led to a series of cross-genocidal processes, first against the Hutus in Burundi in 1965 and 1972, then against Tutsis and moderate Hutus in Rwanda in 1994. Nevertheless, as Longman points out,

> [a]lthough the Western media portrayed the 1994 genocide as a product of "centuries old" intractable divisions between Hutu and Tutsi "tribes," in fact genocide in Rwanda was never inevitable. Genocide was the final product of a strategy used by close supporters of President Habyarimana to preserve their power by appealing to ethnic arguments. Since Hutu and Tutsi continued to intermarry regularly and lived together in relative peace in most communities, the strategy required going well beyond reminding the Hutu of Tutsi dominance during the colonial period to create an atmosphere of fear and misunderstanding.[24]

Not surprisingly, the ICTR found problems in cataloging Rwandan Hutus and Tutsis as "ethnic" groups. As Eric Markusen says, "In many cases, the Tutsis were chosen and killed because of the identity documents introduced decades ago by the Belgian colonial regime, identifying them as such.[25] Did the judges of the UN not, therefore, reinforce the ideology of the murderers by identifying the Tutsis as a distinct group?"[26]

ICTR itself ended up recognizing that "for the purposes of applying the Genocide Convention, membership of a group is, in essence, a subjective rather than an objective concept. The victim is perceived by the perpetrator of genocide as belonging to a group slated for destruction. In some instances, the victim may perceive himself . . . as belonging to the said group."[27]

The Rome Statute and the International Criminal Court

In the event, ICTR and ICTY proved to be disappointing. Not only did many perpetrators manage to escape arrest or reduce their sentences with plea agreements,[28] but the 1948 Genocide Convention proved difficult to apply in practice. International pressure was not enough to change the Convention, but it did give birth to a permanent international tribunal to punish genocide and other serious international crimes: the International Criminal Court (ICC).

The Rome Conference, sponsored by the United Nations, took place in Rome, Italy, from 15 June to 17 July 1998. One hundred and sixty countries participated and the discussions were monitored by over two hundred NGOs. After intense negotiations, one hundred and twenty nations voted to adopt the Rome Statute of the ICC. Seven countries—China, Iraq, Israel, Libya, Qatar, the United States, and Yemen—voted against the treaty, and twenty-one states abstained. The statute came into force on 1 July 2002 and can prosecute only crimes committed on or after that date.

However, despite the fact that many organizations and individuals worked long and hard to establish the ICC, its procedures and performance offer few guarantees against human rights abuses by member states.

Although many scholars and advisers advised against it at the discussion and drafting stages, the definition of genocide adopted in Article 6 of the Rome Statute is copied word for word from Article II of the 1948 Genocide Convention. This has made the concept of genocide unenforceable. Instead, the court has preferred to apply the much more flexible definition of "crimes against humanity" defined in Article 7 of the statute:

Article 7: Crimes against humanity

1. For the purpose of this Statute, "crimes against humanity" means any of the following acts when committed as part of a widespread or systematic attack directed against any civilian population, with knowledge of the attack:
   (a) Murder;
   (b) Extermination;
   (c) Enslavement;
   (d) Deportation or forcible transfer of population;
   (e) Imprisonment or other severe deprivation of physical liberty in violation of fundamental rules of international law;
   (f) Torture;
   (g) Rape, sexual slavery, enforced prostitution, forced pregnancy, enforced sterilization, or any other form of sexual violence of comparable gravity;
   (h) Persecution against any identifiable group or collectivity on political, racial, national, ethnic, cultural, religious, gender as defined in paragraph 3, or other grounds that are universally recognized as impermissible under international law, in connection with any act referred to in this paragraph or any crime within the jurisdiction of the Court;
   (i) Enforced disappearance of persons;
   (j) The crime of apartheid;
   (k) Other inhumane acts of a similar character intentionally causing great suffering, or serious injury to body or to mental or physical health.

The Rome Statute's failure to produce a usable definition of genocide and the replacement to all intents and purposes of "genocide" by "crimes against humanity" is not just a semantic quibble. It means that the ICC can only act in cases where the perpetrators and/or territory involved belong to states that have accepted its jurisdiction. The United States is just one example of a state that is accused of committing crimes under the statute of the court and that has so far refused to ratify the statute. Widening the circle of impunity still further, the ICC has until now only examined cases presented by member states or, in one case, by the Security Council of the United Nations. The court's autonomy to investigate violations seems to exist only on paper.

One consequence is that so far the ICC has focused exclusively on African countries. In three of the four countries where it operates, its actions are directed against members of nonstate organizations reported by the state itself.[29] What is striking in all these cases—beyond the seriousness of the crimes themselves—is that the intervention of the ICC seems to serve no useful function. International criminal law exists to punish crimes committed by the state, not by forces opposing the state, which could equally well be tried under domestic law.

The ICC's involvement in Africa contrasts oddly with its failure to investigate other reported systematic violations of human rights in China, Colombia, Israel, Russia, and Sri Lanka, to name just a few, and alleged human rights violations by U.S. and British troops in Iraq. In some cases, the ICC has justified its failure to intervene on the grounds that the defendants (China, Israel, Russia, or the United States) or countries where violations occur (China, Iraq, and Afghanistan) are not members of the ICC. In other cases, like Colombia, the government claims to be taking action against violations without explaining why no trial proceedings have been started and why killings of political opponents and indigenous groups continue in Colombia to this day.[30]

Finally, the ICC has only confronted one national government—that of Sudan—for the atrocities committed in the western Sudanese region of Darfur and only because the UN Security Council urged it to do so. Of course, the large numbers of victims and refugees, the burning of villages, and destruction of ethnic and political groups are a humanitarian tragedy. But the international arrest warrant issued by the ICC against Sudanese president Omar Al-Bashir in March 2009 has not led to his arrest nor helped to prevent bloodshed in the Sudan. On the contrary, it has been used as an excuse by the Sudanese government to expel international observers and aid organizations assisting the victims. Again, we face the question of whose interests are served by the intervention of the ICC. How do we impose effective sanctions against human rights violators when they control the power and resources of the state?

The Rome Statute and the ICC have not helped to clarify the concept of genocide unless—as William Schabas says—we are willing to relegate the concept of genocide to the history books in favor of the more general and more easily applicable concept of crimes against humanity.[31] However, this would reduce Lemkin's rich concept of genocide as the "destruction of population groups" to the annihilation of civilian populations in general.

The Legal Definition of Genocide: Future Possibilities

Because political groups are not protected by the 1948 Genocide Convention or the 1998 Rome Statute, it is easy to confuse attempts to destroy political groups with the murder of individual politicians or activists. By reducing genocide to crimes against humanity, there is a real danger that we may lose sight of the ways in which the social practices of genocide systematically destroy identity. However, the Convention and the Rome Statute do not completely close the door on new interpretations of genocide. Garzón's perspective of the extermination of political groups in Argentina as the destruction of part of a national group (in this case, the Argentine national group) has proved to be particularly illuminating. In Argentina, the Federal Oral Criminal Tribunal No. 1 for La Plata convicted former police commissioner Miguel Etchecolatz in 2006 and former police chaplain Christian von Wernich in 2007 for crimes against humanity "committed in the frame of genocide." In this landmark ruling, the court considered the systematic nature of the crimes and their effect on society as a whole, urging other courts to use the concept of "destruction of part of the national group" to resolve a number of conceptual and legal issues surrounding Argentina's state terrorism.

According to Lemkin, the main purpose of genocidal practices is to destroy the oppressed group's identity. It makes little difference whether the group is oppressed by a colonial power—as was generally the case in Lemkin's time—or by members of the same national group, as has so often been the case since the 1948 Convention. In the second half of the twentieth century, national armies have repeatedly behaved like armies of occupation in their own countries.[32] The fact that all national genocide laws explicitly forbid the partial destruction of national groups should allow an increasing number of cases to be successfully prosecuted in national courts.

The Conceptual Discussion: Thinking beyond the Law

As we have already argued, defining genocide in terms of the characteristics of the victims has no precedent in modern criminal law and clearly damages the principle of equality before the law. It is now time to consider the implications of such a definition for a historical and sociological understanding of genocide as a social practice.

In legal terms, a homicide is always, in principle, a homicide. For the social sciences, however, some homicides are so extraordinary that they justify the development of a specific name to label them. Sociologists use the terms Holocaust, Shoah, Jurbn, or Judeocide to refer to the systematic annihilation of Europe's Jewish population under Nazism because of the unique characteristics of this historical tragedy. Nevertheless, just as the 1948 Convention's definition of genocide is insufficient to explain the nature of the Shoah, the specific characteristics of the Shoah do not in themselves define the limits of the term "genocide."

In the social sciences, the important element for constructing a concept such as genocide is what we might call the "structural similarities" of unique events. Each historical event is unique so we need to go beyond their specificities in order to categorize social phenomena that are analogous in terms of purpose, design, implementation, and consequences. One issue that tends to overlap with and influence legal definitions is whether different historical processes fit within the same category (e.g., genocide), and when is it necessary to create new terms in order to account for processes that are qualitatively different.

I will now review the main definitions of genocide used by different authors in the social sciences and compare their "structural similarities." I will also consider whether these definitions are useful for describing the systematic killings in Argentina between 1976 and 1983 or whether we need a new term to understand the process behind these specific events.

Historical and Sociological Definitions of Genocide

Not everyone who writes about genocide defines the term explicitly. However, since the appearance of genocide studies as a separate discipline in Europe and the United States in the late 1980s, most authors who study genocidal processes systematically have struggled with the problem of definition.

The first important challenges to the definition in the Genocide Convention are to be found in Vahakn Dadrian, Irving Louis Horowitz, and Leo Kuper. Significantly, all three are authors of comparative genocide studies. In 1975, one of the world's leading authorities on the Turkish genocide of the Armenians,[33] Dadrian, defined genocide as "the successful attempt by a dominant group, vested with formal authority and/or with preponderant access to the overall resources of power, to reduce by coercion or lethal violence the number of a minority group whose ultimate extermination is held desirable and useful and whose respective vulnerability is a major factor contributing to the decision for genocide."[34]

The following year, American sociologist Horowitz defined genocide as "a structural and systematic destruction of innocent people by a state bureaucratic apparatus. . . . Genocide represents a systematic effort over time to liquidate a national population, usually a minority . . . [and] functions as a fundamental political policy to assure conformity and participation of the citizenry."[35]

The South African writer and philosopher Kuper began writing about genocide in the early 1970s. However, in his definitive work, *Genocide: Its Political Use in the Twentieth Century* (1981), Kuper shied away from offering a new definition, for fear of undermining the Convention. Instead, he stated, "I shall follow the definition of genocide given in the [UN] Convention. This is not to say that I agree with the definition. On the contrary, I believe a major omission to be in the exclusion of political groups from the list of groups protected. In the contemporary world, political differences are at the very least as significant a basis for massacre and annihilation as racial, national, ethnic or religious differences. Then too, the genocides against racial, national, ethnic or religious groups are generally a consequence of, or intimately related to, political conflict."[36] Kuper believed that even a limited Genocide Convention was better than none at all; but he also recognized that "it would vitiate the analysis to exclude political groups."[37]

Nearly ten years passed before historian Frank Chalk and sociologist Kurt Jonassohn, both Americans, complained in 1990 that the Convention excluded political and social groups while including nonlethal forms of group destruction. In their view, genocide should be seen as "a form of one-sided mass killing in which a state or other authority intends to destroy a group, as that group and membership in it are defined by the perpetrator."[38]

In 1993, the American sociologist Helen Fein considered genocide to be "sustained purposeful action by a perpetrator to physically destroy a collectivity directly or indirectly, through interdiction of the biological and social reproduction of group members, sustained regardless of the surrender or lack of threat offered by the victim."[39]

In 1994, the Israeli scholar Israel W. Charny argued that "[g]enocide in the generic sense means the mass killing of substantial numbers of human beings, when not in the course of military action against the military forces of an avowed enemy, under conditions of the essential defencelessness of the victim."

Meanwhile, concerned about the exclusion of political groups from the Convention, American political scientists Barbara Harff and Ted Gurr had developed a new concept: politicide. For Harff and Gurr, "genocides and politicides are the promotion, execution, and/or implied consent of sustained policies by governing elites or their agents—or, in the case of civil war either of the contending authorities—that are intended to destroy, in whole or part, a communal, political, or politicized ethnic group."[40]

The difference between genocide and politicide is that victims of genocide are chosen primarily for their community characteristics (ethnicity, religion, or nationality), while victims of politicide are selected mainly for their position of leadership or political opposition to the regime or dominant groups. Harff and Gurr believe that the distinction is valid for the social sciences, but not for law, where the two processes should be considered as equivalent. I will return to the concept of politicide in a moment.

American Jewish philosopher Steven Katz goes further in claiming that only the Jewish Holocaust perpetrated by the Nazi regime counts as genocide. For Katz, the "concept of genocide applies *only* when there is an actualized intent, however successfully carried out, to physically destroy an *entire* group (as such a group is defined by the perpetrators)."[41]

Holocaust historian Henry Huttenbach believes in concise and simple formulations. Thus, he defines genocide as "*the destruction of a specific group within a national or even international population. The precise character of the group need not be spelled out*" (emphasis added).[42] Elsewhere he writes: "Genocide is any act that puts the very existence of a group in jeopardy."[43]

More recently, British historian Mark Levene has warned that disagreements over definitions may make the concept of genocide either so narrow that it excludes virtually all cases or so broad that it includes any type of mass murder. Despite this warning, Levene affirms that "genocide occurs when a state, perceiving the integrity of its agenda to be threatened by an aggregate population—defined by the state as an organic collectivity, or series of collectivities—seeks to remedy the situation by the systematic en masse physical elimination of that aggregate, *in toto*, or until it is no longer perceived to represent a threat."[44]

French political scientist Jacques Semelin advises genocide researchers to distance themselves from the legal and normative definition of genocide. Semelin distinguishes between "destruction in order to subjugate" (where the victims are nearly always defined as political) and "destruction in order to eradicate" (where the victims tend to be ethnic or national). He reserves the concept of genocide for the latter and subsumes both practices under the term "massacre."[45]

If these definitional debates seem tedious, the main features of the definitions can be summarized as follows:

1. Genocide is an action. Therefore, any systematic annihilation of a group because of its characteristics (whatever those characteristics may be) constitutes genocide (see, for example, the definitions by Chalk and Jonassohn, Henry Huttenbach, and Mark Levene).
2. Genocide is the intention to systematically destroy the entire group, and not only a part of it (Steven Katz).
3. Genocide is any systematic annihilation of significant numbers of the population as long as the population is in a situation of "defencelessness" or does not constitute a "real threat" to the perpetrator (see Israel Charny's or Helen Fein's definition).[46]
4. There is a qualitative difference between genocide and politicide because of the characteristics of the victims (see Barbara Harff and Ted Gurr).
5. There is a qualitative difference between destruction/subjugation processes of massacre (where victims are almost always political) and destruction/eradication processes of massacre (where victims are almost always ethnic or national) (see Jacques Semelin).[47]

As mentioned in the Introduction, this book aims to provide a comparative analysis of two genocidal social practices—the Nazi Holocaust and the military repression in Argentina between 1976 and 1983. The Holocaust inspired all the definitions given above and contains them all. But it is not so clear which definition or group of definitions best describes Argentina's case. In the next section we will consider the usefulness of each of these definitions for obtaining a clear understanding of the Argentine repression. We will also consider the wider implications of each definition.

Applying Different Definitions of Genocide to Events in Argentina

1. Genocide as the Annihilation of a Group

This definition is clear and inclusive. The Argentine state defined a group as "subversive." This group was made up of different political organizations (including numerous Peronists and non-Peronist left-wing groups), and individuals (labor unionists, students, neighborhood activists, social workers, teachers, professionals, etc.) who are categorized socially, not politically. What made these people a group, according to the perpetrators, was that they posed a threat to Christian and Western values.

That is to say, although the definition is implicitly political and although, as I have suggested elsewhere in this book, the military government sought to destroy the very fabric of Argentine society (a society based on social autonomy and, particularly, "political autonomy"), the explicit definition of the group was both political ("Western" referred to political alignment with the Western alliance during the Cold War) and religious ("Christian" referred specifically to the official state religion of Roman Catholicism). The annihilation was clearly "one-sided," taking into account that almost all of the armed left-wing groups had been completely defeated by the time Videla's military junta seized power. The destruction was so effective that social autonomy, social criticism, and solidarity were to vanish from the Argentine society for at least two generations.[48]

2. Genocide as the Intention to Systematically Destroy the Entire Group

Steven Katz's definition introduces an element that, to my mind, is too subjective. In relation to the total population of 25 million, the number of people actually murdered was obviously quite small—between 15,000 and 30,000. If, on the other hand, we focus on the consequences of their disappearance, we can argue that annihilation was "practically total," since the behavior for which these people were persecuted (autonomy, political opposition, critical thinking) was eliminated almost entirely from Argentine society for two generations. Even Peronism, which was revived after the military dictatorship, has little to do in terms of policies either with early Peronism (1946–1955) and the Peronist resistance (1955–1973), or with late Peronism (1973–1976).

The word "total" is so subjective that Katz's definition becomes unusable for sociological purposes. If applied literally, this definition might even exclude the Nazi genocide itself—as some Jewish victims did in fact survive. Moreover, assessing "intent" to destroy totally is also a complex task due to the different groups of perpetrators involved in a particular instance of genocide.

3. Genocide as the Annihilation of the "Defenseless"

The critical element in Fein's and, to a certain extent, Charny's definitions of genocide is the "defenselessness" of the victims. Although "defenselessness" is also a debatable category, the Argentine case, in principle, does not seem to fit this type of definition.

Again, the problem lies in how the victimized group is defined. Many of the political groups persecuted by the dictatorship were armed organizations. Their ability to defy state power was always limited, and armed struggle in Argentina cannot be compared with that in Cuba, Nicaragua, El Salvador, or Guatemala, where left-wing armed organizations successfully resisted state forces. Nevertheless, the category of "defenselessness" does not seem to apply to groups that have a philosophy of armed conflict and a military organization, however weak it may be. The process could be defined as one-sided, but that does not imply that the victims were defenseless.

To complicate matters still further, the victims in Argentina included individuals with no clear political affiliation as well as members of different political organizations. Some of these sympathized with various armed organizations to a greater or lesser extent while others repudiated them. The relationship of the victims with those who decided to engage in armed conflict was unclear, ranging from armed sympathizers with left-wing organizations to militants who were strongly opposed to violence.

Most of the murders, however, were carried out by kidnapping victims from their homes, on the street, or at work, and transporting them to concentration camps, subjecting them to torture, and subsequently executing them. This happened regardless of the victim's affiliations and "in a situation of defenselessness," even though many of the victims had, at various times and in various ways, supported the idea of armed conflict. This is what sets the Argentine repression apart from many civil wars fought in the Third World.

Therefore, if we accept this third type of definition, we might say that those victims who were not members of armed organizations qualify as victims of genocide, while those who were members of armed organizations but were kidnapped in a situation of defenselessness fall into an ambiguous category; and finally, a small percentage of the victims—those who died in armed confrontations—do not qualify as victims at all.

This approach, in my view, does more to expose the problems inherent in the concept of "defenselessness" than it does to clarify the Argentine case.

Furthermore, it raises awkward and undesirable questions about the degree of activism of the victims, which may even result in criminal charges against them. The need to prove "defenselessness" reverses the burden of proof, forcing an investigation as to how defenseless the victim actually was.

4. *Qualitative Difference between Genocide and Politicide*

Harff and Gurr apply the term "politicide" not only to political groups but also to anyone who is targeted for opposing a regime. In their view, the Argentine case was one of politicide, not genocide, since "victim groups [were] defined primarily in terms of their hierarchical position or political opposition to the regime and dominant groups."[49] The Argentine repressors clearly persecuted members of groups that engaged in "political opposition to the regime" even if some of these groups—a minority—had never said a word in protest.

We need to question the usefulness of this distinction. Harff and Gurr's work is clearly a response to the exclusion of the "political groups" from Article 2 of the 1948 Convention. Their aim is to analyze different modalities of mass annihilation and a fundamental issue is whether genocide and politicide are different types of persecution or whether politicide is simply a subcategory of genocide. If the two concepts are qualitatively different, then genocide against a national, ethnic, or religious group—or any other specific group, such as a sexual or economic group—must be qualitatively different too.

5. *Subjugation versus Eradication*

I believe that genocide perpetrated against political groups does have its own particular characteristics. If we accept Semelin's distinction between destruction/subjugation processes and destruction/eradication processes as valid, then the Argentine repression conforms to the first type. However, in practice we generally find a mixture of both. In Argentina, the destruction/subjugation processes were mixed with the total "destruction/erradication" of some political movements from the Argentine political arena.

The problem with Semelin's distinction is that only destruction processes, not subjugation processes, count as genocide. This ignores the wider historical context and creates a fragmented picture of genocidal and nongenocidal events, which tends to distort their true meaning. In Argentina, the eradication of political, social, and cultural groups was intended to subjugate society as a whole.

In conclusion, the military repression in Argentina between 1974 and 1983 seems to be best described by the genocide processes Harff and Gurr call "politicide" and by the massacre processes Semelin calls "destruction/subjugation." These different varieties of genocide, however, are often interwoven and difficult to differentiate.

Moreover, as we have already seen, the "Western and Christian" ideology of the Argentine perpetrators was religious as well as political. Now, genocidal processes driven by politics and religion differ in some ways from those driven by national or ethnic conflict. Nevertheless, their "structural elements"—the polarization into "us" and "them," the absolutizing and demonizing of the enemy, the concentration camp system, the dehumanizing of the Other, the destruction of social relationships and other symbolic processes—are very similar.

The concept of "politicide" may be useful for describing a specific type of genocide. However, it could also be used to block reforms—now long overdue—to the 1948 Genocide Convention or to reject national laws seeking to protect political groups. Worse still, it might encourage people to misjudge or even trivialize genocide against political groups, thus granting impunity to the perpetrators.

A Philosophical Discussion about "Being" and "Doing"

It is not only lawyers, sociologists, and historians who have struggled with the problem of defining genocide. Philosophers, too, have made important contributions, particularly to the question of whether different genocide phenomena are comparable and whether the same concept (genocide) can be used to refer to different historical events.

In this chapter we began by examining the question of "structural similarities" from a legal point of view, and we saw that equality before the law is a fundamental concept in modern legal thinking. There is no legal basis or justification for distinguishing between those who are killed because of their ethnic identity or because of their political beliefs. Equality before the law means that all victims are "equal in death."

Moving on to historical and sociological definitions of genocide, I argued that genocide is a technology of power—in other words, a way of managing people as a group—and it is this that makes different instances of mass annihilation similar.

However, these ideas have been challenged by a number of philosophers from different traditions. These philosophers question whether such *structural* "similarities" or "differences" exist or not, and their work has opened up the possibility of exploring new relationships.[50]

All this is linked to a deeper distinction between the annihilation of "being" (the prototypical case being the extermination of the European Jewish population by the Nazis) and the eradication of "doing" (for example, political-ideological annihilation under the military dictatorship in Argentina). The question is whether and in what ways the physical annihilation of "lesser races" is fundamentally different from the eradication of political ideologies and practices. Here, the distinction between being and doing is used in a philosophical sense within the broader question of how identities, in particular collective identities, are formed.

Is There Being without Doing, or Must One Do Something in Order to Be?

The German philosopher Hegel (1770–1831) makes a distinction between nonconscious being (being-in-itself) and conscious being (being-for-itself). Objects such as rocks have only nonconscious being; but human beings have both. For Hegel, "being-in-itself" also refers to the potential abilities a person has not yet manifested. In contrast, "being-for-itself" refers to a person's actual behavior that he or she can incorporate into his or her identity.[51] To take a simple example: no matter how many good ideas I may have for a novel, I can only begin to see myself as a writer once I have written my first book.

Hegel's distinction was adopted by Marx, who argued that under capitalism, workers no longer existed "for themselves" but were alienated by a system of production that took away the fruits of their labor. To continue the previous analogy, workers were like authors whose manuscripts disappeared each day and who never saw their finished work in print. According to Marx, workers could only overcome alienation by collective struggling against the existing social order. [52]

The same distinction between nonconscious and conscious being could also be applied to different types of group identity. In this sense, the main difference between an identity based on ethnicity and one based on a political ideology would seem to depend on how much "choice" the individual has in the matter. Ethnic identity (e.g., being Jewish) is not always voluntary. Although we now know that the concept of race is unscientific, the Nazis defined Jewishness by ancestry whether or not the people concerned thought of themselves as Jewish. Following Hegel's distinction, people could be Jews "in themselves" even if they were not Jews "for themselves."[53] But political and ideological affiliation seems to form part of a consciously constructed identity: political activists "choose" militancy; they accept the risks such activism may bring, actively assuming their identity. They create themselves by "doing" and so they exist as political activists "for themselves."

The Nazis claimed that all Jews were selfish, materialistic, parasitic, and treacherous as a consequence of inborn "degenerative impulses." This sort of "trait theory" suggests a static identity (being-in-itself) unrelated to any particular historical period or way of life. Yet it is doubtful that intelligent Nazis could have believed this.[54] The right-wing historian Oswald Spengler, who was popular among National Socialists until 1934, took pains to explain how Jewish worldviews were the result of a history of exile rather than a product of Darwinian natural selection.[55] Spengler rejected Nazi biological doctrines as unscientific and argued that Western anti-Semitism had grown out of a cultural conflict. In any case, the only way a Nazi could recognize Jewish identity was by observing what Jews actually did. This is apart from the question of whether Jewish identity was more or less conscious, more or less voluntary, and associated or not with a particular social practice.

An obvious question is why the Nazis chose the Jews as their prototypical victims if the Jews were not *doing* something "degenerate" that the Nazis wished to eradicate? Jews were treated much worse than any other prisoner group, including Gypsies, homosexuals, political dissidents, common criminals, and the disabled. The Nazi belief that Jews were a biologically as well as culturally inferior race might explain why the Nazis made no attempt to "reeducate" Jews as they occasionally did with political prisoners, homosexuals, and Gypsies; but it does not explain why they singled out the Jews for persecution in the first place.

In Argentina, the military also believed that "subversive criminals" transmitted ideas and behaviors to their children. However, despite attempts elsewhere to link an extra Y chromosome and aggressive male criminal behavior in the 1960s, the military do not seem to have believed in biological transmission of "subversiveness."[56] This is the only rational explanation for the fact that children born to prisoners in Argentine detention centers were allowed to live. The mothers were killed after giving birth and the newborn babies were "adopted" by families sympathetic to the armed forces. On the other hand, older children were often tortured in front of their parents. Presumably, these children had already been "infected" with subversive ideas and were incurable.

However, just as the Nazis did not persecute Jews simply for "being" Jews, the Argentine military did not only kill people who were fully aware of what they were "doing." Did the French nuns, Alice Domon and Léonie Duquet, who worked helping Argentina's poor and became involved with the Mothers of the Plaza de Mayo, set out to create an identity for themselves at the risk of their own lives? And if so, how conscious were they of this?[57] What about neighborhood representatives or student activists? Even if people made a conscious choice to join a political movement, it is doubtful that many of them knew exactly which day-to-day activities they would be persecuted for.

The question then is to what extent the identity of different victim groups is based on "being" or on "doing," and to what extent identities based on "doing" are consciously chosen. Members of left-wing political-military organizations in Argentina would have known the consequences of armed rebellion if they were caught;[58] however, it is questionable whether other so-called militants were aware of placing themselves in harm's way. Similarly, although middle-class, liberal Jews like Anne Frank's family could not comprehend Nazi prejudice and cruelty, members of the General Jewish Labor Bund in Poland, left- and right-wing Zionists, and even Jewish religious groups did understand that their social practices threatened the Nazi social order.[59] In truth, both the victims of Argentine genocide and the victims of the Jewish Holocaust occupy a continuum between "being" and "doing."

Can the Ideological Ways in Which the Victims Are Constructed by the Perpetrators Constitute a Structural Difference?

Shifting our focus now to the ways in which group identities are constructed by the perpetrators of genocide, we find—at least in principle—two main processes at work. The Nazis essentialized Jews, Gypsies, homosexuals, and other groups as being "subhuman" and a biological threat to the human species.[60] These ideas ultimately derived from Count Arthur de Gobineau's *Essay on the Inequality of the Human Races*, written between 1853 and 1855, although Gobineau himself saw Jews as strong, intelligent people who were very much a part of his "superior race."[61] Once the Nazis had branded certain groups as a threat, it was a short step to identifying different races with different ideologies. For example, the Nazis used the term "Judeo-Bolshevism" to imply that the communist movement served Jewish interests and/or that all Jews were communists.

Argentina's military dictatorship, however, constructed its enemies as "subversives"—an unequivocally political term. Strictly speaking, subversion is an attempt to overthrow structures of authority, including the state. However, the Argentine military's use of the term, although ambiguous, frequently meant something more like "showing political autonomy." Perhaps for this reason both the dictatorship's ideological documents and the news media that supported the military regime regularly spoke of "subversive *criminals*." The term "criminal" justified harsh measures against the social base of armed insurgents in a way that "subversive" did not.[62]

What similarities exist, then, between the Nazi Holocaust and Argentina's National Reorganization Process? European colonialism had constructed the Asian and African Other as something inherently foreign and threatening to the civilized world. Nazism went further by constructing this Other within European societies themselves—an Other that had to be exterminated in order to protect the group as a whole. The same need to protect society as a whole was used to justify genocide in Latin America, when dictators frequently likened Marxism and populism to a social cancer. However, these dictators largely did away with biological metaphors and targeted political autonomy as such. This fact is often missed by those who equate genocide with the Holocaust without realizing that the Nazis' concept of race was an essentialization of their political ideology.[63]

Under Argentina's National Reorganization Process, the shift from "political opponents of the regime" to "subversive criminals" was accompanied symbolically by a shift in the editorial policy in important national dailies such as *La Nación* and *La Prensa*, gradually moving these stories from the political to the crime section of the newspaper. Nevertheless, it was clear that these crimes were different from those that readers had hitherto been accustomed to reading about. There was talk of "separating the sick from the healthy," and restoring "health" to the social body, as well as "harsh treatment of criminals" that would be secret, illegal, and all-embracing.

The voluntary nature of militancy thus became irreversible. Renouncing one's political ideas and solidarity with former colleagues was no guarantee of survival. Once the victims fell into the hands of the genocidal apparatus, their fate was no longer in their own hands. The repressors in the Argentine concentration camps repeatedly said: "Now we are God and we decide over life and death." So, although there was no attempt to legitimize persecution with racial metaphors, the Argentine perpetrators did not accept voluntary repentance, either. Nor were most of those who provided information under torture able to save their lives or those of their families, despite the fact that the few who "reappeared" were shunned as traitors by former friends, making them victims twice over.[64]

Raphael Lemkin broke the deadlock in the Genocide Convention negotiations by arguing that political groups lacked the cohesion or permanence of other groups. But differences in cohesion and permanence do not stand up to philosophical scrutiny. Anne Frank and her family probably had as much in common with the Jewish partisans of Eastern Europe as the French nuns, Alice Domon and Léonie Duquet, shared with members of the Montoneros guerrilla organization. And if "subversive criminals" were as permanently irredeemable for the Argentine perpetrators as the Jews were for the Nazis, it is difficult to believe in an essential and structural differentiation between victim groups.

Conclusions

It is clear that problems of definition are central to any discussion of genocide and genocidal processes. Without claiming to have any definitive answers to these questions, I will now offer some provisional definitions to help with the work in hand.

From a legal point of view, any definition of genocide should respect the principle of equality before the law and the customary law that has emerged from the history of relations between human communities. In other words, genocide should be defined in broad and general terms as *the execution of a large-scale and systematic plan with the intention of destroying a human group as such in whole or in part.* In this sense it would be identical to the systematic annihilations carried out by the Ancient Greeks and Romans or by the Mongols.

I will use the concept of "genocidal social practices" to clarify differences between modern genocide and earlier processes of destruction. By "genocidal social practices" I mean a technology of power that is intended to destroy social relations based on autonomy and cooperation by killing a significant portion of society (significant in numbers or influence) and that then attempts to create new social relations and identity models through terror.

Genocide is not the only way to transform societies, but it has been a very successful method during the twentieth century, along with revolution. However, although revolutions have also destroyed and reorganized social relations, they have not necessarily done so through mass annihilation. This is the main difference between revolution and genocide.

In the following chapters I will examine the precise nature of the social relations and identity models destroyed and the new social relations and patterns of identity brought into being by two historical instances of genocidal social practices: the prototypical genocide committed by the Nazis, and the genocidal social practices occurring in Argentina between 1974 and 1983.

If we look at victims' subjective experiences of the Nazi Holocaust or of Argentina's systematic killings—in other words, if we take what philosophers call a "phenomenological approach" to these events—we end up in both cases with a similar catalog of horrors: concentration camps, deportations, torture, and human perversity. I have argued that it is this "equality before death" which makes it impossible to legally limit the crime of genocide to certain groups.

Another danger of viewing the Nazis' genocide as irrational—a persecution based on blind racial hatred—while seeing Argentina's genocide as rational—a confrontation of ideologies—is that the supposed rationality of one case defines the irrationality of the other, and vice versa. The Jews had done *nothing* to justify their fate, so the Argentine "subversives" *must* have done something to justify theirs. If all this sounds a bit far-fetched, it is because plenty of nonsense has been written in the past: "the Nazis only killed Jews"; "the Nazis did not kill for political or ideological reasons"; "Jews did not take part in politics"; "Jewish identity is genetic"; and "there is no explanation for the Holocaust."

The sanctification of the Holocaust in contemporary Jewish thinking as "incomprehensible" diminishes processes of disappearance and annihilation viewed as "understandable"—especially political murders—by blaming the victims. It is almost as if an unconscious and therefore innocent "being-in-itself" is accusing a conscious and clearly political "being-for-itself." If we accept that logic, then the historian's job—like that of the sociologist, the philosopher, or the political scientist—becomes primarily one of deciding in which direction to tip the scales: innocent or guilty.

On the other hand, using the term "genocide" to refer to two different historical processes does not mean that the two processes are the same. It does not mean ignoring the enormous socioeconomic and ideological differences between the Germany of the 1940s and the Argentina of the 1970s. The same is true of the Armenian genocide of 1915 to 1923, the repressive policies against political and ethnic groups in the Soviet Union under Stalin, counterinsurgency wars in Indochina and Algeria, the annihilation of the communist opposition in Indonesia and East Timor, the annihilation of "class" enemies by the Khmer Rouge in Cambodia between 1975 and 1979, "ethnic cleansing" in the former

Yugoslavia, or the extermination of nearly one million people in Rwanda in 1994.

I do not deny in any way the difference between the factory-scale murder and incineration of millions of people under the Nazis and the extermination of tens of thousands of people on an almost cottage-industry scale under the Argentine military juntas. What these two cases have in common is that the perpetrators sought to annihilate their enemies both materially and symbolically. Not just their bodies but also the memory of their existence was supposed to disappear, forcing the survivors to deny their own identity, as a synthesis of *being* and *doing* defined like any other identity by a particular way of life. In this sense, the disappearances outlast the destruction of war: the effects of genocide do not end but only begin with the deaths of the victims. In short, the main objective of genocidal destruction is the transformation of the victims into "nothing" and the survivors into "nobodies."

2

Toward a Typology of Genocidal Social Practices

Then there was neither this grief
nor the thankless condemnation of looking back.
Then exile did not matter
and I did not seek comfort for loneliness.

–Victor Heredia, "Then"

Many writers have sought to define the essential features of the Nazi genocide. Rather fewer have attempted to understand how genocidal social practices have varied across different societies during the twentieth century. Fewer still have moved beyond comparative analyses of this sort to consider genocidal social practices as a social process—in other words, as *a sequence of social changes* accompanied by *predictable* changes in social relations, attitudes, and values, albeit with distinctive local variations.

In fact, in the sixty years following Raphael Lemkin's pioneering study in 1944, only eight authors presented any new classifications of genocide: Frank Chalk and Kurt Jonassohn, Israel Charny, Vahakn Dadrian, Helen Fein, Leo Kuper, Roger Smith, and Barbara Harff. In the first part of this chapter I will critically analyze these eight models before going on to suggest a new way of organizing and categorizing genocidal social practices that includes what I call "reorganizing genocide." As we will see, this type of genocide is the link between the two historical events that are explored in this book: the Nazi genocide from 1933 to 1945 and Argentine state terror from 1974 to 1983.

Eight Typologies of Genocide

No sooner had Lemkin coined the term "genocide" than he became aware of the need to distinguish between different types of genocide. For Lemkin, genocide was a "new word . . . to denote an old practice in its modern development."[1] So, it was necessary to differentiate, say, the massacre of civilians by the Mongols in the Middle Ages from the massacre of the Armenians by the Turks during World War I, particularly if one intended to describe both events as genocide. The two scholars who made the greatest effort to develop a coherent typology of genocide before 2005 were Frank Chalk and Kurt Jonassohn. Chalk and Jonassohn's classification, published in their classic book *The History and Sociology of Genocide: Analyses and Case Studies* (1990), is summarized below. However, before looking at it in detail, it is worth remembering that Chalk and Jonassohn pointed out in a later article that other typologies are possible, depending on what kind of factors are examined. These factors could include ways of relating between different groups within a society, power relations between different societies, the means employed to carry out mass annihilations, or the causes, intentions, or results of each genocidal process.[2] Chalk and Jonassohn chose the purposes of the perpetrators as their organizing principle, and in fact all eight models examined below are based either on the causes, intentions, or results of genocide.

In his study, Lemkin divided genocides into three different types according to their purpose:

1. Those seeking to destroy a nation or group completely. He considered this kind of genocide to be typical of the ancient world.
2. Those seeking to destroy a culture by assimilating its members rather than by killing them. This was later separated from genocide and given the legal name of "ethnocide."
3. Those seeking to destroy both the group and its culture. Lemkin considered the Nazi genocide as a prototypical instance of this third type.

However, although Lemkin's distinctions are interesting, Chalk and Jonassohn have rightly pointed out that Lemkin did not realize that the prototypical form of genocide in the twentieth century involved a society destroying a portion of *its own citizens*. Indeed, we might add that Lemkin was unable to see this despite his own experience of Nazism, which was the basis of his theoretical work.[3]

A critical reading of Lemkin and others such as Hervé Savon, Irving Louis Horowitz, and Vahakn Dadrian caused Chalk and Jonassohn to reformulate their own ideas several times. In 1990 they distinguished four types of genocide, according to the intentions of the perpetrator:

1. To eliminate a real or potential threat to society
2. To spread terror among real or potential enemies
3. To acquire economic wealth
4. To implement a religious belief, a scientific theory, or an ideology

It is clear that Chalk and Jonassohn's categories will be more useful than Lemkin's for the purposes of our study, even though they focus exclusively on intentions, thus diverting attention away from the underlying *causes* of different genocides. The causes are more obscure but may prove more instructive once they are fully understood.

In contrast to Chalk and Jonassohn's relatively complex definition of genocide, Israel Charny's study in 1994 defined genocide quite simply as the mass killing of defenseless victims, whether intentional or otherwise. Charny was thus forced to consider a much wider range of situations. In fact, he distinguished six main types of genocide, linked to *how* the genocidal practice is carried out:

1. Genocidal massacre (mass murder on a smaller scale)
2. Intentional genocide (an explicit intention to destroy a specific targeted victim group). Charny subdivides this into
   a. Specific intentional genocide—against a specific victim group
   b. Multiple intentional genocide—against more than one specific victim group, either at the same time or in closely related or contiguous actions
   c. Omnicide—simultaneous intentional genocide against numerous races, nations, religions, etc.
3. Genocide in the course of colonization or consolidation of power
4. Genocide in the course of aggressive ("unjust") war (killing of civilians in military actions)
5. Genocide as War Crimes against Humanity
6. Genocide as a result of ecological destruction and abuse

Charny's classification is perhaps undermined by its sheer scope, but the definitions of types 1, 2, and 3 are, in my view, extremely useful for distinguishing different instances of genocide according to their intentionality and the nature of the practices involved. This sort of analysis would clarify whether it is appropriate to use the term genocide to describe types 4, 5, and 6, or whether these are better described as "crimes against humanity." As we will see, Charny's classification is helpful in constructing a new typology just as his definition of genocide proved helpful in the previous chapter for defining the concept of genocidal social-practice genocide and fixing its limits.[4]

Although he also considered the question of intentionality, Dadrian constructed a typology more related to the *results* of genocidal practices. His classification in 1975 consisted of five categories:

1. Cultural genocide (Lemkin's "genocide by assimilation"). In my view, this could be included under the category of "ethnocide."
2. Latent genocide as a by-product of war. Dadrian gives the bombing of civilian populations in wartime as a typical example, which makes it similar to Charny's type (4) "killing of civilians in military actions" or the broader concept of crimes against humanity.
3. Retributive genocide: massacres that aim to punish a minority that challenges a dominant group. Dadrian states that a minority is not necessarily

a numerical minority. It may be any group that is socially subordinate in the balance of power.

4. Utilitarian genocide: that which is done with the purpose and result of gaining control of economic resources. It is thus related to Charny's type (3) "genocide in the course of colonization" and Chalk and Jonassohn's type (3) "to acquire economic wealth."
5. Optimal genocide: aimed at the total extermination of a population. Prototypical cases would be the Armenian genocide and the Nazis' attempt to exterminate the European Jews.

Unfortunately, Dadrian's types have too many overlapping variables (causes, outcomes, intentions) and so more than one category could be applied to the same historical event. In particular, "optimal genocide" can include any of the other four categories.

In contrast to Dadrian, in 1979 Helen Fein made a fundamental distinction between genocidal social practices carried out "before" and "after" the founding of the modern nation-state. Fein subdivided genocides committed "before" the emergence of the nation-state into two types: religious and ethnic. With respect to genocide committed "after" its emergence, Fein distinguished among three types:

1. To legitimize the existence of the state
2. To eliminate an indigenous group blocking the way to state expansion
3. To respond to a rebellion against the state[5]

We will return to the question of the nation-state later in this chapter, where I will argue that it is the emergence of the nation-state that marks the turning point in the development of modern genocide.

Despite being one of the first scholars to question the restrictive definition of the 1948 Genocide Convention, Leo Kuper—like many later critics—believed in the need to defend legality. This led him to base three of his five categories of genocide on the Convention's definition, while he groups the other two under "related or similar atrocities" because they are outside the scope of the text approved by the United Nations. His first three types, which correspond to the categories of genocide of the Convention, are

1. Genocides aimed at settling religious, racial, and ethnic differences
2. Genocides designed to terrorize the peoples conquered by a colonizing empire
3. Genocides designed to enforce or fulfill a political ideology

Kuper also distinguishes two types of "related atrocities":

4. Mass political killings
5. Attempts to destroy an economic class (including those that occurred under communism and "real socialism")[6]

Kuper's notion in type (1) of genocide as "dispute resolution" is questionable, and types (3) and (4) are difficult to tell apart. Nonetheless, Kuper's is the only classification of genocide that explicitly includes attempts to destroy a social class—as defined in the Marxist sense of a specific relationship to the means of production and the type of work done. But perhaps this type is only applicable when the people who embody those social relations are *physically* annihilated, as happened in Cambodia during the 1970s. However, the Cambodian genocide was in many ways unique, and, in any case, it is doubtful that social reorganization without the *physical* elimination of individuals embodying certain ways of relating to others counts as full-blown genocide or even as a genocidal social practice.

Although the possibility of genocide obviously increases under any totalitarian regime, the key question for Marxist thinkers and communist regimes is whether "the disappearance of the bourgeoisie" actually involves killing the middle classes or simply transforming them into manual workers. Marx, Lenin, and Gramsci all believed that the bourgeoisie must cease to be bourgeois by surrendering ownership and control of the means of production. None of them advocated anything more than expropriation and loss of social privileges. Conversely, physical destruction does not of itself guarantee that others—whatever their class origins might be—will not perpetuate the same social structures. Moreover, physical destruction is incompatible with Marxist humanism—although it is true that this philosophy only developed after Khrushchev's famous denouncement of Stalin at the Twentieth Congress of the Soviet Communist Party in 1956.

Arguably, the most powerful communist leaders of the twentieth century, Joseph Stalin and Mao Zedong, did not resort to killing as a strategy for political, economic, and social reconstruction, despite persecutions and even mass killings under both regimes.[7] For Pol Pot and the Khmer Rouge, however, the elimination of a materialistic, individualistic, and pro-capitalist urban population was a way of building socialism. In 1973 Pol Pot had noted that urban areas quickly eliminated socialism and reverted to their old ways as soon as the Khmer Rouge retreated from the cities. When he came to power in 1975, Pol Pot acted on the assumption that the social relations existing under capitalism could be destroyed only by annihilating those who embodied these relationships. The Cambodian genocide is therefore a clear ethical warning to socialist thinkers because—like Stalinism and Maoism—it was supported by a socialist ideology, expectations of social improvement, and the struggle for justice.

Continuing with our analysis of typologies, in 1999 Roger Smith made a basic distinction (derived from Kuper's work) between "external genocide" directed at other peoples, and "domestic genocide," which targets members of the society itself, a distinction that I will use in other parts of this book. Smith identified five types of genocide, which can be applied to both "external enemy" and the "internal enemy," namely:

1. Retributive genocide: where an invader punishes a conquered people or a society punishes members who represent a (possible) challenge to authority. It is used mainly as a rationalization (e.g., the Nazi genocides). Smith's prototypical example is the early military campaigns of Genghis Khan.
2. Institutional genocide: politically sanctioned mass murder in ancient and medieval times. It works without a challenge from the victims and is in fact intended to prevent retaliation. The prototypical example would be the Crusades.
3. Utilitarian genocide: where deaths enable the acquisition of land and other resources or improve the standard of living of the dominant people or class. Many examples can be found in the period of colonial domination and exploitation of indigenous peoples from the sixteenth to nineteenth centuries (and in Latin America into the twentieth century).
4. Monopolistic genocide: a tool for the elite to monopolize and centralize power, the most frequent cause of genocide in the twentieth century and early twenty-first century. Smith cites the genocides in Cambodia, Pakistan, and Armenia, although some cases seem to overlap with the next category.
5. Ideological genocide: the desire for a perfect society leads to the extermination of those considered "impure"—for example, the Crusades, Nazism, Stalinism, and Cambodia. Smith claims that ideological genocide is the chief category but fails to justify his assumption that ideology played only a minor role in premodern genocides but is at the core of modern genocides (particularly "domestic" genocide).[8]

Smith's categories provide some interesting insights (for example, the ideas of retributive genocide and utilitarian genocide). But, like Dadrian's types mentioned earlier, they tend to overlap, and this reduces their usefulness for comparative purposes.

Finally, Barbara Harff distinguished four basic types. In each case the main distinguishing feature is the type of social practice prior to the genocidal process, something that none of the other models takes into account and that proves to be extremely helpful.

1. Postwar and postimperial genocide: resulting from war and/or the weakening or collapse of empires. The disintegration of the Ottoman Empire led to the Armenian genocide during World War I, while the defeat of the German Empire in World War I gave rise to the Nazi genocide during World War II. The massacres following Genghis Khan's military campaigns of expansion would be a different example.
2. Postcolonial genocide: old ethnic and/or religious grievances resurface after decolonization, sometimes (but not always) leading to attempts to

form break-away states. Harff cites South Sudan, Biafra, Bangladesh, Burundi, and East Timor as prototypical cases.
3. Postcoup and postrevolutionary genocides: refers to annihilation by the right-wing or left-wing governments following a regime change. Harff includes Stalinism and Pol Pot's regime, as well as Latin American dictatorships.
4. Genocides of conquest: refers mostly to the annihilation of indigenous peoples in America, Australia, Africa, and Asia during the period of European colonization or in the new nation-states founded by European settlers.[9]

Harff's typology is very clear and provides a new perspective on the different processes leading to genocidal social practices. Although the processes she describes are not necessarily the main *causes* of genocide, the clarity and coherence of Harff's approach make it invaluable for constructing a typology of genocidal social practices.

Toward a Typology of Genocidal Social Practices

The aim of this chapter is to critically assess the most important typologies of genocide published to date in order to develop a new classification of genocidal social practices as specific ways of destroying and reorganizing social relations.

In my analysis of Kuper's typology, I argued that "modern genocide" requires the physical—not just symbolic—destruction of a human group. Following Fein's distinction between genocidal social practices carried out "before" and "after" the founding of the modern nation-state, I will define "modern genocide" as any genocidal social practice related to the destruction of a human group since the late fifteenth century, especially those involving Europeans or European settlers. "Modern genocide" is founded on four historical events:

1. The beginning of the first protomodern state in Spain with the marriage of Isabella of Castile and Ferdinand of Aragon in 1469.
2. The expulsion of Jews and Muslims from Spain (in 1492 and 1501, respectively) to achieve religious and political unity.
3. The simultaneous discovery of America by Europeans in 1492, followed by debates about the humanity of the Indians (e.g., did they have souls?). The debate had already commenced in the mid-fifteenth century with the beginning of the African slave trade and was to continue for nearly four centuries with regard to the populations of Africa, Asia, and Oceania.
4. The consolidation of the Inquisition and the logic of "interpellation" through the persecution of "witches" and "heretics." (Interpellation is the way in which ideological state apparatuses cause people to tacitly accept a particular view of themselves and of the world.)

Accordingly, I will consider deaths resulting from military conquests in the ancient and medieval world as forms of "pre-state genocide" (although the Crusades are perhaps a transitional case because of their strong ideological component).

Within modern genocide, or genocidal social practices, I will distinguish four basic types:

1. Constituent (foundational) genocide: aimed at destroying ideologically "unacceptable" populations and/or political opponents in a new nation-state.
2. Colonial genocide: the annihilation of indigenous populations, primarily to seize their land and natural resources and/or to subjugate them as a labor force. This differs from other types of "modern" genocide in that it clearly targets people perceived as being from outside the colonizers' society.[10]
3. Postcolonial genocide: specifically refers to the destruction of the local population by the colonizer during the struggle for national independence. However, if genocide results from power struggles between indigenous groups after independence, it should be classed as type (a).[11]
4. Reorganizing genocide: refers to destruction aimed at transforming hegemonic social relations *within* an existing nation-state. As we will see, this mode is dominated by the logic of concentration camps, so another name for this fourth type could be "concentration camp genocide." However, the term "reorganizing" includes other aspects that are not necessarily present in the "concentration camp" definition.[12]

Let us now examine each of these four types of genocide, or genocidal social practices, in more detail. The first type—constituent (foundational) genocide—is based on the assumption that genocidal social practices are an integral feature of modernity, rather than an irrational departure from it or a hangover from the past.[13] In most cases, the emergence of a new nation-state in Europe and the Americas (between the fifteenth and the nineteenth centuries) or in Africa (in the twentieth century) gave rise to a new social order within its territory.

Argentina was no exception. After seventy years of civil wars following the May Revolution of 1810 until the definitive formation of the Argentine state in 1880, the new nation annihilated three large population groups: (1) indigenous peoples, particularly through military "campaigns" in Patagonia and the northeastern region of Chaco (1870–1884); (2) black descendants of African slaves—who comprised up to 50 percent of the population in some provinces at the time of independence; the men were used as cannon fodder in the Argentine War of Independence against Spain (1810–1818) as well as in the War of the Triple Alliance against Paraguay (1865–1870), and—because most Afro-Argentines lived in appalling conditions—they bore the brunt of the cholera epidemics of 1861 and 1864, and the yellow fever epidemic of 1871; (3) *caudillos*, or provincial leaders, many of them half-castes or *mestizos*, who still supported local autonomy over centralized power.[14]

In short, constituent (foundational) genocide aims to define or redefine the power relations in a particular territory by crystallizing or realigning latent power structures, or by creating them from scratch.

The second type—colonial genocide—targets people perceived as being *outside* the colonizer's own society. This form of genocide was particularly common during the so-called Scramble for Africa (1881–1914), a period of rapid colonization by the European powers. Prototypical examples would be the annihilation of the Herero people of South-West Africa by Germany between 1904 and 1907, and the Italian atrocities against civilians during the conquest of Abyssinia (1935–1940). However, similar cases can be found at earlier periods of history, for example during the Spanish colonization of the Americas.

This form of genocide is related to constituent (foundational) genocide, but it is also different in several ways. It is part of the logic of territorial conquest under capitalism and serves an entirely economic purpose. Consequently, not all capitalist colonial domination involves genocide. Rather, genocide develops as a response when indigenous peoples actively resist or otherwise hinder or obstruct the economic development of a colony. Often they are condemned to annihilation through confiscation of their land and destruction of their livelihood, leading to starvation or malnutrition. Some of these practices survived in the twentieth century and can still be found in the twenty-first century in the few regions of the planet that are not completely controlled by global capitalism, such as some tribal areas in the rain forests of the Brazilian Amazon and Paraguay.[15]

The third type—postcolonial genocide—is found across a wide range of historical and political contexts. Typical examples are the counterinsurgency wars in Indochina, Algeria, and Vietnam between 1945 and 1975. The operating principle was similar: a link between the old colonial rule and the new circumstances of the Cold War.[16] In the global war on communism, counterinsurgency doctrine drew on the ethnopolitical figure created by the Nazis—the Judeo-Bolshevik—to denigrate colonial populations, using images that fused political and racial stereotypes.

Some of these images reappear in the fourth and last type—reorganizing genocide—and especially in the case of Guatemala. Central America was never officially annexed by the United States as Indochina and Algeria were by the French. However, the U.S. government assumed an active role in expanding capitalism throughout the region in the 1950s. Guatemala, Nicaragua, and El Salvador became informal colonies run by groups of family oligarchies—for example, the "fourteen Salvadoran families."[17] Land belonging to indigenous peasant communities was cleared to make way for large-scale agricultural estates and the production of export crops. Those who resisted eviction were branded as communists and murdered in United States–supported counterinsurgency operations. That was how—especially in Guatemala but also in El Salvador—the discourse of the elite came to equate "indigenous" with "subversive."[18]

During the Cold War, South America depended less obviously on the United States than did Central America. Although the Southern Cone countries (Argentina, Brazil, Chile, Bolivia, Paraguay, and Uruguay) clearly underwent reorganizing genocides in the 1970s and 1980s, there was no appeal to racism to stigmatize the victims—a fact that was later used to deny the genocidal nature of the killings.

Reorganizing genocide acts specifically on existing social relations. However, the disappearance of those who embody certain ways of relating to others would not be enough to prevent similar relationships in the future if it were not for the simultaneous use of denouncers/informers to provoke mistrust among friends and neighbors, thereby destroying grassroots solidarity as well as political opposition. Under reorganizing genocide, murder is a means to an end rather than an end in itself. The real aim is to "reorganize" society by breaking down "relations of reciprocity" among its members—a theme that is developed at length in the next chapter—and replacing them with new forms of political, economic, ideological, and cultural power.

Reorganizing Genocide and the Logic of the Concentration Camp: Destroying and Reorganizing Social Relations

This book focuses on a specific type of genocidal social practice that I have labeled as "reorganizing genocide" because its purpose is to restructure the society of an existing nation-state *from within*. This restructuring aims to modify social bonds and relationships, social conventions, aspects of daily life, forms of political mediation—in short, to transform the concrete and abstract operations of power within a given society.

If the technology of power that characterizes the modern world is the destruction and reorganization of social relations, the instrument through which this type of genocide operates is the concentration camp. Concentration camps appeared in the late nineteenth century as temporary measures within wartime states of emergency and were used by the British in South Africa to prevent civilian noncombatants from helping the Boer guerrilla forces during the Second Boer War (1899–1902). However, although more than 26,000 women and children died of disease and malnutrition in these camps, it was the Nazis who first realized their potential as instruments for spreading terror. According to the Italian political philosopher Giorgio Agamben, "The entire Third Reich can be considered a state of exception that lasted twelve years. In this sense, modern totalitarianism can be defined as the establishment, by means of the state of exception, of a legal civil war that allows for the physical elimination not only of political adversaries but of entire categories of citizens who for some reason cannot be integrated into the political system."[19] Agamben considers the concentration camp as the "nomos of modernity" in the sense that the modern nation-state—even under democracy—cannot survive without centers in which normal legal guarantees and protections are suspended and basic rights are denied. The Nazis' innovation was to include the concentration camp as part of a strategy for transforming society as a whole.

One way that reorganizing genocide differs from, say, foundational or colonial genocide is that the metaphor of a *struggle between nations* is replaced by medical metaphors. The Nazis themselves claimed that in killing Jews and other population groups, they were removing a tumor from the body of Germany. Nevertheless, it should be remembered that the Nazis committed other types of genocide as well. As Guillermo Levy and Tomás Borovinsky have rightly pointed out, Nazism is not a unitary political and social phenomenon.[20] On the contrary, it is a historical knot that is difficult to disentangle, including now the myth of having founded a new state—the Third Reich, which was to last for a thousand years; the colonial expansion of Germany, which had been late in achieving statehood; and a strategic plan to reorganize Europe and the Soviet Union as well as Germany itself along racial lines.

All this was possible because Nazi racism was "politicized racism." It was the Nazis' willingness to repress communism that persuaded Hindenburg and the conservative elite to help them into power, and German communists were among the first people to be sent to concentration camps. However, between 1933 and 1936, the Nazis' list of political dissidents came to include not only communists, socialists, and anarchists, but dissidents and oppositionists from within National Socialism itself, together with homosexuals, Jehovah's Witnesses, and of course Jews, who were to become the main target of Nazism once war broke out. In the period 1936–1938, the emphasis was still on punishing political, "social," and common criminals, sexual deviants, and conscientious objectors, but the images of the "thieving Gypsy" and the "Judeo-Bolshevik," a figure that will be explored in later chapters, were gradually racializing crime and criminalizing race.

With the German invasion of Poland in September 1939 and the Soviet Union in June 1941, racism played an increasingly central role in Nazi policies. Nazi discourse was now directed not only against Jews and Gypsies, but against other "non-Aryan" peoples, especially Slavs. The Slavs occupied territory that the Reich needed for its expansion in the East and were treated in much the same way as colonized peoples had been treated during the Scramble for Africa. However, the Jews—and more specifically the ethnopolitical "Jewish Bolshevik"—were killed because they were seen as a threat to the German social body. As the Reich expanded, the "reorganizing" character of Nazism required not only the material annihilation of the Jewish Bolshevik but the symbolic annihilation of Jewry and Jewishness from all the occupied territories.

So what was the essential Jewish characteristic the Nazis wished to eradicate from Europe? As Zygmunt Bauman has pointed out, before the modern state of Israel came into being in 1948, the Jews were a people "straddling modernity" with one foot in each country and their soul in humanity.

It was precisely the Jews' internationalism and humanism, together with their failure to form a nation-state of their own in an age of nationalism, which meant—in the Nazis' view—that they could not be absorbed into the new order. Also, the socialist movement had been historically internationalist and so, in Hitler's mind, Judaism and communism were inseparable. The Nazis felt they were waging an ideological crusade to save Europe and Western civilization from the "Asian barbarians" of the Soviet Union and their allegedly Jewish leaders.

The genocidal "reorganization" of society first practiced by the Nazis utilized techniques that would later be developed during the counterinsurgency campaigns against guerrilla and national liberation movements in the 1950s and 1960s before the military seized power in Argentina in 1976 with the aim of "reorganizing" Argentine society. Unlike the Nazi genocide, the so-called Dirty War in Argentina was, in fact, a politically motivated genocide that made no attempt to hide its goals behind the nineteenth-century concept of race and so did not need to waste time and resources persecuting ethnic minorities. That the Argentine military were clear about their goals from the outset can be seen in the name they gave to their new regime: the "Process of National Reorganization." So it was that in the Republic of Argentina, an already existing nation-state that had been built—like most nation-states—on genocide, the de facto government of the military dictatorship proposed to "re-found" the state on a new social, political, and cultural basis. The tool chosen to carry out this reorganization of society was the concentration camp.

"Process of National Reorganization" has been rejected as a euphemism by many historians. Instead, they prefer the terms "military dictatorship" or "Dirty War" to define this period in Argentina's history. However, both these alternatives are actually more confusing and euphemistic than "Process of National Reorganization." There were many military dictatorships in Argentina during the twentieth century. However, none of the previous dictatorships proposed a "social reorganization" of this magnitude. Similarly, "Dirty War" is a misnomer that wrongly implies a civil war in which casualties are more likely to be soldiers than civilians.[21]

One commonly accepted way of understanding the period from 1974 to 1983 (which conventionally starts with the military coup of March 24, 1976, but in fact really begins with Perón's death in July 1974, or earlier) is that it was the culmination of a series of military suspensions of civilian government (1930,

1943, 1955, 1962, 1966). But this denies the qualitative abyss between the Argentine military's political project in the 1970s—national and social reorganization—and its previous policies and practice, even though, in some cases, the same people were involved in both.

The specific details of the Nazis' and the Argentines' genocides will be analyzed in detail in later chapters. However, in the process we should not to lose sight of the strategic objective of this book, which is to unravel possible continuities between these two events in order to understand modern genocide, a phenomenon that drove Raphael Lemkin to create a new name for it despite the presence of mass killings throughout history.

If a new word was needed in the twentieth century to describe a new type of annihilation, perhaps it was because the reorganizing genocide of the concentration camps lies, as Agamben has rightly pointed out, at the heart of our social order, forming the "hidden matrix" of modernity.

3

Reconciling the Contradictions of Modernity

Equality, Sovereignty, Autonomy, and Genocidal Social Practices

> Ulla bar Koshev was sought by the [Roman] government. He fled to Lod, to the house of Rabi Joshua ben Levi. [Roman troops] came and surrounded the town. They said: If you do not hand him over we will destroy the town. R. Joshua ben Levi went up to him [Ulla], persuaded him [to submit], and handed him over. The prophet Elijah, of blessed memory, had been accustomed to reveal himself to R. Joshua ben Levi; but he stopped visiting him. R. Joshua fasted many fasts and Elijah appeared again. [In answer to why he had stayed away, Elijah said:] Shall I reveal myself to betrayers? He replied: But have I not acted upon a rabbinic teaching? Elijah replied: Is this a teaching for pious men?
>
> –Jerusalem Talmud (Terumot 8:4)

In recent years a growing body of literature across various disciplines has been concerned with the concept of modernity. Writers in areas as diverse as law, history, sociology, philosophy, aesthetics, and design now routinely use it—often in quite different and even contradictory ways. For the purposes of this discussion, modernity means a power system together with a set of specific practices (whose precise details vary according to historical context) for destroying and reconstructing social relations. However, even in this restricted sense, modernity is still a broad enough notion to have different (and even contradictory) manifestations. These practices, or "diagrams of power," as Michel Foucault calls them (see chapter 1), act together as a "technology of power" to construct hegemony—in other words, to establish the dominance of one social group over another. They can be used not only to control populations but to reconstruct their very identity.

This chapter starts from Foucault's analysis of the theoretical and political features of the modern power system.[1] I use this perspective to explore the disturbing notion that genocidal social practices have arisen during the modern period as a part of a new technology of power. Thus, although such practices are not inevitable, they are always latent in modernity—what Zygmunt Bauman calls a "logical possibility."[2] We will also examine some of the contradictions that arose as modernity became consolidated as a system of power and the role that genocidal social practices have played in attempting to solve these contradictions.

Broadly speaking, the emergence of modernity as the hegemonic system of power gave rise almost immediately to a series of contradictions around three main issues: *equality*, *sovereignty*, and *autonomy*. These issues reflected structural changes in the ways Europeans experienced and represented the world (and therefore themselves) during the transition from feudalism to capitalism in the eighteenth century, while the contradictions resulted from a mismatch between the explicit discourse of the new system of power and the way power was exercised in practice. In time, these contradictions began to have dysfunctional or, at least, unexpected effects that threatened to undermine the legitimacy, consensus, and rationality of the system itself. It was the need to reconcile these contradictions that caused the technology of power to evolve.

Here I will consider contradictions related to all three of the main issues. However, I will focus mostly on the question of autonomy as it is more directly connected with the role of genocidal social practices within the power structures of the modern world.

The Contradictions of Modernity

The Issue of Equality

From the last quarter of the eighteenth century onward, the bourgeoisie competed with the nobility for power within the emerging nation-states of Europe. Traditionally, feudalism and Christianity had divided society into three castes or "estates"—nobility, clergy, and commoners—each with different duties and privileges. Later, thinkers such as Jean Jacques Rousseau, Adam Smith, Immanuel Kant, and Karl Marx developed the ideas of earlier liberals such as Locke and Montesquieu in an effort to legitimize the aspirations of the rising middle classes by giving legal and symbolic status to the notion of human equality.

The notion that all men were citizens with rights (rather than privileges that could be taken away by an absolute monarch) rested on the assumption that all men were equal (at least symbolically, if not economically). However, although the Declaration of the Rights of Man and of the Citizen of 1789 declared fundamental rights, not only for French citizens but for "all men without exception," it did not recognize women or slaves as citizens. Thus, in a sense, the declaration and other works that followed subverted the possibility of social empowerment and greater autonomy in social relationships.

In *The Social Contract* (1762) the French philosopher Jean-Jacques Rousseau famously noted that "man is born free, and everywhere he is in chains."[3] As the notion of equality became more widely accepted in Europe after the American and French revolutions, philosophers also became increasingly interested in explaining the causes of human inequality. Rousseau himself believed that individual liberty should be subordinated to the "general will" of the community. However, he considered that human beings do not have the intellectual capabilities to rationalize the general good, and so the "general will" is impossible to determine. However the Scottish social philosopher and economist Adam Smith (1723–1790) believed that the best way to benefit society as a whole is by acting in accordance with one's own self-interest. Smith accordingly advocated self-regulating markets free from state intervention. Adam Smith explained differences in wealth or power in terms of the accumulated work of previous generations. This helped in understanding how inequalities had arisen, but it could not justify the policies of inequality that continued to be applied by modern nation-states. How then could discriminatory state policies be justified?

One attempt to resolve the contradiction between "natural equality" and actual inequality was the doctrine of racism. This questioned the notion of natural equality and tried to set limits on citizenship. The German philosopher Immanuel Kant (1724–1804), for example, stated in his *Observations on the Feeling of the Beautiful and the Sublime* (1764) that "the Negroes of Africa have by nature no feeling that rises above the trifling . . . even though among the whites some continually rise aloft from the lowest rabble, and through superior gifts earn respect in the world. So fundamental is the difference between these two races of man, and it appears to be as great in regard to mental capacities as in color."[4] In line with other thinkers of the time, Kant held that Adam and Eve had been Caucasian and that other races had developed because of a degeneration caused by environmental factors, such as climate and poor food.[5] Kant argued elsewhere that we cannot simply take the precepts of natural law from our hearts. The "good use of reason" was also required.

The nineteenth century, however, gave rise to a more radical form of racism. Although he grew up in an aristocratic, Catholic milieu among people who despised the ideals of the French Revolution, Joseph Arthur Comte de Gobineau (1816–1882) openly challenged the Judeo-Christian doctrine that all human beings shared common ancestors in Adam and Eve. It is in his book *An Essay on the Inequality of the Human Races* (1853–1855) where Gobineau developed his theory of the Aryan master race.

Meanwhile, the English biologist, philosopher, and sociologist Herbert Spencer (1820–1903) was busy elaborating a developmental theory of species and race, which he published in 1855 in his *Principles of Psychology*. It was

Spencer who coined the expression "survival of the fittest" to explain Darwin's concept of natural selection, and it became the cornerstone of Social Darwinism, a social theory that power and wealth of individuals and even whole nations is a consequence of their genetic endowment.

The German physician Gerhard Wagner (1888–1939) pushed this cynical theory to its logical conclusion during the Nazi era. Dr. Wagner was the leader of the National Socialist German Physicians' Federation (NSDÄB) when Hitler came to power and became leader of the Reich Physicians' Chamber in 1935. On September 12, 1935, Wagner announced in a speech that the Nazis would soon introduce a "law for the protection of German blood" preventing mixed marriages between Jews and 'Aryans." This is how he justified his proposal:

> The doctrine of equality also denied racial boundaries and especially in the case of Europe the boundaries between Europeans and Jews. The result has been a growing mixture with Jewish blood, completely foreign to us. This growing illegitimacy was bound to bring direct consequences . . . because the special racial characteristics of the Jewish people . . . made such a mixture extremely harmful. By contrast, National Socialism has begun to recognize once again that the foundation of all cultural life is the natural and God-given inequality of men and it draws the necessary conclusions from this. Politically, the guiding idea is to promote a hierarchy based on the inherently different value of different individuals; as a consequence of this, responsibility in all areas has once again become possible. Biologically speaking, this means fighting racial degeneration in order to favor the able-bodied and healthy over the unfit as well as rejecting mixed blood or the influence of any alien race.[6]

Although Gerhard Wagner was mainly concerned with eradicating "life unworthy of life" by sterilizing the mentally handicapped and preventing "the infiltration of Jewish blood into the German national body,"[7] the Nazis quickly expanded this definition to include Gypsies, Slavs, Blacks, American Indians, tribal groups, colonized peoples, "mulattos," Arabs, Muslims, Jehovah's Witnesses, homosexuals, political dissidents, and the homeless, among others. Thus, scientific racism—whether based on the earlier degeneration theories or later evolutionary theories—undermined one of the most enlightened and fertile concepts of the modern age: the notion of natural equality.

Once a belief in racial hierarchy had become politically respectable, it was a short step from positive eugenics—for example, giving awards to mothers of Aryan children and discouraging contact with "inferior races"—to negative eugenics through forced sterilization and, later, mass annihilation.[8] However, although the Nazis took such policies to extremes, other countries shared these ideas. Racial segregation was widespread in the United States until the 1960s; as early as 1924, the State of Virginia passed laws criminalizing marriages between "whites" and "coloreds" and introducing forced sterilization of "mental deficients" and the "mentally ill." In some European colonies, racist theories led to the extensive exploitation and murder of unequal Others.[9]

The Question of Sovereignty

Although the term "sovereignty" commonly refers to independence and self-government, here it is used in the more literal sense of the power or right of a sovereign to rule. According to Foucault, one of the main ways of disciplining populations in the modern world is through biopower—in other words, "technologies of domination [that] act essentially on the body, and classify and objectify individuals."[10] Foucault argues that it is "the emergence of biopower that inscribes [racism] in the mechanisms of the State . . . as the basic mechanism of power, as it is exercised in modern States."[11]

The feudal technology of power was based on the sovereign's right to "kill or let live." In accordance with the doctrine known as the divine right of kings, feudal kings derived their right to rule directly from God and were not accountable to their subjects. But the modern need to justify power rationally gave rise to a new technology based on the protection of life rather than the threat of death. Rulers were expected to improve the quality of life of their citizens through improved public health, education, and justice in return for which the population surrendered a good deal of its freedom. But this in turn gave rise to a new problem: how to justify the "need" to kill when the state was, almost by definition, expected to guarantee life?

The solution was as follows. In the seventeenth century the term "body politick" described a politically organized group of people under a single government. In the modern era, this medical metaphor was extended to include the notions of "normal" and "pathological" groups of people, thus undermining the doctrine of natural equality and replacing it with notions of social hygiene derived from scientific racism: the pathological must be eradicated to defend the normal. Murder, genocide, and extermination were thus justified as ways to preserve the human species from physical and mental degeneration, and the legitimacy of state murder was reinstated under the formula "live or let die."

Of course, it is impossible to discriminate against large numbers of people, let alone murder them, without causing moral outrage in a population brought up to believe in equality and the sanctity of life. But these moral barriers can usually be broken down by portraying others as a threat to public health and safety that requires drastic measures. This argument is commonly used by the perpetrators both during and after the event to justify looting, rape, torture, and murder.

A government that brands certain groups as parasites that cannot be taken on board its political and cultural project is on a fast track to genocide. The genocidal process tends to move through predictable stages: first branding and harassing the victims, then isolating and weakening them before ultimately destroying them. And this process is experienced as "purification." Branding distinguishes the "sick" from the "healthy"; harassment desensitizes the perpetrators, preparing them to commit worse atrocities; isolation destroys the victims' social ties, making them dependent on their captors, who can then break their physical and psychological resistance more easily. Finally, the "social cancer" is removed as the victims are made to disappear, both physically and symbolically. The social body has been cured: biological images help the perpetrators to explain the inexplicable, not only to a hypothetical "moral other" but also to their private consciences.

The Nazis took the desire for political, genetic, and ethnic cleansing to extremes. Their attempt to create a racially pure society shook the very foundations of the post-Enlightenment technology of power. But the same logic was used until recently by Latin American governments to eliminate their political opponents and can be found today among those that exclude, harass, and murder African immigrants in France and Germany or street children in Brazil. Unfortunately, the outrage caused by the Nazi genocide does not seem to extend to these cases. All too often emphasis on the uniqueness of the Holocaust diverts attention from a technology of power that underpins many other modern states.

The Question of Autonomy

As mentioned earlier, feudalism assigned people to different social classes according to their birth and gave each class different privileges and obligations. The modern concept of autonomy was necessary for building social relationships based on equality. The absolute right of the feudal monarch was replaced by the need for consensus based on a responsible use of reason. Within the modern liberal paradigm, Jean Jacques Rousseau is the most extreme exponent of the bourgeois liberal vision of equality and the "social contract" as a source of legitimate authority, while Immanuel Kant emphasizes the role of reason in human action and human autonomy as a goal to be achieved.

I have suggested how discriminatory social and economic policies can be legitimated by a hierarchical and naturalist vision of social reality. But this only happens when such a vision is imposed on us by others or, as Kant put it, "heteronomously." The medieval Christian Church exercised a tight control over the ways the world could be understood, including the natural world. Because the Church defended a closed system of knowledge in which phenomena had allegorical, metaphysical, and mystical meanings, any challenge to its authority could have disturbing philosophical, metaphysical, and even epistemological consequences. Galileo was imprisoned in 1637 for saying that the

Earth moves around the Sun because this implied that man was not the center of the universe.

In the late eighteenth and early nineteenth centuries, it was the Roman Catholic Church's perceived opposition to scientific research and technological innovation that drove liberals to secular thinking and "instrumental reason," even though the latter often reduced human beings to mere objects of manipulation.[12] Secular thinkers challenged the belief—born in the monasteries of Europe—that man is incapable of self-determination. However, equality and natural liberty implied a model of power as well as a commitment to individual freedom. In particular, the concept of *autonomy*, so necessary for modern scientific development, was to prove difficult to achieve in political terms.

Autonomy comes from the Greek *auto-* "self" *nomos*, "law" (i.e., "to give oneself one's own law") and refers to our capacity for self-determination. However, there have been many debates in modern philosophy as to what this actually means. Autonomy is often defined in opposition to natural (or eternal) law, which, according to Saint Thomas Aquinas (1225–1274), is a God-given knowledge woven into our nature that is meant to govern our lives.[13] In contrast, nineteenth-century liberals held that because individuals have different interests, laws should be based on a consensus about what will benefit the greatest number of people. Giving oneself one's own law thus means accepting that the law is a human construction, created freely through reason and *consent*. However, the destruction of traditional structures and truths that allowed the middle classes to achieve social and political power in the nineteenth century was to create serious problems for bourgeois governance in the twentieth century.

Both Rousseau and Kant considered that autonomy was threatened not only by the existing *social order* of nobility and Church but by the *natural order* of instincts and impulses. Thus, Rousseau argued that a citizen could only pursue his true interest by acting unselfishly even if this benefited somebody else in the short term, while Kant also pointed out the danger of basing decisions on irrational thoughts or obsessions. But the biggest problem was with the social contract itself. Although Rousseau and Kant argued for a state that was both rational and voluntary, they generally identified the *common good* with the postcontract status quo—the bourgeois state—which excluded most of the population from power. The property qualification for voters meant, for example, that in the so-called golden age of British parliamentary democracy of the mid-nineteenth century, only 7 percent of the population could vote.

In fact, the social contract on which the bourgeois state was supposedly founded was a metaphor. The original consensus—if such a thing had ever existed—had long since vanished and was simply an assumption, as Rousseau himself recognized in his *Discourse on Inequality* (1754). The bourgeois state itself was founded on deep social inequalities. Marx used the term "original accumulation of capital" to describe the role played by earlier colonial conquests and plunder in the rise of industrial capitalism in Europe. This accumulation, which predated any social contract, had permitted both private ownership of the means of production and the existence of a mass of "free" laborers, that is, former agricultural laborers and hand-loom weavers now unemployed because of more efficient, capitalist methods of farming and textile making. As Marx noted, "freely negotiated" contracts between buyers and sellers of labor were "free" only in a formal sense since the buyer owned the factory, the raw materials, and the tools, while the seller, without work, faced starvation.

Even the miseries of unregulated capitalism, however, could not persuade people to give up the egalitarian and libertarian ideals of the French Revolution. Despite the restoration of the monarchy, the Church, and a landowning aristocracy in France and the Napoleonic Empire after Napoleon's defeat at Waterloo in 1815, the forces of conservatism would never recover the absolute authority they had enjoyed under feudalism. The new autonomy of the bourgeoisie created not only a new relationship with knowledge through science and technology but also new forms of political and social interaction that were gradually adopted by the disenfranchised working classes. These new forms of association were based on what the Swiss psychologist Jean Piaget (1896–1980) called "reciprocal relationships between peers," that is, the ability to see others as equals.[14] Moreover, autonomy did not just mean individual autonomy but autonomous social groups and organizations, such as trade unions and friendly societies, which were independent from the state.

More recently, the concept of autonomy has come under attack from several quarters. Feminists, for example, have pointed out that liberal notions of autonomy ignore the ways that individuals are situated in a community. Nevertheless, besides serving as an ideological linchpin of bourgeois societies, the concept of autonomy has also proved to have humanistic and revolutionary potential and is fundamental in explaining the revolutionary movements of the nineteenth and twentieth centuries.

Autonomy becomes an instrument of social control only when it is granted to some and denied to others. It is easy to understand why this occurs. If the principles of equality and freedom, in the form of autonomy, were taken to their logical conclusion, the modern liberal order would be overturned by the innumerable wretches of this world. By exercising their right to self-determination, these "outsiders" would impose a more egalitarian order and consensus. Hence we have the constant conflict between capitalism and democracy, which has given rise to all sorts of solutions from limited franchise democracy, through various paternalistic and dictatorial regimes, to fascism and the corporative state.

Society in the bourgeois state was organized through a network of disciplinary institutions. Prisons, factories, workhouses, asylums, hospitals, universities, schools, and even the family were all designed to keep the newly acquired autonomy in check. Unless the population was constantly monitored and divided, autonomy tended to produce profound social unrest. Often, the disciplinary network was not enough to stem the tide of self-determination among different political, social, and ethnic groups. A clear example is the Revolutions of 1848, which spread to over fifty countries in Europe and Latin America and led to the abolition of serfdom in Austria and Hungary. But throughout the nineteenth and twentieth centuries, tensions between authority and autonomy were never far below the surface.

Reorganizing Genocide

Earlier we saw how racism had made it possible to solve the contradictions associated with equality and sovereignty. However, during the nineteenth century, the discourse of racism was still not able to confront the notion of autonomous social relations—a notion ultimately founded on *mutual respect.* It was not until the twentieth century that a new and horrifying solution to this problem emerged. Although it acquired its most extreme form under the Nazis, the use of *reorganizing genocide* as a tool of social engineering was to transform many modern states. The medical metaphors of ethnic cleansing and social hygiene were much more than a scientific justification of racist policies. They implied a profound destruction and reshaping of social relations.

Here, I should make clear that *reorganizing genocide* is different from other types of genocide (pre-state, constituent, colonial, postcolonial) in that it aims to destroy both materially and symbolically "the enemy within." The Others to be exterminated are no longer barbarians or savages living in Europe's colonies or in the frontier territories of the Americas—alien peoples construed as both exotic and inferior. Instead, it is our next-door neighbors—sometimes more educated and civilized than ourselves—who are stigmatized as part of a massive conspiracy to undermine the biological health of the species.

In other words, the Others have to be eliminated because they are *dangerous* but not necessarily because they are *inferior*—at least not in the sense of being backward. And, at the same time, reorganizing genocide does not simply target a social force or social group. It aims to eliminate a specific type of social relationship, namely, peer relationships. These relationships between equal partners are based on mutual solidarity and are independent of any externally imposed authority.[15]

Reorganizing genocide comes to the fore with the Nazis, although it plays a marginal role in some of Stalin's policies. One controversial hypothesis (explored later in this book) is that the presence of such peer relationships was the common thread linking the often very different victim groups of Nazism. Once one starts to think in terms of relationships of autonomy and free association, a common identity among these victim groups begins to emerge.

The victims of Nazism were socially autonomous in various ways: culturally, politically, sexually, and in the workplace. Even though they came from very different cultural and social backgrounds, the inmates of the Nazi concentration camps (particularly during the period 1933–1938) all had one thing in common: they all behaved in ways that were "undisciplined" according to mainstream institutions and ideologies.

Once introduced by the Nazis, reorganizing genocide reappeared in various parts of the world throughout the rest of the century. Under the military dictatorship in Argentina after 1976, reorganizing genocide took an unusual and particularly dramatic form. As we will see in later chapters, the destruction of autonomous social relations remained an *implicit* goal of Nazi policy, one that can be deduced from the ways the Nazis construed their victims. However, the issue of autonomy becomes *explicit* under Argentina's military dictatorship.

One official document clearly stating that people were being victimized for making use of their autonomy was a pamphlet distributed in 1977 by the Argentine Ministry of Education entitled "Subversion in the Field of Education." This pointed out "the evident offensive in the area of children's literature, the aim of which is to send a type of message starting from the child and which may enable him or her to become self-educated on the basis of liberty and choice." The same official pamphlet states that "the intention of Marxist publishers is to offer books to accompany children in their struggle to delve into the world of things and the world of adults, to help them not to be afraid of freedom, to help them to love, to fight, to assert themselves, to defend their ego against the ego which parents and institutions try to impose upon them on many occasions, consciously or unconsciously victims of a system which has tried to make them in its own image."[16]

This point of view was shared by General Acdel Vilas, who headed Operation Independence against the ERP (Ejército Revolucionario del Pueblo, or People's Revolutionary Army) in the province of Tucumán starting in December 1974. Although the ERP murdered dozens of soldiers, policemen, government officials, and executives of foreign companies during the early 1970s and "occupied" a third of the province of Tucumán in 1974, the use of state terror tactics by the army during Operation Independence was the first attempt in Argentina to carry out a reorganizing genocidal social practice. Here is how Vilas explained the meaning of the term "subversion": "If the military allowed corrosive elements—psychoanalysts, psychiatrists, Freudians, etc.—to proliferate, stirring up people's consciences and questioning the roots of the nation and the family, we would be defeated. . . . From then on every teacher or student that proved to be enrolled in the Marxist cause was considered subversive and, as could hardly be otherwise, he [*sic*] was subjected to the appropriate military sanctions." There are dozens of similar statements on record, and many of them will be examined in detail in the chapters devoted to Argentina. Here I simply wish to point out the explicit way in which autonomy was constructed as dangerous by the Argentine military. This hostility toward autonomy even led to a ban on the teaching of Cantor's set theory in university math classes since conservative Christian theologians saw it as challenging traditional views about the nature of God.

Symbolic Enactments

As mentioned in chapter 1, a key characteristic of reorganizing genocide is that the perpetrators seek to annihilate their enemies not just materially but also symbolically, forcing the survivors to deny their own identity. Their disappearance from memory is maintained by what I have called *symbolic enactments*—the ways through which postgenocide discourse distorts the nature of the victims and denies that the social relationships in which they took part ever existed.[17]

By symbolic enactments I mean a process of reformulation or redefinition of the history and, most importantly, of the collective memory of past events. Although the majority of victims in Argentina did not take part in acts of violence and were killed quite simply because they acted "differently," public opinion after Argentina's return to democracy in 1983 was soon divided between those who maintained that "they [the victims] must have done something wrong" and those that replied "they had done nothing." This debate about the victims' possible guilt or innocence distracted attention away from the real reasons for their disappearance. At the same time, it maintained the effects of terror and prevented the survivors from reappropriating their old way of life.

In his commentary on the "Wolf Man," Freud proposed a concept that describes this process well: *repudiation.*[18] Unlike repression, which removes uncomfortable experiences from consciousness but leaves them intact, repudiation allows them to remain conscious, but empties them of meaning. In Argentina, it was collective repudiation rather than repression that allowed uncomfortable memories of helplessness and the guilt of survival or collaboration to be erased by lies, silence, and terror.

The Role of Betrayal in Remodeling Social Relationships

An important feature of modern genocidal societies is that the definition of "subversive" is often left ambiguous in order to justify arbitrary arrests and detentions without trial. Moreover, even though the perpetrators presumably know why they have arrested a particular person and not another, in practice the grounds for the arrest may not be made clear either to the victims or to their families. This was especially true in Argentina between 1976 and 1983 but also occurred in Nazi-occupied Europe. This ambiguity is no accident. It is one of a series of interlocking techniques designed to undermine solidarity and create an atomized society with submissive relationship to power.

Another way in which genocidal regimes undermine solidarity is through the uncertainty created by the use of informers. Once a person can be arrested for almost anything, even for listening to foreign radio broadcasts, the best way to escape being accused of a particular activity is to denounce a neighbor for doing the same thing. Denunciations are encouraged by all modern genocidal regimes because of their effectiveness in destroying social networks. In a society where anyone might be an informer, nobody knows for sure who can be trusted.

However, fear is not the only factor at work. It is true that in Nazi-occupied Poland, many Poles—and even some Jews—became paid informers in order to survive and help their families to survive. However, Robert Gellately's research into the records of the Gestapo shows that most informers were unpaid. The vast majority of denunciations were made by neighbors, acquaintances, co-workers, and even relatives, many of whom were motivated by greed, jealousy, or a desire for revenge rather than by fear.[19] Others were sadists enjoying power over the life and death in the name of loyalty to the regime. Whatever the different motives for betrayal, however, the population ended up forming a social order in which, paradoxically, the only "reliable" interlocutors were the Gestapo and the security services.

It is interesting to note how the Argentinean perpetrators of genocide adapted "divide and rule" techniques developed by the Nazis. In the field of education, for example, parents were encouraged to denounce teachers and students, and students were encouraged to denounce one another. In a document entitled "Instructions for Detecting Signs of Subversion in Your Children's Education" distributed by the military government in 1976, parents were warned to watch out for words like "dialogue, bourgeoisie, proletariat, Latin America, capitalism." Although words such as bourgeoisie or proletariat are commonly associated with Marxist thinking, the word "dialogue" implies a type of social relationship that goes well beyond any ideological or partisan boundaries.

In Nazi Germany the traditional German academic approach to education was dumbed down to a more emotional level. Uncritical acceptance of Nazism's racist and xenophobic outlook was regarded as essential for character building and, as one German teacher noted, "those pupils who are in positions of leadership . . . often display unmannerly behavior and laziness at school."[20]

In Argentina, however, the approach was different. "Instructions for Detecting Signs of Subversion" also argued that "group work . . . , which has replaced personal responsibility, can be easily used to depersonalize the child, accustoming him to being lazy and laying him open to indoctrination by students previously selected and trained to 'pass on' ideas."[21] Now, group work seems to be much less a Marxist strategy than a way to generate cooperation among peers. By banning group work in the name of "personal responsibility," the Argentine military showed they understood that promoting individualism is just as effective for social control as regimentation.

Another "divide and rule" technique that the Argentine military learned from Nazism was collective punishment. Together with denouncements, collective punishments were described by survivors of Nazi concentration camps as one of the most effective techniques for destroying solidarity among inmates.[22] This disciplinary mechanism was actively promoted by the Argentine military dictatorship in schools, as can be seen in the Ministry of Education's curriculum materials for "Moral and Civic Education," which also taught pupils the "importance" of informing on fellow pupils.[23]

In short, the informer is a product of genocidal societies, even though other societies have found less violent ways of producing the same exacerbated individualism. The mechanism of betrayal encourages people to see their peers as enemies and the institutional power as their ally. It applies the logic of market competition to moral relations, with each individual competing for the approval of the authorities, much as companies compete for contracts. This mercantile logic, which turns others into mere objects or commodities and destroys trust, solidarity, and associational power, invades all areas of social practice even after the perpetrators are no longer in power. This explains the tremendous difficulty that postdictatorial Argentina has found in organizing groups to undertake collective action, at least until the economic crisis of 2001.[24]

Postmodernism and Autonomy: Authenticity as an Alternative Strategy for Deconstruction (A Digression)

Although an important focus of this chapter has been the use of informers to destroy autonomy, it is worth taking a brief look at an alternative and equally effective power strategy that has also—although not always—been applied in postgenocidal societies since the Second World War.

The spread of mercantile individualism as a result of the Industrial Revolution and the birth of the human sciences—particularly psychology—at the end of the nineteenth century gradually produced a new "turn" in the concept of autonomy. As mentioned earlier in this chapter, two rival notions of freedom coexisted throughout the nineteenth and early twentieth centuries: the contractarian-liberal notion of the bourgeoisie and the revolutionary notion of the French Revolution. Both had humanistic and universalist connotations. However, by the mid-twentieth century, they were being challenged by the narcissistic concept of "authenticity."[25]

With the advent of the consumer society, the concept of autonomy gradually ceased to mean "giving oneself the law" for the common good, and came to signify a self-indulgent pursuit of pleasure. The American hippie movements and the May 1968 protests in France, which equated free sex with a release from repression—and thus with autonomy—finally undermined the notion of morality as something separate from individual desires and wishes. This hedonist approach to morality is strongly linked to the logic of neoliberalism. Being autonomous is understood as "doing as I please." Liberation becomes so individualist and so dependent on buying and owning things that its revolutionary quality is not only watered down but effectively transformed into a means of domination.

Autonomy becomes equated with release from all forms of discipline, and, at the same time, release from responsibility for injustice and suffering in the world, from our mutual obligations with peers (since these conflict with our immediate desires), and from rules of civility and respect for others—thus blocking any possibility of organized social action. "Giving oneself the law" is transformed into "I am the law." It becomes a form of absolutism that is no longer monarchical ("I am the state") but individual and hedonistic ("I am reality"). The current profusion of spiritual self-help books is accompanied by the logic of "consuming experiences."[26] Social relations are transformed into a marketplace of sensations. The "other" ceases to exist as an end in him- or herself and is seen only as a means toward ego gratification and self-satisfaction.

This is a strange way to rid oneself of Judeo-Christian guilt—through an even more demanding and complicated system of self-monitoring (although without the traditional self-control). It is not based on fear of divine punishment, but on a sort of mandatory wish fulfillment defined in terms of consumerism and perceived as the deepest and most legitimate expression of self—an authenticity that must be discovered and satisfied, a core self that is ultimately a desire to consume either goods or feelings.

In contrast, the French Jewish philosopher Emmanuel Levinas rejects the notion that other people are simply objects in our subjective worlds. Levinas argues that our subjectivity does not exist independently but is formed in and through our subjection to others. In particular, I am subjected to the *faces* of others (especially the faces of the weak—orphans, widows, the poor, or the refugees) that speak to me emotionally before I can even begin to reflect on them. My emotional response turns me into a "being for others"—in other words, a moral being with responsibility for the suffering and the disadvantaged—as opposed to the "being for oneself" of postmodern hedonism. Thus, autonomy begins, ironically, with our subjectedness to others, which is a form of "heteronomy" or external control quite different from the stifling submission to authority in genocidal societies.[27]

Some Political Consequences of Blocking Autonomy

The postmodern approach to autonomy based on the notion that everyone should be a "law unto himself" has led to fragmentation in the political sphere—even in protest movements. Small isolated groups and individuals prefer to forsake the possibility of effective social action rather than give up their uniqueness and authenticity (conceived of in essentially individualistic terms) by making common cause with the rest. Instead of becoming more self-critical, which is a necessary part of the process of forming autonomous relations with others, they develop a defensiveness that operates at two levels:

1. They defend *their truth* by setting themselves up as political avant-gardes that are more visionary than ordinary mortals. Other people are just another obstacle to overcome in their evangelizing mission.
2. They defend *their identity* through the group. New social movements and "identity politics" that developed in the 1960s and the 1970s (feminism, civil rights, gay liberation, Green, etc.) fail to break out of their narrow circle and make contact with the reality and suffering of others. On the contrary, they cling to their need to solve *their* community problem, thus facilitating the maintenance of the status quo with its model of society and modes of conflict resolution.[28]

The continuing emergence of new social groups—increasingly smaller, more specific, and more enclosed—reflects the growing number of social sectors overwhelmed by global capitalism and finance. While such resistance to the various negative impacts of globalization is healthy in itself, it tends to miss the wood for the trees.

Gramsci identified three levels or stages of political development, each with its own form of political action. At the first stage—the "economic-corporative" level, people come together to defend specific interests. Joining a labor union for fear of downsizing or pay cuts is a good example of this. At the second stage—the "economic-political" level, a sense of solidarity develops between groups sharing similar economic interests, as when several labor unions call a general strike. Finally, at the third stage—the "state-hegemonic" level—groups are welded into a political party with long-term political, social, economic, and moral goals capable of inspiring and mobilizing larger sections of society.[29]

Gramsci thus recognizes that action at the "economic-corporative" level is totally insufficient for bringing about broader social change. Such short-sighted views of reality, currently glorified as media commodities, can arouse feelings of rebellion but lack the wider humanistic vision required to create a freer and more ethical society. Social movements acting at the economic-corporative level are more like consumers trying to defend themselves within the free-market system (except that their interests are moral rather than commercial). Their inability to find common causes becomes an obstacle to collective action. Their emphasis on difference becomes divisive.

Genocide, Autonomy, and Humanism

Attempts to understand genocide go far beyond the sometimes morbid accounts of mass murder or even necessary acts of justice and/or remembrance for the victims. Genocidal practices are social engineering aimed at destroying relationships of equality, autonomy, and reciprocity within a given society and substituting for them power relations based on the destruction and/or reformulation of autonomy and identity. This shapes political practices in the postgenocidal society.

Genocide is a cold-blooded, rational policy, with social and political effects that go beyond the disappearance of the victims, no matter how many are killed. Understanding the longer-term objectives as well as the material and symbolic effects of genocide is a necessary step to reshape the model of postgenocide social relations, a model that leads to moral destruction.

PART TWO

Historical Foundations

The Nazi Genocide

The purpose of this section is to raise some sociological questions about the different ways in which genocide has been theorized. In fact, sociologists had little to say on the subject before the 1990s. Since then, however, things have changed and European, U.S., Israeli, and Canadian sociologists, historians, philosophers, and theologians have produced some remarkable work in this area. In this section we will be considering the theoretical and political implications of these different approaches.

Part II is divided into three chapters. Chapter 4 addresses arguments put forward by some philosophers and historians that the Holocaust is indescribable, unparalleled, and unique. It also looks at how genocidal social practices have been narrated and at the symbolic and conceptual implications of different narrative techniques. Chapter 5 discusses some historical and causal models that have been used to explain the Nazi genocide and their relation to the various hypotheses developed in this book. Finally, chapter 6 addresses the social relationships involved in genocidal practices, focusing on the Nazi era. It considers genocidal practices as a means of destroying and reorganizing social relations, using the Nazi genocide to show how genocide works as a social practice beyond the case in question.

4

Discourse and Politics in Holocaust Studies

Uniqueness, Comparability, and Narration

Ways of Narrating the Holocaust and Their Consequences

Before considering different theoretical explanations of the Holocaust, we need to examine the various discourses that have grown up over the years as writers have attempted to get closer to their subject matter. Because the destruction of European Jews involved a radical break with previous social practices, social relations, and methods of killing, we also need to understand the material and symbolic implications inherent in different ways of "representing" the Holocaust.

The first historical accounts written after World War II were concerned with how the Holocaust fitted—or did not fit—into the past and future of German and European society. During the postwar period, the dominant scientific ideology was still positivism, and positivism saw history as an ascending curve of civilization and progress. People asked, then, to what extent genocide was a logical consequence of European history and to what extent it represented a break in the continuum of history.[1]

Above all, the question that obsessed thinkers during these postwar decades was, "What made the Holocaust possible?" Perhaps this was the wrong question to ask or perhaps the early narratives simply left much to be desired. In any case, I will now examine some widely accepted approaches developed in response to this question in order to clear the ground for the next chapter, which deals with causal models of the Nazi genocide in a more strictly historical and sociological sense

Demonization and Irrationality: Driving Away the Specter of Genocide

One of the first widely accepted explanations of the Holocaust was developed during the 1950s and 1960s by non-Germans[2] before later being revived by

Daniel Jonah Goldhagen, whose book *Hitler's Willing Executioners* has been the subject of much scholarly and popular debate.[3] This perspective could be defined as a complex and subtle denial of the idea that genocide is a constituting force in modern societies—an idea I have already discussed in previous chapters.

Before the late 1980s, the most frequent view of the Holocaust was that the planners, the perpetrators, and their accomplices were manifestations of pure evil. This demonizing approach was taken to a greater or lesser degree by historians such as Lucy Davidowicz and Yehuda Bauer, among many others.[4] But it was Goldhagen who revived it in the late 1990s, when *Hitler's Willing Executioners* became a best-seller in the United States and Europe.

The demonization of the Nazis—also present in films and literature about the Second World War—served as a subtle device to ward off the specter of genocide lying at the heart of modern civilization. Portraying the Germans as barbaric hid the fact that most European societies of the period practiced material and symbolic racism. Goldhagen's position, however, is that the Holocaust was first and foremost a "German" rather than a "modern" phenomenon. In his view, the perpetrators were suffering from a "disease" that can only be understood by reference to German history. In a tortuous transposition of Christopher Browning's classic book, *Ordinary Men* (1998), Goldhagen tries to explain how "ordinary Germans" could become perpetrators without any moral qualms or mercy.[5]

Goldhagen's position became popular precisely because it stresses Germany's "unique" anti-Semitic culture. This, together with the sheer scale of the Holocaust, allows readers to distance themselves from questions of wider responsibility. Genocide can be written off as a pathology anchored in a particular time and place. There is nothing about the here and now to suggest that the reader is in any way involved in or affected by genocide. In this view, memory is nothing more than an obligation to the dead: the victims deserve compassion and the perpetrators deserve hatred and disbelief—but all this happens in the abstract. Because it has nothing to do with us, it is an "alienated memory."

This kind of metaphysical condemnation of genocide is brilliantly expressed in the catch-phrase "never again." The problem, however, with this post-Holocaust injunction is that it not only leaves the subject implicit ("*what* never again?"), but also the reason ("*why* never again?"). More explicit condemnations are avoided because the social conditions that breed genocide are (re)constructed each day in our contemporary nation-states.

Foucault uses the term "normalization societies" to describe modern societies undergoing a demographic explosion that the authorities then attempt to regulate through biopolitics.[6] By demonizing the perpetrators of the Holocaust as madmen and monsters, we turn a blind eye to the "normalization" taking place in our own societies. By pathologizing genocide, and in particular the Holocaust, we create a "soothing" narrative that leaves our own strategies for constructing identity and otherness intact. Manuel Reyes Mate condemns such smug condemnations of evil because they avoid the need for self-questioning that might lead to a vision of genocide as something more complex, nuanced, and dangerous than the congenital wickedness or folly of a particular group of perpetrators, a people, or a nation.

Appeals to congenital or cultural pathology are an attempt to avoid confronting that component of modern societies that cannot speak its name. For even if genocide is not strictly speaking inevitable, it is certainly true to say that a "genocidal temptation" lies at the heart of all modern societies, and this problematizes the ways in which we shape our identities both individually and collectively: the "me" and the "us." However, if we can believe that genocide is a product of madness or supernatural evil existing outside any social frame of reference, it becomes a fairly simple matter to control the bad and the mad by locking them away in prisons and psychiatric hospitals or even—as has happened in the twenty-first century—by dropping bombs on them.

Since the late 1960s, demonizing theories placed a growing emphasis—particularly in the United States and Israel—on the "uniqueness" of the Jewish Holocaust.[7] Supporters of this view claimed it was impossible to compare the genocide committed against the Jewish people with any other modern social process. Some Jewish theologians even condemned comparisons on religious grounds, arguing that they demean the sacredness and dignity of Holocaust victims. They began to shun the term "Holocaust" in favor of the Hebrew word *Shoah* ("catastrophe") in order to exclude the Nazis' non-Jewish victims.

This claim that the Holocaust was "unique" has had immense symbolic significance. Scholars who questioned the uniqueness of the Holocaust—as distinct from those who deny its existence—have been publicly denounced in an attempt to silence or punish them. Indeed, the concept of uniqueness has proved more powerful than any narrative. Its supporters are willing to resort to legal action on the grounds that any attempt to compare the Shoah with other historical events is an act of anti-Semitism, intended or otherwise.

But ignoring the causal and structural similarities of the Shoah with other processes tends to preserve the essential characteristics of our "societies of normalization": control from above, discipline, obedience, control of time and space, norm-referencing, informing on neighbors, and alienation. The inevitable appearance of genocidal social practices in such societies is then seen as "exceptional."

Uniqueness and Comparability of Genocidal Practices: The Debate about Uniqueness

To argue that a historical event cannot be compared with any other goes against the most elementary principles of historical and sociological analysis as well as the methodology of the social sciences in general. Although all historical events are unique, this does not mean they cannot be compared. In fact, comparative studies are expected to examine both similarities and differences. This dual focus helps to develop new theoretical concepts and, at the same time, to understand the limitations of theory when faced with the specificity and idiosyncrasy of historical events. The fact that each historical event has its own unique political, social, economic, and cultural dimensions is less an obstacle than a stimulus to comparative studies.

However, *uniqueness* has been the dominant narrative of the Holocaust—at least in academic circles—for over forty years, thanks to the Jewish ethnocentrism of many genocide scholars. At the same time, a resulting dearth of historical and sociological analysis has been accompanied by an unspoken but no less serious contempt for other victimized populations. This implies that the suffering of other groups is less important and even less genuine—a view that represents a real failure, not only in academic but also in political terms.[8]

One of the main elements of confusion caused by uniqueness theories can be explained by Dadrian's distinction between singularity and exclusivity. Dadrian says, "While genocide in itself and by itself is a unique experience for any victim group, it is entirely plausible to grant certain types of genocide the attribute of uniqueness within the broader and generic category subsuming that phenomenon."[9] In other words, uniqueness theorists start from the fact that history never repeats itself exactly in order to argue that different historical events are unrelated in any way whatsoever. Worse still, they proclaim that since the Holocaust was unprecedented and the Jews were its victims par excellence, the term "genocide" cannot be applied to any other event. In their view, any attempt to compare the Holocaust with other historical processes trivializes the Holocaust and is tantamount to genocide denial. So, perhaps a better name for this ethnocentric (or just plain egocentric) attempt to monopolize the term genocide would be *onlyness.*

Arguably, the most extreme uniqueness theorist is Steven Katz—who insisted on restricting the term "genocide" to the Shoah. However, others, such as Lucy Davidowicz and the early Yehuda Bauer, might also be included. In his later works, however, Bauer has recognized the genocidal nature of the Armenian massacres and other historical events.[10]

Without returning to the debate in chapter 1 on how genocide should be defined, it is worth examining the arguments of these uniqueness theorists in more detail. Accordingly, I will now consider what authors as different as Vahakn Dadrian, David Stannard, Israel Charny, Ward Churchill, Leo Kuper, and Benjamin Whitaker (in his well-known report to the United Nations) have to say about the uniqueness of the Shoah as a concept for deciding what genocide scholars are allowed to say and do.

Types of Argument and Their Consequences

In this section, arguments about uniqueness will be analyzed on two different levels: the factual level, that is, whether they are based on historically verifiable truths; and the level of implications for methodology, that is, whether a particular type of uniqueness rules out comparisons with other processes or events. A third level—the symbolic effects of uniqueness theories on narrative construction—will be discussed at the end of the chapter, where I will examine the consequences of resorting to different "story lines" about the Holocaust.[11]

Let us begin, then, with the first argument supporting the "exclusive singularity" or uniqueness of the Jewish Holocaust: the number of victims. Typically, this argument might sound something like this: "Six million victims make the Shoah a unique crime in the history of mankind. Neither before nor afterward have so many people died in this way."

Even at the factual level, this claim is questionable. The indigenous peoples killed on the American continents in the nineteenth century alone numbered at least ten million (the exact figure varies according to the source, but in any case it far exceeds the number of Jews who fell victims to the Nazis). Moreover, between a million and a million and half Armenians were murdered in the second decade of the twentieth century, and between one and two million Cambodians were annihilated in the second half of the 1970s. This raises the question of how many million victims are required before the criterion of exclusivity applies. Is an accounting system necessary to determine whether genocide has taken place? And if so, do victims who died in Europe score more points than those who died elsewhere? Enzo Traverso has partly exposed this ethnocentric fallacy by suggesting that Europeans were much less afraid of genocide when it took place in their colonies than when the Nazis brought it into their own backyard.[12]

If numbers are a key consideration in determining our choice of research methods, what happens when there are "only" tens or hundreds of thousands of deaths, as in the Latin American genocides carried out during the era of the National Security Doctrine or the genocides of Indonesia, Rwanda, or former Yugoslavia? Can the number of victims really be definitive in these cases when often entire cities, towns, or villages were razed to the ground and their inhabitants completely annihilated? Is there really a quantitative way of distinguishing between qualitatively different social processes and, if so, how many deaths are needed to join the exclusive club of genocide victims: 10,000? 100,000? 1,000,000?[13] If this last question sounds sarcastic, it is meant to be. By treating extermination as something concrete or material, this obsession with numbers objectifies and dehumanizes the deaths of the individuals who were annihilated.

The second argument used to support theories of uniqueness is a variation on the first one: qualitative differences in social processes are based not on total numbers, but on the percentage of casualties compared to the total population. To paraphrase the essential point made: "Two out of every three European Jews were killed by the Nazis." This claim is also debatable at the factual level since the total number of European Jews on which the percentage is based can and has been estimated differently. So, here we have another subtly perverse number game played with casualty figures. Moreover, even if we accept two out of three as an accurate estimate, other genocides have had even higher death rates. In the nineteenth century, many of the indigenous peoples of the Americas lost up to 90 percent of their populations, while in the twentieth century, the Armenians in Turkey and the Roma in Europe both lost over two-thirds of theirs.

But of course the total number of Jews depends on cultural, religious, and genealogical considerations—unless, of course, we accept the Nazis' definitions of Jewishness, which rather defeats the purpose of Genocide and Holocaust Studies. And how do we calculate the casualty rate in Argentina? As a percentage of the total population? As a percentage of the total membership of left-wing groups? Or as a percentage of the total number of political activists? Notice that the percentage increases dramatically as we move from overall population to political activists.

Returning to the Holocaust, the Jewish death rate was much higher in some parts of Nazi-occupied Europe (e.g., in Lithuania) than in others (e.g., in Denmark), and it was even higher in the death camps (although similar rates would apply to other victim groups in the camps). Conversely, if one takes into account the Jewish population living outside of Europe, the percentage becomes lower. So what is the purpose of calculating percentages?

This second argument, besides being conceptually flawed, is ethically harmful. Calculating "victim rates" belongs with nineteenth-century eugenics or Lombroso's theory of the born criminal rather than with a critical approach to the social practices of genocide. Scholars cannot behave like bookkeepers, calculating a profit-and-loss account in which dead bodies are treated as investments and moved around to maximize the moral payback. This is totally unacceptable in a field like genocide studies, where a commitment to ethical and moral standards is paramount.

The third argument is more coherent in its theoretical and methodological approach since it focuses on the *method* of killing. The ways in which the victims are murdered could well be the basis for defining different types of genocide. However, we would need to see if the method of killing is sufficient *in itself* to make a historical event unique and incomparable—or at least to warrant the use of the term "genocide."

Let us pause for a moment to consider how this argument conceptualizes the term "technology." Uniqueness theories tend to make a fetish of technology (in the sense of investing it with magical powers) only to include it within the less important category of *techniques*. They are not interested in the "technology of power"—that is, the power structures and social processes involved in managing people as a group, which *are* important when distinguishing between different types of extermination. They concentrate only on the techniques for killing (gassing, shooting, starvation, forced marches, etc.). In other words, they fixate on the tools rather than the process in which the tools are used. They see the Holocaust as unique because it is the first and only case of genocide using industrial-scale killing factories rather than the "cottage-industry" methods that had been the norm until then and that continued to be used after the Holocaust.

Even on the factual level, however, this argument is disputable. First, it could be argued that several post-Nazi genocides—for example, some of those that occurred in Latin America—have shown a similar level of technology in the sense of using modern techniques and even "high-tech" forms of kidnapping and disappearances. For example, many Argentine victims were dumped into the sea, bound and sedated, from military aircraft.

One thing that did appear for the first time, however, and which made the Holocaust unique, was a new technique for disposing of the bodies. As the scale of killing increased, the problem of what to do with the dead was solved with the creation of the six death camps scattered across Poland. This was murder on an industrial scale.[14] The death camps were a significant historical development and deserve specific attention in order to determine similarities and differences with earlier and later processes. Nevertheless, this does not mean that there is any qualitative difference between the Holocaust and other instances of genocide at the deeper level of the technology of power.

As mentioned earlier, a fixation on methods and instruments of murder rather than a willingness to examine the social practices in which they are used may lead to a fetishizing of such methods in which the instrument comes to define the practice. This type of reification is rooted in historical accounts of the Industrial Revolution which supposedly originated in various tools developed during the eighteenth century, even though many of these tools already existed as "inventions" long before capitalism and industrialization made their use economically viable.

The main methodological problem with this approach, then, is not that it leads to factual and historical inaccuracies (because it does not) but that it puts tools at the center of social processes In the case of the Holocaust, rather than focusing on the design of the gas chambers, we need to consider what kind of social relationships can turn death into an industrial process. Considered as a technology of power, the Holocaust is no different from many other instances of genocide that followed it. But it does differ structurally from the constituent (i.e., nationbuilding) and colonial genocides that preceded it.

In chapter 2, I argued that genocide is a distinctly modern phenomenon, or a product of modernity, which can be classified into four clearly differentiated types or stages according to the technology of power used: (1) *constituent* genocide was used to create modern nation-states; (2) *colonial* genocide oppressed those living materially and symbolically outside colonial society; (3) *postcolonial* genocide repressed rebellions and uprisings in regions undergoing decolonization; and, finally, (4) reorganizing genocide attempts to radically restructure society. If the Holocaust was one of the first reorganizing genocides in history, it was not the gas chambers or crematoria that made it so, however important these were as technical innovations.

I will return to this point in later chapters, but it is worth stressing here that technical and technological differences do not invalidate comparative analyses but are rather factors to be included in them.

The fourth argument used to support theories of uniqueness refers to intentionality. "The Holocaust was the first organized effort to systematically wipe out an entire ethnic group," this argument might run. Steven Katz makes extensive use of contemporary statements to explain why the genocide of indigenous peoples was "unintentional." But proving this again becomes a game of numbers. In trying to establish death rates and causes of deaths, Katz confuses different historical periods, treating the seventeenth, eighteenth, and nineteenth centuries as a single entity. In this view, most indigenous peoples died of diseases that were not intentionally transferred to America by the conquistadores. Therefore, there was no manifest intent to kill.

However, many historians would disagree that the Nazis clearly and explicitly intended to exterminate the Jewish people from the very beginning. Historians like Philippe Burrin and Karl Schleunes argue that this decision only emerged as the Nazis implemented their technology of power, and the "Final Solution" was adopted only after considering a series of alternative proposals.[15] The decision to kill all the Jews had not yet been taken in 1933, much less in 1923. It was through trying out various options that the Nazis edged closer to genocide, and once the decision had been taken, implementation followed swiftly.

It is more difficult to say when this fourth type of argument applies. Intent may be a criterion for defining a genocidal practice, and indeed it is one of the three essential elements of genocide, together with acts and victim groups, under the United Nations Convention on Genocide. But historians cannot determine an intention to commit genocide on the basis of documentary evidence alone. They need to look closely at people's actions and the outcomes of these, bearing in mind the specific features of each case, even though such an approach may entail subjective judgments about what is or is not important.

Uniqueness theorists have used a comparative approach to argue the exclusive nature of the Holocaust. Yet, paradoxically, they compare the

Holocaust with the slaughter of indigenous people in the New World or the Armenian population of the Ottoman Empire during World War I, both of which were clearly sequences of actions rationally planned by the perpetrators to obtain the result of genocide, even if it is extremely difficult to find written orders in either case. On the other hand, we should remember that the absence of Hitler's signature on any document ordering the "Final Solution of the Jewish problem" does not make his or the Nazis' intention to annihilate the Jews any less certain.

To sum up, the four types of argument considered above suggest a political need to justify uniqueness (or "onlyness," as its trivialized version has been called) rather than an attempt to understand a technology of power in theoretical terms. Some uniqueness theorists seem bent on denying that any historical event other than the Holocaust of the Jews deserves the name of genocide. Events in Latin America during the 1970s or for homosexuals persecuted by the Third Reich can be safely dismissed by appealing to arithmetic ("tens of thousands are not enough cases"), while colonial genocide is best denied by questioning the techniques used or the perpetrators' "intent." As for cases like the Nazi extermination of the Roma, no argument seems to apply very well. So, these cases are either excluded from the discussion or their causality rates are minimized.

Problems and Limits of Comparative Studies: Transgressing the Taboo of Uniqueness

However, challenging the dogma of uniqueness and breaking the comparative analysis taboo creates another problem for social scientists, that is, the need to clearly define the concept of genocide lest it become so all-embracing that it explains nothing. Breaking down the dogma of sacredness is necessary but not sufficient for a critical analysis of the social practices of genocide.

To hold that genocidal social practices are–at least potentially—an essential element of modern societies is not to say that any form of violent state repression is necessarily a genocidal social practice or that all mass killings constitute genocide. Neither does it mean that all genocidal processes develop in the same way, or lead to similar results. In particular, genocide should not be used as a term of condemnation for social problems such as hunger and exploitation resulting from neoliberal economic policies in Latin America, Asia, or Africa or any other kind of state repression, however reprehensible these policies may be.

To paraphrase Helen Fein, we need to guard against the anti-uniqueness approach caricatured in the catchphrase "if this is awful, it must be genocide"—a parody that aptly depicts the way the term genocide tends to be trivialized. For even if Fein, in her criticism of Charny and Kuper, goes too far in trying to limit the use of the term "genocide"—or, more precisely, proposes the *helplessness* of the victims as a rather unconvincing defining variable (see chapter 1)—she is right to point out that not every massacre constitutes genocide.[16] The need to avoid jumping to false conclusions about uniqueness does not mean accepting a populist watering down of concepts to the point where they can mean anything and nothing. If genocide is part of a technology of power, then only some—but not all—social practices can be termed genocide. We need to be clear on this point because there is a real danger that in confronting uniqueness theories, we may swing to the opposite extreme and minimize or play down the Holocaust and/or other genocides by equating them with war.

Ernst Nolte's work is a classic example of Holocaust minimization in which the concept of genocide is diluted by comparing the Holocaust with the Soviet revolution. Far from trying to analyze the genocide that was latent during certain periods of Stalin's rule, Nolte depicts the Holocaust as an extension and a consequence of Soviet genocide.[17] But Nolte undermines his own comparative study by failing to define the different types of practices he is referring to, their special characteristics, and their intended purpose within the given social order. In short, he fails to define his terms or contextualize genocide within a specific technology of power. Stalin developed an unusually harsh and repressive regime, particularly during the 1930s. He used many of the techniques of persecution later adopted by the Nazis—including concentration camps—and he annihilated ethnic, political, and national groups using social practices comparable to genocide. This opens up a legitimate debate on whether the concept of genocide can be applied to the millions of people murdered under Stalin. But this question cannot be answered without looking carefully at the similarities and differences between Nazism and Stalinism. The same is true of the Holocaust and the Argentine "Process of National Reorganization," which are the main focus of this book. What is clear is that genocidal processes may have quite different causes. On the other hand, authors like Nolte seem to be looking for a way to shake off German guilt about the Nazi era.[18]

Perhaps the biggest headache for researchers interested in genocidal social practices and the sociopolitical models that underpin these is not so much how to categorize Stalin's purges and executions, but how to label the clearly genocidal policies of another supposedly socialist state: Cambodia during the Khmer Rouge period between 1975 and 1979.[19] But whichever historical events we are comparing, we need to account for similarities—for example, the role of modernity in the development of genocidal social practices—as well as differences, for instance, how genocidal social practices were carried out in capitalist societies, such as Nazi Germany, as compared to societies trying to build socialism, such as Cambodia. These considerations in no way prejudge the magnitude of the atrocities in question or the suffering of the victims.

It is also important to note that the uniqueness debate can have totally different implications depending on where and when it takes place. In Germany, for example, historians like Nolte have attempted to confront uniqueness in order to minimize German responsibility, a trend that requires careful ethical and epistemological analysis. In contrast, various Jewish groups in Israel and the United States have used uniqueness to give the State of Israel a sense of moral superiority that supposedly justifies human rights violations against the Palestinian people. In the rest of the world, uniqueness has tended to be used as a way of minimizing mass annihilations of other peoples as these will always be "dwarfed" by the magnitude of the Nazi genocide. In short, theoretical and conceptual debates are always situated historically, so we need to participate in such debates responsibly, bearing in mind their possible ethical and political consequences. But only by breaking the taboo of uniqueness does it become possible to analyze genocide. Of course, there is always the risk of making genocide sound more "mundane," of including it in the broader category of "oppression" or making its different manifestations less distinctive. All these are constant temptations social scientists will have to fight against once the notion of comparative analysis has been demystified.

The Problem of "Narratability" and the "Unspeakable" in Experiences of Genocide: A Reflection on Ways of Remembering

An important point to consider here is whether it is at all possible to portray events of such magnitude and horror. Elie Wiesel has frequently stressed the impossibility of telling ("silence is forbidden, it is impossible to speak . . . those who have not experienced it, will never know how it was, those who know, will never say, not everything, not what it really was like").[20] This feeling is shared by other survivors like Jorge Semprún, who contributed to making Kant's concept of radical evil part of the hegemonic discourse of remembrance ceremonies. Wiesel's and Semprún's approach can be summed up in George Steiner's terse observation that the best if not the only way to talk about genocide is by remaining silent.

Steiner, a brilliant literary critic and professor of literature, seems to be echoing Theodor Adorno's often quoted but much misunderstood assertion that "to write poetry after Auschwitz is barbaric"—a statement that Adorno himself later questioned and qualified. In the event, the Romanian poet Paul Celan, who lost both parents in the Holocaust and whose uncle died in Auschwitz-Birkenau, showed that he *could* write poetry after Auschwitz and even tried to remake language in order to narrate the supposedly unspeakable.

Holocaust scholars who subscribe to the idea of the "unspeakable" tend to superimpose personal experience and theoretical analysis in different ways. But most argue that their theoretical analysis is worthless unless the reader can understand or personally identify with the experience: those who were not there cannot talk because they do not understand, and those who were there will never be understood. Only silence can speak the unspeakable.

Some also claim that the unspeakable is incomprehensible because it transcends (or overflows) human categories for grasping reality. They argue that the scale of the Shoah, its recognizable pattern of horror, and the despair in "human nature" it produced in the survivors make it into a single event. But, they add, the reality of the Shoah is buried in the individual memories of the survivors and is not transferable to those who did not experience it.

This notion of the unspeakable has profound implications because it raises questions about the "limits of representation." Theologians and philosophers have asked to what extent all explanations of social phenomena are, by their very nature, subjective reconstructions and whether such reconstructions can ever recapture lived experience as such. Here, the question is whether the testimony of the survivors can ever be adequately expressed in words.

This notion of the unspeakable, however, can be a serious obstacle to constructing counterhegemonic perceptions of genocide. A notion that began by making genocide sacred has in many cases emptied it of any real meaning, albeit unintentionally. Walter Benjamin has pointed out that memory should be understood as a story told from the viewpoint of the defeated (as opposed to history, which is written by the conquerors).[21] So, if the survivors' testimony is reduced to the category of the incomprehensible—the unspeakable—this simply encourages the use of natural science methods to understand social reality. By relegating the testimony of the survivors—their "memory" in Benjamin's sense of the term—to the realm of metaphysics, we become estranged and alienated from their reality and we are deprived of the opportunity to examine it from a historical or sociological point of view. In this way, the philosophical notion of *intransmissibility* creates political alienation. As we have seen, the link between the two is uniqueness theories, which prevent the analysis of historical experience. But this connection is neither direct nor obvious.

However, a word of caution is in order here. I am not claiming that *all* testimony is directly representable or directly transferable. Nor am I arguing that *all* philosophers who question the limits of representation—often in a rich and profoundly suggestive way—support the idea of the unspeakable. What I am trying to say is that by excluding eyewitness testimony we run the risk of confusing "reality" with an external, supposedly "objective" approach based on documentary sources. This notion of objectivity is so strong that many genocide historians—without subscribing to any sort of uniqueness theory—have denied the importance of eyewitness testimony from survivors on the grounds of its alleged unreliability. However, when nearly all the documents are produced by *genocidaires* as in the case of the Holocaust, there is a real risk of confusing "reality" with the vision of the perpetrators.

The documentary approach thus becomes another obstacle to developing a sociological understanding of experience. It reduces the probability that social relations will be analyzed as such and normalizes documentary accounts of them. In this sense, debates among historians about the role played by Nazi leaders in the Holocaust can be truly astonishing. Some historians are so trivial in their approach that they reduce this problem to the existence or not of a Nazi decree of annihilation—as if one of the greatest social upheavals and transformations in human history could be reduced to a piece of paper.

In short, the notion of intransmissibility has tended to break the link between eyewitness testimony and historical reconstruction, producing two rather different discourses, both of which get in the way of sociological analysis. One of these discourses stresses subjective experience but considers it to be nontransferable, while the other emphasizes history in the abstract, ignoring personal experiences and therefore making it impossible for us to understand how genocidal social practices work in practice.

A fundamental principle of modern political thought—which comes from Niccolo Machiavelli via Antonio Gramsci and Michel Foucault, among others—is that a social practice must first be thoroughly understood before it can be successfully confronted and eradicated. First, it must be demystified and its multiple, complex, and nuanced causal relationships laid bare. This means analyzing the social relations that are central to the practice rather than indulging in metaphysical speculations about the "true" nature of reality.

However, this analysis requires survivors to identify personal experiences rather than simply talking about themselves, which is typical in historical-political reconstructions. This being the case, it is obviously even more difficult for a person to take possession of and talk about the "unspeakable." When does silence become a strategy that prevents people from recovering and owning their experience? What connection exists between a speaking subject and the genocidal practice he or she is speaking about?

About the Modes of Narration: "Owning the Past as It Flashes Up in a Moment of Danger"

Hayden White considers Art Spiegelman's comic book *Maus*, together with the testimony of Primo Levi, to be the most effective representations of the Holocaust.[22] Although his approach has angered many Holocaust scholars, White has managed to establish a way of understanding the unspeakable that, unlike Steiner's injunction to remain silent, does not suppress memories of trauma—does not create a split between history and testimony—but opens up limitless possibilities of representation.

In particular, White presents the idea of infinite narratability in an incisive and provocative manner. Infinite narratability—the idea that a story can be told from any number of different points of view—results partly from the essential openness and interconnectedness of historical events.[23] Glossing over the distinction between the "speakable" and the "unspeakable," White argues that it is impossible to give a definitive account of any historical phenomenon—not just of genocide. Whatever historical genre they choose, historians are forced to bridge an abyss between an ever-elusive historical event and their inescapably subjective retelling of that event.[24]

Consequently, White rejects Berel Lang's idea of an "intrinsic genre" that should predominate in the literature on genocide. Lang recommends a nondistancing, "intransitive" approach for narratives about the Holocaust, whether historical or fictional.[25] More precisely, he proposes that "each Jew should tell the story of the genocide as though he or she had passed through it."[26] In contrast, White argues that every literary genre contains an essentially subjective gaze and so allows for committed storytelling.[27]

Beyond individual recommendations or preferences, the significance of the Lang-White debate is that it highlights the theoretical and political consequences of choosing a particular narrative genre. These consequences do not derive from the subject matter but from the narrator's intention. If applied literally, the nondistancing, or "intransitive" storytelling method proposed by Lang would be as clumsy and tedious as the memory of Funes the Memorious. In this fictional story by Jorge Luis Borges, first published in 1942, Ireneo Funes acquires the gift—or curse—of remembering absolutely everything. Funes is incapable of generalization or abstract thought so he needs a whole day to remember the previous day. Funes is one of those rare people we nowadays call autistic savants. Neuroscience, however, shows that most people's memories work quite differently.[28]

On the other hand, if all representation is reconstruction, a selection of events turned into "scenes" whose purpose is to "re-present" a unique story, the feasibility and effectiveness of the story depend on the scenes selected and the narrative framework in which they are placed. This is even truer of stories that are supposedly untellable. In short, historians and social scientists can neither remain silent nor resort to extensive first-person narratives. On the contrary, although this proposal may sound shocking to some conservatives, their task is not so different from that of a poet or novelist.

And this brings us to the key issue in this chapter: the inherent *implications* of different ways of depicting the Holocaust. Just like any other literary device used by historians, stereotyping the Nazis (and other perpetrators of genocide) as demons or madmen, or sanctifying the Shoah as unique, incomparable, even indescribable, has implications for storytelling. Different narrative forms, in turn, will produce different responses to the social practices involved in genocide: empathy and ownership, or revulsion, alienation, and dehumanization.

Davidowicz and Goldhagen do not find monsters in the documents they analyze. Rather, they transform the perpetrators into monsters through their narratives. When Steiner calls on us to remain silent, somehow he cuts us off from other ways of imagining experience. Katz does not find all Holocaust survivors to be identical. He has to invent arguments to persuade us that the survivors' experiences are identical in that they are "unique." He has to build a chain of reasoning so that his conclusion—that the Jewish Holocaust cannot be compared with other instances of mass murder—is not seen for what it really is: a stubborn denial of the suffering of other victims.

Tzvetan Todorov distinguished two ways of remembering the experience of genocide: literal and exemplary memory.[29] He argued that literal memory—individual narratives of atrocities and suffering—may well be "true," but that it does not help the survivors to face the future with renewed strength or hope. Instead, survivors run the danger of losing contact with present reality and becoming stuck in their victim status. Moreover, exhaustive factual descriptions of the type recommended by Lang are ultimately as impossible as they are pointless. It is impossible to connect events in literal memory. At best, one can evoke fragments. Gradually but irreversibly, these fragments lose their meaning, become alienated, and eventually fade from memory.

On the other hand, exemplary memory is potentially liberating as it allows the survivors and others to move from the particular to the general, from the events to the pattern. Exemplary memory is not just about my loved ones, my loss, but also about yours and everybody's. It attempts to learn from the past in order to give meaning to the present and the future. Walter Benjamin wrote in his critique of Ranke, "articulating the past historically does not mean recognizing it 'the way it really was.' *It means appropriating a memory as it flashes up in a moment of danger*. . . . The only historian capable of fanning the spark of hope in the past is the one who is firmly convinced that *even the dead* will not be safe from the enemy if he is victorious. And this enemy has never ceased to be victorious."[30]

As explained in the Introduction, this book sets out to compare two historical events. The connection between these events is neither direct nor obvious. On the contrary, it is in some extent "contrived" in order to see what we can learn about the way genocide constructs, destroys, and reconstructs the social fabric. However, even though the events chosen are not closely related in time and space, they have not been picked at random: the criteria for their selection are conscious and explicit. I could have examined other events, but I decided to compare these as they flash up in my moment of danger in Buenos Aires at the beginning of the twenty-first century.

The relationship between them is ultimately constructed through discourse—a discourse that is as legitimate as any of its kind. I am not writing in Bangladesh or Denmark but in Buenos Aires, a city haunted by survivors, perpetrators, and witnesses of the Nazi genocide as well as Argentina's own "Process of National Reconstruction" (with one generation between them). Buenos Aires is still suffering the effects of terror and betrayal in social relations, is still anguished by silenced memories and memories with which the population is bombarded each day, by discourses relating to one or the other of the two genocides, to both or to neither.

I assume there is a continuum between the events we call genocide, a continuum that goes beyond the actual events themselves and is related to a particular form of social planning and engineering (and therefore to a particular way of redefining social relationships) that has tended (and still tends) to lead to our moral demise.

With this in mind I will now move on to discuss the causes and effects of the Nazi genocide. I will attempt not only to discover the logic that led to the Nazi genocide but also to expose the symbolic effects of genocide and the role that discourse plays in maintaining them. Although we can never completely undo the effects of genocidal social practices, I hope this will go some way to mitigating them.

5

The Problem of Explaining the Causes of the Nazi Genocides

Comparative analysis does not exempt scholars from trying to understand the causes of the Nazi genocides and the conditions that made them possible. On the contrary, without such an understanding, they would find it impossible to establish the structural similarities and differences between these and other genocidal processes—or to know whether two events were comparable at all.

This chapter examines some of the many social science perspectives that provide causal models for understanding the Nazi genocide. However, this examination is simply a "contribution" (as Ian Kershaw would say) to understanding a phenomenon of almost unimaginable scope and complexity.

I would be pleased if this critical survey—together with the hypotheses suggested in the next chapter—sheds light on some of the lesser known aspects of the Nazi genocide and encourages others to explore them in new ways. However, this is just one approach to understanding Nazism—one that by no means exhausts this complex subject.

Partly as a result of my own theoretical affinity with the pioneering work of Raul Hilberg and Hannah Arendt, and partly because of the relevance of their work to the issues under discussion, these two authors take up a large part of this chapter. Like Hilberg and Arendt, I view the Nazi genocides as a social practice linked to the logic of modernity and its scientific, political, and bureaucratic development. This approach does not exclude ideas from other relevant perspectives that might be useful for carrying out further analysis.

Finally, before we embark on this chapter, it is worth pointing out that it is in no way intended be a survey of the thousands of important works on the Nazi genocides. Its purpose is simply to identify clearly and draw together the main theoretical threads running through this book.

Hilberg, Arendt, and the Question of the Irrationality of Evil and the German *Sonderweg*

The explanation of the so-called *Sonderweg* (special path) as a view of German history was widely accepted by historians in the first two decades after the Second World War, at least outside of Germany.[1] Works in this line of research attempted to explain how it was possible that, in the heart of an enlightened Europe, in a country that prided itself on being the cradle of modern philosophy, a phenomenon of this kind was able to develop.

In the 1960s, however, two authors challenged the prevailing consensus. It is true that several members of the Frankfurt School—Theodor Adorno, Max Horkheimer, Franz Neumann, and Walter Benjamin—had already hinted strongly at a possible connection between Nazism and modernity. However, in 1961, Raul Hilberg published a book that was to become canonical over the next twenty years.[2] In *The Destruction of the European Jews*, Hilberg discusses the role played by bureaucracy in the process of annihilating European Jewish communities. A monumental achievement for its time, its publication was followed almost simultaneously by the appearance of Hannah Arendt's notes on the trial of Adolf Eichmann, the Nazi lieutenant colonel responsible for transporting millions of Jews to concentration camps. In her book, entitled provocatively *Eichmann in Jerusalem: A Report on the Banality of Evil*, Arendt describes the perpetrators as "terribly and terrifyingly normal" and, more importantly, argues that genocide is latent in all "normal" Western civilized societies.[3]

Adorno had already suggested in *The Authoritarian Personality* that individual personality traits and collective psychic structures found among Nazis were equally common in a society like the United States.[4] But the work of Hilberg and Arendt marked a turning point in our way of thinking about the relationship between Nazism and modernity.

The commonsense understanding of the time, even among legal experts, was that Nazism had been an exceptional departure from the upward path of human progress, but that it did not, in itself, invalidate the notion of indefinite progress. But Hilberg and Arendt pointed out that genocide—or at least the potential for genocide—was the rule rather than the exception in the contemporary world. Far from being signs of progress, such features of modern life as bureaucratization, task division, routines, and depersonalization were essential, although not sufficient, for the mass extermination of populations.

Significantly, neither work was well received when it first appeared. Arendt's essentially journalistic work came in for severe criticism in academic and political circles because she portrayed Nazi perpetrators as ordinary human beings, thus challenging the image of insane and irrational Nazis, far removed from our everyday world. Dozens of works were published attempting to discredit the views and interpretations of Arendt on Eichmann and the perpetrators, and her work was banished from "serious" reading lists on Nazism in Israel and the United States, and even in France.[5]

It was another thirty years before a historian, Christopher Browning, was able to develop a similar line of argument in *Ordinary Men: Reserve Police Battalion 101 and the Final Solution in Poland.* Browning's book, which traces the history of a battalion of German Order Police operating in Poland during the German occupation, marks a fundamental turning point in the way we view the Nazis. Browning found that this group of 500 men in their thirties and forties had started out as just that—ordinary men.[6] Only a few of them were members of the Nazi Party and fewer still belonged to the SS. And yet they went on to shoot (or transport to Treblinka death camp) at least 83,000 Jewish civilians.

By the 1950s, self-exculpatory accounts of the Nazi era had become the norm in Western society. These constructed Nazism as an exclusively German pathology, completely at odds with the recent history of the West. This model was challenged by Hilberg, Arendt, and Adorno, who placed Nazism within the mainstream of Western societies as a potential that exists in every one of them. This also raised thorny questions about the degree of commitment, complicity, empathy, or indifference of many governments and much of civil society in the Europe of the 1930s and 1940s.

If Arendt was placed on academia's index of banned books about the Shoah, Hilberg proved even harder for most intellectuals to swallow and was largely ignored. For the generation that had lived through the Nazi era, the demonization of Germany and a collective memory of irrationality functioned as a survival mechanism, making self-exculpation possible together with a sort of closure. It was only the next generation that was able to question the contradiction inherent in such an approach—the fact that millions could have taken part in an irrational event and yet nobody was willing to discuss the extent to which *they themselves* had participated in it. Once people were aware of the inconsistency, they were able to read Hilberg's book with fresh eyes.

People in postwar Europe were able to lay their ghosts to rest by claiming that the Nazis were irrational, but their children could not help noticing this contradiction again and again. There is no other way that we can understand works such as those of Ernst Nolte, whose success was built on the inadequacy of conventional explanations of the Nazi genocide.[7]

Hilberg, Arendt, and Adorno are, then, the forerunners of a debate that only began to come to the forefront in the 1980s, when a new generation of scholars was growing more and more dissatisfied with established causal explanations of Nazism. Zygmunt Bauman, Christopher Browning, and Enzo Traverso, among others, attempted to give a deeper answer to the question of why Nazism happened by mapping its European genealogy and its place in the formation of modern nation-states.[8]

Bauman's controversial *Modernity and the Holocaust* was a first attempt to describe systematically the modern nature of the Nazi genocide and its founding and formative role in shaping the modern world.[9] Consequently, Bauman's book was criticized and minimized when it first appeared in 1989, although less so than Arendt's work a quarter of a century earlier. Traverso's *The Origins of Nazi Violence*,[10] coming over a decade after *Modernity and the Holocaust*, placed Nazism on a time continuum that began with colonial genocide. In the words of Traverso, "The Germans did nothing but apply in Poland, the Ukraine, the Baltic countries, and in Russia the same principles and methods that France and the United Kingdom had already adopted in Africa and Asia."[11]

Compared with what Arendt, Adorno, or even Bauman had suggested, Traverso's proposals smacked of demystification and even heresy. Traverso had brought Nazism in from the cold, so to speak, turning it from a story of anti-Semitism writ large into a decisive event in world history. Nazism could now be seen as a key element (although just one) in a way of constructing identity and otherness that began with the inquisitorial activities of the Catholic Church in the seventeenth century and the development of the nation-state (first along confessional lines and later along nonconfessional ones).

Obviously, techniques for objectifying and dehumanizing people (which, of course, are directly connected to genocide) could not be the same in Europe as in Europe's colonies. This discrepancy is one of the many keys to interpreting the uniqueness of Nazism, its lines of cleavage with respect to other European racist thinking, and its genocidal consequences. But cleavage does not imply a complete break. If Nazi racism had its origins in Europe, we need to ask which mainstream European logics of power it is related to. This is a core question for understanding how and why Nazism mutated into genocide. This perspective was later developed in a whole line of analysis that connects genocide and colonialism, as it does in works by Dirk Moses, Donald Bloxham, Dominik Schaller, and Juergen Zimmerer, among others.

The Concept of Totalitarianism

In the past, most scholars who asked about the causes of the Nazi genocides were influenced by the emergence and subsequent evolution of the concept of totalitarianism. Although this term was regularly used in Mussolini's Italy during the 1930s, first by fascists and then by their opponents, it was Hannah Arendt who popularized it in her book *The Origins of Totalitarianism*,[12] even if later usage owes little to her analysis. Hannah Arendt's concept thus predates Hilberg's *The Destruction of the European Jews* (1961) by at least a decade.

Although some of Arendt's analyses are interesting, the concept of totalitarianism in the hands of authors like Carl Friedrich, Dwight MacDonald, Arthur Koestler, and Zbigniew Brzezinski, among others, has become—to paraphrase Slavoj Žižek[13]—an "ideological antioxidant" covering up the connections between genocidal social practices and modern Western civilization. In tracing the history of the concept of totalitarianism, Traverso proposes a periodization beginning with Mussolini's fascists describing themselves as totalitarian and then their identification of fascism and bolshevism as the only "real" forms of politics.

As Traverso shows, the concept of totalitarianism was established in the English language shortly afterward by antifascist European exiles living in America. However, it only acquired real significance—and, at the same time, became a conceptual trap—during the Cold War, when it was used to equate Nazism and Stalinism, thus rescuing and glorifying "anti-totalitarian" liberal democracy.[14] It is interesting to note how comparisons between Stalinism and Nazism were used to support this liberal perspective as well as to underpin Ernst Nolte's Holocaust revisionism.

Žižek's irony about ideological antioxidants helps us to understand how the concept of totalitarianism produces a logical disconnection between the modern Western world and genocidal social practices. These practices began in the nineteenth century and continued into the twentieth as first the British and the French and later the Italians and the Germans attempted to legitimize European colonialism and the domination and extermination of indigenous populations. In the cases of Germany and Italy, these included Germany's war of extermination against the Hereros in Southwest Africa between 1904 and 1908 and Italy's colonial war in Ethiopia in the 1930s. An intermediate point of cleavage between colonial and constituent genocides can be found in the Armenian genocide as a step toward creating a modern pan-Turkish nation-state out of the scattered territories of the Ottoman Empire between 1915 and 1918.

Franz Borkenau, writing at the outbreak of the Second World War, was one of the few theorists to use the concept of totalitarianism in a different sense. He tried to understand totalitarianism "not as a German aberration or as an expression of Slav barbarism, but as the authentic fruit of modernity."[15]

If the concept of totalitarianism is too limited to account for historical processes, Žižek undermines it still further by noting how it dissolves the structural relationship between Nazism and modernity—or even between Nazism and capitalism. The concept of totalitarianism hijacked that of democracy in ways that had little to do with the history of "democratic" European states (first England and France, and later Italy and Germany). It portrayed the Europe that rises in the Rhine or Loire and ends at the Pyrenees as the "cradle" of modern, Western, democratic civilization, pitted against a wild world of totalitarian barbarism, which tended to be progressively more Eastern and Slavic and less Germanic. Paradoxically, a racist model thus emerged as a "counterbalance" to the ideology of racism, with the peculiarity that it was defended by liberal democrats (such as Carl Friedrich, Zbigniew Brzezinski, and Karl-Dietrich

Bracher) and social democrats (drawing on the work of ex-communists such as Arthur Koestler and George Orwell).[16]

And so Europe fell into its own trap. The United States—as the stronghold of Western democracy and leader of the free world—then claimed the right to judge and evaluate the "reformed" European states (and, increasingly, the whole planet) on their "level of democracy," their "freedom," and their "respect for human rights." Indeed, the success of the concept of totalitarianism as a form of symbolic representation of the Nazi genocide has not been sufficiently appreciated.

The United States carried out more repressive, racist, and xenophobic military interventions than any other country on the planet during the second half of the twentieth century. These ranged from the Bay of Pigs invasion and Vietnam, through Guatemala, Grenada, and Panama, to the invasion of Iraq and Afghanistan. And yet the United States was able to present itself as a bastion of democracy and pluralism. This image can only be understood as part of a successful symbolic reworking of the Nazi genocide in which earlier processes of derationalization, demonization, and a resort to the metaphysical construct of evil helped to produce the opposite pole of "health" and "normality" in modern, liberal, Western civilization.

Thus, the concept of totalitarianism has been more successful than even Žižek recognizes. It has become the key notion for recycling the Nazis' racialization of politics, turning their technology of power into a kind of antifascist "racialization of politics." In this way, antitotalitarian thinking can be seen as a new synthesis. It is no longer the fascist blend of anti-Marxist left and "revolutionary" right; rather, it is a fusion between an anti-Marxist left and a right whose populism has dissolved and been transformed into a "revolution from above" in the name of world civilization and the fight against totalitarianism.

The concept of totalitarianism is the best example of how social processes eventually develop into symbolic representations. Hegemonic discourses give meaning to experience so that it can be understood and fixed in one form or another. However, the military defeat of Nazism—with the millions of deaths on the Eastern Front and the emergence of local, antifascist resistance movements throughout Europe, from Italy and France to Yugoslavia and Greece—did not triumph at the symbolic level. After the fall of Nazism, the notion of totalitarianism became a symbolic wall stronger than the Berlin Wall itself in preventing a return to the principle of the self-determination of peoples.

In the words of Žižek, and paraphrasing the advertising slogan of Celestial Seasonings Green Tea, the "beneficial role" of totalitarianism as an "antioxidant" has been to "inhibit the free radicals and help the social body to maintain good political-ideological health."

Marxism in the Face of Genocidal Social Practices

If the liberal right was able to reinvent itself as an enemy of fascism through the concept of totalitarianism, Marxism sadly minimized and trivialized the specific nature of the Nazi genocide. Apart from a few fleeting insights by Leon Trotsky and Antonio Gramsci and a later reworking of fascism by Ernest Mandel, many Marxists tended to subsume Nazism under the category of fascism, defined by Georgi Dimitroff at the Seventh Comintern Congress in 1935 as the "open terrorist dictatorship of the most reactionary, most chauvinistic, and most imperialist elements of finance capital."[17]

Examining what various fascist regimes had had in common—which was much more than the so-called totalitarian regimes—did not help Marxist thinkers to distinguish the Nazis' radically new genocidal policy from the brutality of fascist regimes, or to comprehend the differences between mass movements in Italy and Germany and repressive military governments in Spain and Portugal and, later, in Latin America.

For Trotsky, on the contrary, the Nazi genocides cast doubt on the classical Marxist position that the political idiosyncrasies of different modern nation-states were irrelevant. Although Trotsky still saw Nazism in the early 1930s as a "feudal ideological residue exhumed by a declining capitalist society," by the late 1930s the fate of Jews under the Nazis seemed increasingly to confirm the alternatives posed by Rosa Luxemburg at the beginning of the twentieth century—socialism or barbarism. "Today decaying capitalist society is striving to squeeze the Jewish people from all its pores; seventeen million individuals out of the two billion populating the globe, that is, less than 1 percent, can no longer find a place on our planet! Amid the vast expanses of land and the marvels of technology, which has also conquered the skies for man as well as the earth, the bourgeoisie has managed to convert our planet into a foul prison."[18] Despite these insights, Marxism tended to view Nazism as an exceptional and archaic form of barbarism—a vision similar to that described earlier, which demonized Nazism as an atavistic regression running counter to the development of the modern world. Ernest Mandel was one of the few Marxists able to build on the insights of Trotsky. In a highly suggestive work on the meaning of the Second World War, Mandel noted that "the roots of genocide are not to be found in traditional petit bourgeois and peasant Judeophobia, but rather in the racist and colonialist culture of imperialism, whose murderous nature has already been made clear by the slave trade and the extermination of indigenous populations in Central and South America by the Conquistadores. The historical roots of Auschwitz must therefore be discovered in Western civilization, its culture and its social relations."[19]

For fifty years Trotsky's insights were ignored by a hegemonic Marxism which, servile to the geopolitical needs of the Soviet Union, subscribed to the "demonizing" visions of the Nazi genocide.[20] It was not until 1994, three years after the collapse of the Soviet Union, that Traverso used these strands in his book *The Marxists and the Jewish Question* to develop the European genealogy of Nazi violence as an offshoot of imperialism and colonialism.

The shortcomings of Marxism as a theoretical framework for explaining genocidal social practices shows what happens when theory is subordinated to geopolitical interests and how, in turn, theoretical dogmatism becomes an obstacle to political struggle. Although large numbers of Marxists were killed or persecuted by the Nazis, Marxism had problems in thinking critically about genocidal practices until the 1980s, when the rediscovery of Antonio Gramsci and Walter Benjamin, among some other classic heretics, together with the breakup of the Soviet Union, allowed the emergence of new Marxist writers (such as Arno Mayer, Enzo Traverso, and Tony Barta, among others), who tried to approach the issue of genocidal social practices from this perspective, an endeavor that has only just begun.

Michel Foucault and the Concept of "Society of Normalization"

Here I will take an unorthodox look at some of the ideas of Michel Foucault, paying special attention to the symbolic dimension of social practices. I will consider above all his analysis of what he identifies as a new form of social relations, a new technology of power generated by the rise of capitalism, which he incisively calls the "the normalizing society."

According to Foucault, "the normalizing society" has two complementary facets: the disciplinary and the statistical. *Disciplinary norms* help to build average, productive bodies capable of ensuring the average performance required by industry—in other words, cogs for the industrial machine. *Statistical norms,* on the other hand, help to build healthy bodies by defining average life expectancies, average strengths, and norms of hygiene that guarantee productivity. Statistical norms regulate human life: they are used to control fertility (through birth control) and mortality (by providing care), to detect epidemics, and to construct urban health networks. They give governments the power to lengthen and enhance citizens' lives.[21]

Within the normalizing society, the "majority" no longer has the derogatory overtones of the "mass" as it did in the feudal technology of power. Instead, it has become synonymous with "normalized subjects" belonging to the complementary categories of population and citizens. In contrast, the concept of "minority" has become associated with segments of the population that cannot be "normalized": the disabled, the sick, the insane, thieves, idlers, groups that—for economic, political, or cultural reasons—do not fit with the concepts of nation, citizenship, and property. These concepts of the "normal" together with the binary pair "normal-pathological" and the concept of "degeneration" allow us to build the image of the "nonstandard Other" as a danger to the population.

Thanks to the demystification of Nazism by Hilberg, Arendt, and Adorno, the concept of the "normalizing society" makes it easy to understand how genocide became a constituent practice of modernity. The origins of modern genocide can be traced back to the challenge posed to the egalitarian contractualism of the eighteenth and nineteenth centuries by a new order of values based on inequality. The idea that not all human beings are equal leads to the need to make those who are different "disappear"—either by forcing them to conform to the norm or, if this is not possible, by murdering them.

The concept of the normalizing society inevitably leads us to consider how the various continuums of normality/abnormality are constructed. To understand this important and complex question, I will refer now to the debate between Arno Mayer and Christopher Browning, to which I will add Zygmunt Bauman's reflections on the subject as well as some ideas of my own.

From Christopher Browning's "Racialism" to Arno Mayer's "Politicism": Jewish or Jewish-Bolshevik?

As mentioned earlier, Nazism was demonized by most historians during the two decades following World War II. However, as this vision gradually lost ground, historians polarized into two camps, which Tim Mason has aptly called the intentionalists and the functionalists.[22] The intentionalists focused on the intentions of the Nazi leaders, especially those of Hitler himself, in bringing about genocide, seen as the result of a master plan. In contrast, the functionalists were much more cautious, considering genocide as a latent possibility inherent in Nazism. In this view, genocide was not the inevitable result of the Nazis' ascent to power in 1933 because it existed at that time only as a *potentiality*. Rather, genocide emerged from the structural features of Nazism—in other words, from its subsequent political, economic, and social development. Although functionalists may emphasize different contributing factors—the war the Nazis' political ups and downs, their lack of success on the Eastern Front, and the failure of their resettlement plans—all agree that the destruction of the Jewish people did not become inevitable until 1942.

At this point, I especially wish to highlight a debate involving two of the many historians who have decided to tackle the problem of "causal explanation" directly from a functionalist perspective. Here, I am more interested in the way these historians weave the facts into complex and comprehensive models for historical understanding than in determining the precise moment that the decision was taken to implement the "Final Solution," which was the focus of their debate. Of course, several other authors have set out to achieve similar goals, but the Mayer-Browning debate will help to clarify some issues that are crucial to my own hypotheses.

The first author I will examine is the Princeton researcher Arno Mayer. In his essay *Why Did the Heavens Not Darken? The "Final Solution" in History*, Mayer sees the Nazi genocide as part of the Nazis' counterrevolutionary war against Judeo-Bolshevism. Mayer thus seeks to reinstate the Nazis in world history by placing them at the center of a class struggle that erupted in Europe in the first half of the twentieth century.[23]

The second author I will comment on is the researcher Christopher Browning. Especially in *The Path to Genocide*, Browning explicitly challenges Mayer's hypothesis by prioritizing Hitler's racist discourse and his proposed reorganization of Europe along racial lines. Refreshingly, Browning does this without attempting to demonize or pathologize the Nazi leadership. Instead, he analyzes the racist proposal for redesigning Europe and its consequences at the level of social relations.[24]

As a foil to this discussion, I will also consider the work of Polish sociologist Zygmunt Bauman, who draws equally on Karl Marx and Max Weber in attempting to understand the place occupied by the Jews in interwar Europe and why they were the special target of Nazi annihilation, linked not only to the issue of class struggle or racist policies, but the more global and complex problem of how identity is constructed in the modern Western world.[25]

Arno Mayer's Vision

Explicitly eschewing the intentionalist approach, Mayer places the Nazis in a historical sequence that combines the concepts of "ideological crusade" and "total war." He traces the idea of an ideological crusade back to the European Christian crusades against Jews and Muslims between 1095 and 1270, highlighting the crusaders' role as "liberators" and their overobjectification of the Other. Similarly, Mayer traces the term "total war" to the Thirty Years' War between European Catholics and Protestants from 1618 to 1648.

In Mayer's view, the Nazi genocide was a combination of a *total war* (which he placed between 1914 and 1945—in other words, another thirty years' war beginning and ending with the two world wars) and an *ideological crusade*, this time against those who subverted the modern order (not in religious but in ideological terms). This was the crusade against communism by the capitalist West. Nazism, from this point of view, represents the heyday of counterrevolution in Europe, waging a war of annihilation only in Eastern Europe and the Soviet Union, quite unlike its conventional military campaigns in Western Europe.

Mayer argues in his book that conventional approaches to the Judeocide have obscured some very important evidence, such as the order given to the *Einsatzgruppen*—mobile killing units, as distinct from regular army units—by Reinhardt Heydrich during the German invasion of the Soviet Union in 1941 (Operation Barbarossa) to eliminate "all high-ranking members of the Communist party, all 'people's commissars,' all Jews in service to the party." This policy had its direct antecedent in the Nazi persecution of German political dissidents and their internment in concentration camps between 1933 and 1935. Mayer examines the image of the "Judeo-Bolshevik" constructed by Nazi propaganda in order to understand Nazi genocidal social practices and the role played by the concentration camps in Germany, where communist opposition was repressed *before* the anti-Semitic campaign began.

It was this anticommunist ideological crusade that won the Nazis the support of the German elites and the silence of the European elites until the invasion of Poland in September 1939 led to war with Britain and France. Until that moment, they had allowed Nazism to grow and consolidate in order to keep communism in check. The Nazi battles with the West were part of the struggle for political hegemony but, Mayer insists, not a war of annihilation.

But why, then, the obsession with Western Jews and not just with Judeo-Bolsheviks? Why is a racial rather than a political metaphor used to justify the war of annihilation? Mayer sees the racist thinking of Hitler, Goebbels, and other Nazi leaders as "irrational" even if it also served the interests of Nazism. We should not forget that in the premodern period both the ideological crusade and total war had religious components, which the Nazis revived in the figure of the Jew—but this does not go far toward explaining the Nazi genocide as such.

For Mayer, the Nazis constructed a syncretic ideology with a confusing overlap of antimodernism, anticommunism, and racism. This syncretism is synthesized in the figure of the Jew. However, this does not explain the phenomenon itself—only its symptoms, its ideological expression. Mayer argues that from a Nazi perspective even conservative Jews are seen as "Judeo-Bolsheviks."

Finally, Mayer argues that the Nazis decided to annihilate European Jewry only after failing to eradicate the ideological politics of communism and Judeo-Bolshevism during the invasion of the Soviet Union. Mayer tries to demonstrate that decisions about the total annihilation of the Jews were taken when the results of Operation Barbarossa started to become uncertain or directly adverse, "since we cannot annihilate the Bolshevik enemy, let us at least annihilate its Jewish face."

Provocative and heretical, Mayer's essay has the merit of placing the Nazi genocide within a historical sequence, restoring its place—where it is perhaps not alone—within world history and not on its edges.

Christopher Browning's Vision

As mentioned earlier, Browning explicitly challenges Arno Mayer—and in fact one of the chapters of his book is an open response to Mayer's essay. For Browning, Mayer's chief mistake is to locate the Jewish genocide (which Mayer calls "Judeocide") as a "by-product" of the Nazis' anticommunist ideological crusade. That is, Browning's main problem with Mayer is that the latter's general framework for explaining the Nazi genocide makes no allowance for the distinctiveness of this Judeocide. Was Hitler's madness to blame? Or was it just a secondary cause? Was it a symptom? Can it be explained simply as a hate reaction once it was clear that the invasion of the Soviet Union and its mission to destroy communism had failed?

In Browning's view, Mayer denies the distinctiveness of Judeocide by transforming it into a spin-off of a higher-order set of practices described within a more general explanatory framework. Thus, Mayer ignores the central innovation in the Nazis' technology of power, which is their racist worldview.

The attempt at European reorganization along racial lines is seen by Browning, unlike Mayer, not as the crazy project of a few deluded leaders supported by a self-interested European (as well as German) bourgeoisie but as a viable political project and the basis of Nazi politics and even Nazi geopolitics. The annexation of territories to the east of Germany to create *Lebensraum* ("living space") for the Reich can only be explained from this logic, and not as a derivative of the Nazis' ideological crusade against communism. Browning does not deny such a crusade existed, but he argues that the Nazis' political project was separate from the wishes and priorities of the European bourgeoisie. The Nazis aimed to progressively resettle and partition populations in the East, according to their degree of "racial impurity," Aryans being the purest, then Slavs, and finally Jews. "Inferior races" would be relocated in Asia (although in 1940 Himmler seriously contemplated sending the Jews to the island of Madagascar), leaving *Lebensraum* in Europe for the development of the "superior races."

It was the failure of this geopolitical project and measures taken to resettle Jews on a Jewish reservation in the Lublin district of Poland between late 1939 and mid-1940 which led to the Final Solution. If there was nowhere left in the world for them to live, then the solution was to remove them from this world to a "nonplace" by transforming them from "subhumans" (*Untermenschen*) into "nonhumans" (*Unmenschen*).

For Mayer, Nazi ideology uses the figure of the Jew in its struggle against communism. For Browning, however, Hitler only hated what he saw as the "Jewish characteristics" of communism—its emancipatory, egalitarian, and internationalist side. Hitler's struggle against communism was intended to forge strategic partnerships with the European bourgeoisie. His long-term plans, however, were more linked to a racial reorganization of Europe rather than an ideological one. In Browning's view, the Nazis believed that ideology was underpinned by race and not the other way round.

If Mayer sees Nazi racism as a tool, Browning sees it as an end in itself and the main focus of Nazi policies. Ultimately, we cannot choose between these two explanations unless we know to what extent Nazism believed its own myths, and to what extent observables account for social processes. Browning takes Nazi anti-Semitism much more seriously and relocates it at the very center of their *Weltanschauung*. Even though the Nazis came to power in an anticommunist struggle supported by the German elites, their ultimate goal was not to fight communism but to redesign Europe along racist lines. This explains their obsession with hunting down all Jews wherever they were—whether in eastern, western, northern, or southern Europe.

Could Zygmunt Bauman Add Something to This Debate?

Commendably, Bauman has developed a perspective that explains the processes by which power was consolidated in Europe while, at the same time, accounting for the specific nature of the "Judeocide." In his work he rethinks the role of the Jews in twentieth-century Europe both in relation to the ideological struggle between capitalism and communism and from the wider perspective of "biopolitics" (in the Foucauldian sense of the word). He does this by focusing on the reality of Jewish life during this period: the role of Jews in the new model of identity formation of nation-states of modern Europe. Bauman builds a metaphor to explain this place that is a nonplace, a people lying astride of modernity.

In a model of power that defines identity in national terms, excluding all other features, what place remains for a people spread across the length and breadth of Europe without a state of their own? In the era of nation-states, the Jews were a stateless nation that unlike other peoples, claimed to be members of various European nation-states without giving up their identity or sense of cultural belonging. This was a characteristic the Jews shared with another major cultural victim of Nazism: the Gypsies (i.e., the Sinti and Roma peoples).

Here I wish to add my own ideas to the model proposed by Bauman, and also comment on the Mayer-Browning debate, including the role of the Jews and the Gypsies as the main victims of the Nazi extermination camps. Under any regime seeking to reduce ethnic, religious, cultural, or ideological diversity in order to create a unified nation, those seen as having "divided loyalties" will immediately be accused of subversion.[26] Not only the Nazis but indeed the whole of the European bourgeoisie strongly rejected the Jews' internationalism, their emancipatory traditions, and their ethical egalitarianism, as well as balking at the Roma people's notions of cultural autonomy and communal property.

In July 1938, just eleven days after Hitler annexed Austria, U.S. president Franklin D. Roosevelt convened an international conference at Évian-les-Bains, France, to discuss the growing number of Jewish refugees fleeing from Nazi persecution. Representatives from thirty-two countries and twenty-four voluntary organizations attended, but when the United States and Britain refused to take important numbers of Jews, most of the other countries followed suit, leaving around half a million Jews trapped in Germany alone.

It is difficult to explain the refusal of the various governments to welcome Jewish refugees simply in terms of "indifference" to their fate. The truth is that no modern nation-state wanted Central European Jews because of their subversive potential (their internationalism and wandering, their conscious or unconscious challenges to the identities of the modern world based on exclusion). In the words of Hitler: "We're doing what all of Europe wants to do, but would never dare to admit to it."

However, by glossing over this issue, later representations of Nazism proved useful to both Europe's leaders and many members of Jewish communities living in Europe. Europe's politicians could wash their hands of the Holocaust, putting all the blame on Nazi Germany, while Europe's surviving Jewish communities could try to forget the modern anti-Semitic stigma—particularly after 1948, when the Jewish people were "normalized" by having their own state, the State of Israel—created by and for the Jewish nation.

How do we explain the silence of the European leaders before the war or the absence of bombing raids to destroy the Nazi death camps and railways leading to them once the war had begun? Was it necessary for Europe's leaders to stir up ancient and lethal hatreds again, a victimizing paranoia that always sees the Other as an enemy? How, also, do we explain the persistence of anti-Gypsy laws in much of Europe after the Second World War? Or the reappearance of hate and discrimination against the Roma in twenty-first-century France, Spain, and Italy?

In this sense, the figure of the Jew—and also that of the Gypsy—was quintessentially opposed to the ways identity was constructed in the modern Western world. It was not the bolshevism of certain Jewish workers and intellectuals or the physical appearance of Central European Jews and Gypsies that disturbed the Nazis, but their universalism, their multiple identities, and their diasporic wandering. This is how, with the help of various historical circumstances, Jews and Gypsies became prototypical figures of discrimination and persecution.

It was the social ubiquity of European Jews that made them such easy targets everywhere (not just in one place) for the ideological crusade described by Mayer. The Jews were not a social class: they were to be found among the European bourgeoisie (as an assimilated minority that was discriminated against, but present nonetheless) as well as among the middle and working classes. This made it relatively simple for the Nazis to stir up various class hatreds.

Tony Barta and the Concept of "Relations of Genocide": Social Relationship or Social Practice?

In 1987, the Australian researcher Tony Barta—whose specialty is not Nazism but the annihilation of indigenous peoples in Australia—developed a new Marxist approach to the phenomenon of genocide by creating the concept of "relations of genocide."[27]

Based on a novel interpretation of the Marxist concept of "relations of production," Barta explores how they can become "relations of destruction" and, in particular, the specific type of destruction involving genocide. For Barta, the common sense and way of life of the Australian settler population were based on the disappearance and destruction of the colonized population (either directly through murder or indirectly through the destruction of their livelihood).

Barta suggests that the Australian settlers' behavior was not a random phenomenon. Rather, destructiveness was a central element in the relationship between modern Western colonialism and Otherness. In other words, when capitalism reached its colonial phase (what Lenin called its "imperialist phase"), production and economic growth could only be maintained through "genocidal relations" with the colonized populations. Thus, capitalism condemned the colonized to material and symbolic extinction by destroying their way of life, treating and thinking about them like objects, ignoring them, or rendering them invisible.

Even today, portraying genocide as a "social relationship" is a highly subversive approach given the prevailing hegemonic view in the field of genocide studies. It raises far-reaching questions about the way Western modernity has organized the planet and relations between its inhabitants.

Although Barta raises searching questions about the consequences—both past and present—of colonialism, his approach is less useful for analyzing domestic or reorganizing genocides, which form the subject of this book. Nevertheless—even if Barta is unaware of it, accepting the notion of genocide as a "social relationship" may somehow lead us to "naturalize" this social relationship as a stage in a historical sequence that is difficult (if not impossible) to reverse.

Revisiting some of the ideas developed in chapter 1, I will now explain the difference between genocide as a "social relationship" and genocide as a "social practice," that is, as a specific way of destroying and rebuilding social relationships. It is clear that destruction itself is not in itself a *relationship* but a *practice* that destroys certain social relations—for instance, cooperation, solidarity, reciprocity, and autonomy—and makes other ways of relating hegemonic, for example, subordination, betrayal, individualism, and authenticity. Unlike Barta, I am arguing that genocide is the cause (and not the effect) of a profound transformation in social relations.

Toward a Provisional Synthesis

In this chapter we have examined various suggestions to the effect that the Nazi genocides form an integral part of European history and, therefore, of world history. The topics we have discussed include the connections between genocide and modernity suggested by Hilberg, Adorno, and Arendt; the different views regarding totalitarianism; attempts by Gramsci and Mandel to place Nazism within the Marxist model of understanding social reality; the genealogy established by Traverso tracing the Nazi genocides back to colonial annihilation processes; the debate between Mayer and Browning about the "meaning" of the annihilation of the Jewish population in Central Europe; Bauman's perspective on the role of the Jew in the modern West—with my own contributions to this debate; and the concept of genocidal relations, as developed by Tony Barta.

Was Nazism a latent potential in or an inevitable consequence of modernity? Was it an expression of class struggle? A peculiar mode of social relationship in the imperialist phase of capitalism? A projection onto European soil of the dominant modes of constructing Otherness in Europe's colonies? A counter ideological crusade in the context of a total war? A racist redesigning of Europe's geopolitical map? Or was it a dispute over how to construct identity and Otherness in Western modernity?

I do not claim to be the final arbiter between these competing visions and debates. Nevertheless, together they suggest ways of thinking about historical phenomena. For example, can we understand the genocides of the 1970s and 1980s in Latin America as a continuation of the Nazis' ideological crusade against communism? One only has to remember calls during this period from the Argentine and Chilean military for a "Third World War" or the Catholic Church's involvement as a central player in the "crusade"—in this case—to defend "Western Christianity." And can we place genocide in Rwanda and the Balkans or the more recent wars in Iraq and Afghanistan and the present conflicts in Sudan and the Middle East, together with global threats from "Islamic terrorism," in a new racist reorganization of the planet? What connection do these have—if any—with Nazism? How do we relate attacks by Western powers on southeastern Europe, in the Middle East, or in Central Africa with the fact that European powers dominated these parts of the world from the late nineteenth until the mid-twentieth centuries? What about European and American interventions—even those carried out for supposedly humanitarian purposes or invoking a "responsibility to protect"?

These visions and debates also suggest ways of thinking about sociological issues. For example, what figures are challenging our ways of constructing identity in the postmodern world? Does changing the victim change the type of destructive process we are analyzing? Isn't killing in the global south just as problematic as killing populations in central and western Europe? Has the emergence and international recognition of a Jewish state put a definite end to a way of constructing the negative Other, or have the Jews simply been replaced as objects of discrimination by Arabs, Latin American and Asian immigrants, handicapped people, or people with different sexual identities? Do we need to be reminded, perhaps, that some of these groups were also victims of the Nazis and others prior to the Nazi era?

Each of the approaches we have examined raises questions of a different kind. Nevertheless, such questions allow us to construct a vision of history with which to foresee and—who knows?—perhaps change and even improve our uncertain future. This is a perspective that, like Walter Benjamin, is trying to catch the memory of the Nazi genocide "as it flashes up at a moment of danger" (see chapter 4).

I think that some of us—and by "us" I mean not only my own generation but the younger generations as well—have grown a little tired of appeals to "absolute evil" in the context of genocide studies. Evil is a metaphysical concept that distracts us from the processes involved in genocide. It lets the accomplices of genocide sleep soundly in their beds and alienates the experience of genocide from those who continue to suffer its material and symbolic consequences. It creates spheres of ownership in which "Judeocide" is a Jewish problem, "Armenicide" is an Armenian problem, and "Gypsycide" is only a problem for the Roma people. It allows us to return home with a nice warm glow inside after expressing our empathy with the victims and condemning their executioners—Germans, Turks, or whatever—who might just as well have come from another planet. Evil permits us to close our eyes and not think about all those who suffer unheard today while we repeatedly recall the horrors of the past in banal and bombastic ceremonies that sanctify horror without trying to understand what made it possible. Meanwhile, yesterday's victims are metamorphosed into those of today—and we continue behaving in the same old ways.

Unless we are willing to eschew political correctness and explore new and perhaps heretical ideas—for we will surely make mistakes along the way—we will continue repeating the same cautious and uninspiring lectures, and have the same sad, solemn, and banal memorials—all of which have a sedating and soothing effect and possibly even allow us to feel smug about ourselves, but which are intellectually and socially useless for the task of confronting genocidal social practices.

6

Reshaping Social Relations through Genocide

After examining some basic approaches to the Nazi genocides, in this chapter I will offer a six-stage model of genocidal social practices, emphasizing their ability to construct, destroy, and reorganize the social fabric. This is not a historical timeline of the Holocaust, of which there have been many, nor does it attempt to analyze the successive vagaries of Nazi ideology. Rather than a succession of important events, it treats the Nazi genocides as a series of interrelated and overlapping processes.

My aim here is to highlight the progression of events necessary for implementing such a phenomenon of mass destruction, a process that begins by sapping the victims' strength and undermining "moral empathy" for the victims in the face, for example, of public humiliation, before moving on to harsher measures and finally to legitimizing large-scale killing by the state as a state policy. This model is based largely on the Nazi genocides, but the aim is to construct a model that can be applied to other genocides carried out by modern states.

I have already argued at length that racism is both a symbolic and a material contrivance allowing the state to take the lives of its citizens thanks to a biological discourse that makes the victims responsible for a gradual "degeneration" of the race—a race whose "genes" must be protected at all costs. Thanks to this biological rationale, a state that evolved to guarantee and protect the life of its citizens is "forced" to implement a machinery to destroy life—the lives of those who threaten the "health" of the wider population.

However, we will gain a better comprehension of genocidal social practices if we also examine the testimonies of survivors of Nazism. Many of their stories—particularly those of psychologists like Bruno Bettelheim and Victor Frankl, of philosophically minded writers like Primo Levi, and of political militants such as Jaika Grossman, Schmerke Kaczerginsky, and Marek Edelman—allow us to understand genocide as an attempt to destroy the social fabric and, especially, to replace critical thinking and active solidarity with authoritarian control and individualism.[1]

Destruction and Reorganization of Social Relations

In his studies of children's rule games, the Swiss psychologist and philosopher Jean Piaget distinguished three broad stages of moral and social development related to children's awareness of rules. The first was *pre-moral judgment*, in which rules are not understood (up to the age of four or five years old). The second was *morality of constraint* or "heteronomous morality," in which children accept the rules and authority of adults as permanent and inflexible (from five to ten years old). A third stage was *morality of cooperation*, or "autonomous morality," wherein rules are mutually agreed upon, and can be changed by mutual consent (from the age of ten). At this autonomous stage, children's thinking is no longer constrained by authority, and children can discern new solutions to problems—what Piaget refers to as the construction of knowledge, as distinct from its social transmission.

Piaget believed that a true sense of justice emerges only through "constructive" cooperation with peers, "thus adult authority, although perhaps it constitutes a necessary moment in the moral evolution of the child, is not in itself sufficient to create a sense of justice. This can develop only through the progress made by cooperation and mutual respect between children to begin with, and then between child and adult as the child approaches adolescence and comes, secretly at least, to consider himself as the adult's equal."[2] He also claimed that a morality of cooperation was necessary for what he termed "reciprocity"—that is, for evaluating in-groups and out-groups as being of equal worth, despite one's own in-group attachment—and for an equitable distribution of wealth and resources in society. In Piaget's words:

> In conclusion, then, we find in the domain of justice, as in the other two domains already dealt with, that opposition of two moralities to which we have so often drawn the reader's attention. The ethics of authority, which is that of duty and obedience, leads, in the domain of justice, to the confusion of what is just with the content of established law and to the acceptance of expiatory punishment. The ethics of mutual respect, which is that of good (as opposed to duty), and of autonomy, leads, in the domain of justice, to the development of equality, which is the idea at the bottom of distributive justice and of reciprocity.[3]

Not surprisingly, critics have claimed that the games of marbles on which Piaget based his theory of moral development do not represent children's whole perception of morality. Piaget's theory has also been criticized for assuming moral universals, whereas moral and social development in non-Western cultures may differ from those of the children that Piaget and his collaborators studied. Nevertheless, in sociological terms, the emergence of cooperative relations of reciprocity and solidarity obviously depends on members of a given society being able to perceive others as equals.

On the other hand, as Robert Paul Wolff has pointed out, "Insofar as a man fulfills his obligation to make himself the author of his decisions, he will resist the state's claim to have authority over him."[4] For this reason, history provides numerous examples of attempts to block and dismantle nascent relations of cooperation by stigmatizing nonconformists as Others. Stigmatization works through binary oppositions, such as believer/heretic, civilized/primitive, normal/pathological, in which one pole always dominates. The binary logic of imperialism, in which white/civilized/moral/teacher/colonizer (and so on) is collectively opposed to black/uncivilized/immoral/pupil/colonized (and so on), is just one example of how "negative Otherness" is applied and extended.[5] This process disempowers and alienates the "Othered" from their experience by forcing them to identify with stereotypes, as described in Frantz Fanon's classic study of racism and colonization.[6]

The stories of the victims bring to light the efforts of the Nazis, time and again, to break their victims as human beings, to destroy their solidarity, their dignity, anything they could be proud of; they reveal the Nazis' constant need to transform their victims into what their biological discourse (the most negative vision of the Other ever created until then) depicted them to be: a degraded, degenerate version of the human species.[7] There are numerous testimonies of this kind. For example, Primo Levi writes:

> Then for the first time we became aware that our language lacks words to express this offence, the demolition of a man. In a moment, with almost prophetic intuition, the reality was revealed to us: we had reached the bottom. It is not possible to sink lower than this; no human condition is more miserable than this, nor could it conceivably be so. Nothing belongs to us anymore; they have taken away our clothes, our shoes, even our hair; if we speak they will not listen to us, and if they listen, they will not understand. They will even take away our name: and if we want to keep it, we will have to find ourselves the strength to do so, to manage somehow so that behind the name something of us, us as we were, still remains.[8]

How, then, have modern states managed the move from stigmatization to extermination? Michel Foucault argues that one of the key technologies of power of the modern nation-state is *biopower*. According to Foucault, biopower emerged in the mid-eighteenth century with the aim of defending the life and health of populations; it is exercised at the collective level through regulatory control, and at the individual level through discipline and punishment.[9] For example, the state might use prenatal programs to increase birthrates ("the biopolitics of the population") and, at the same time, punish "deviants" who engage in nonreproductive sex ("the anatomo-politics of the human body").[10] Foucault claims that in a modern, normalizing society, these two levels are essentially complementary. According to Foucault, "If genocide is indeed the dream of modern power, this is not because of the recent return to the ancient right [of monarchs] to kill; it is because power is situated and exercised at the level of life, the species, the race, and the large-scale phenomena of the population."[11] However—and this cannot be stressed too strongly—in any discussion about definitions, *the political purposes of extermination must remain hidden.* As Foucault explains, "In the biopower system, in other words, killing or the imperative to kill is acceptable only if it results not in a victory over political adversaries, but in the elimination of the biological threat to and the improvement of the species or race."[12]

In this sense, genocidal social practices not only attempt to destroy individuals as subjects "for themselves" by alienating them from their experience, but also to strip them of control over their own bodies. The choice of victims and the methods used in genocidal social practices are always political, and are meant to eliminate all forms of physical autonomy in subjects with a history of self-determination. From this perspective, it is no surprise that the Nazis' main goal—from the moment the victims were chosen—seems to have been the elimination of all forms of bodily freedom as well as all trace of social and personal autonomy.

Robert Gelatelly divides the Nazi repression prior to the death camps into four main periods:[13]

1. Between 1933 and 1934, communists and members of other leftist political parties were placed in "*preventive custody*"—in other words, they were imprisoned without trial in concentration camps. Gellately estimates that about 100,000 prisoners passed through these camps, of which over 65 percent were members of the German Communist Party. Between 500 and 600 inmates were killed in these two years by summary executions or as a result of living conditions in the camps.
2. After a drastic reduction in the use of concentration camps during 1935 and much of 1936, the Nazis found a new target: the "asocial." Dr. Werner Best, a lawyer and chief legal adviser to the Gestapo, defined asocial as "*every attempt to impose or maintain any theory besides National Socialism,*" which was "*a symptom of sickness, which threatens the healthy unity of the indivisible volk organism*"[14] In his instructions to the Kripo (*Kriminalpolizei*, criminal police) of April 4, 1938, Himmler defined as asocials those "who demonstrate through behavior which is inimical to the community, but which need not be criminal, that they will not adapt themselves to the community."[15]

The Kripo developed increasingly specialized branches to handle different types of "asocials," including homosexuals, drug addicts, abortionists and their clients, adulterers, and "crimes of opinion," constituted by the mere possibility of critical judgment about Nazism or any of its policies. This was coupled with a policy of "crime prevention" that operated by sending "potential" criminals, ex-prisoners, beggars, prostitutes, and even the unemployed to prison or concentration camps. Of the 5,000 to 15,000 prisoners interned in concentration camps between 1936 and 1938, most were "asocials" rather than communists or political opponents.

3. The Nazis simultaneously developed policies of persecuting physically and mentally handicapped people, starting with the sterilization law of July 14, 1933, and culminating in the murder of 70,000 psychiatric patients and handicapped children in the Aktion T4 operation between 1939 and 1941. The persecution of homosexuals, though less well documented, produced between 5,000 and 15,000 victims.
4. From June 1938 onward, racial policies gradually predominated. At first, these affected only Jews and Gypsies, but after the German invasion of Poland in 1939 policies became increasingly anti-Slav, particularly with regard to the Polish population and—after the invasion of the Soviet Union in 1941—Russian political prisoners and Russian POWs. The Nazi-organized pogrom of November 1938 known as *Kristallnacht* culminated in the arrest of between 20,000 and 30,000 Jews, 1,500 of whom were sent to concentration camps accused of being "asocials." About a hundred of these Jews were murdered and the rest were released after a few weeks, but not for long. Simultaneously, Himmler ordered the arrest of at least 200 unemployed people in each police district of Germany. The detainees were used as "free labor" in labor camps as a way of encouraging others to work. In 1939 there were just over 40,000 concentration camp inmates, but with the creation of these new labor camps and the outbreak of war, these figures increased enormously, making Nazi camps a radically new experiment.

The evolution from concentration camps to labor camps and then extermination camps, each with their own policies of systematic annihilation, will be analyzed later in this chapter. However, the general trend can be interpreted as follows.

Before World War II the Nazis persecuted those who behaved or expressed themselves physically in ways they considered politically subversive or "abnormal." Persecution even extended to those dedicated Nazis who tried to maintain some autonomy and a critical voice within the Nazi movement, as happened with the *Sturmabteilung* (the paramilitary wing of the Nazi Party or SA), and later with certain splinter groups within the *Schutzstaffel* (Protection Squadrons, or SS). More generally, anyone who objected to Nazi militarist or racist policies, or who refused to take their place in the world of work or the law, who was a homosexual or practiced interracial sex with Jews, Gypsies, or Slavs, could become a target. However, by 1938 the great enemy of the Reich had become the Jews.

In the immediate prewar period, the Nazis saw the Jewish ghettos of Eastern Europe as the "breeding ground of all the Jews in the world."[16] That is why they argued that to "stop the Jews was to stop communism."[17] Central European Judaism in the late nineteenth and first half of the twentieth century was, in the eyes of the European bourgeoisie, a subversive mode of identity construction, characterized by a culture that based decision making and action on critical thinking. This was a culture that valued the rabbinical discussions in the Talmud and the ethical thinking of the Haskalah, the Jewish Enlightenment movement of the eighteenth and nineteenth centuries that challenged Kantian ideas. Its "assimilated" versions were to be found in Marx, Freud, and Einstein, who had effectively deconstructed the scientific thinking of their time, and in the Jewish-influenced Marxism of Walter Benjamin, among other thinkers.

Toward an Attempt at Periodization

In the six-stage model of genocidal social practices developed below—one which is largely based on the Nazi genocides, as mentioned earlier—we will see state-sponsored murder used to destroy the capacity for self-determination both of other "races" and of the mainstream population. The first step involves identifying the break that made later genocidal practices possible. This was the moment when the Nazis managed to limit expressions of autonomy in politics and the workplace, in religious beliefs and practices and in private life, stigmatizing any who used their bodies, cultural heritage, or intellect in ways that deviated from the Nazi worldview.

In this sense, Foucault's ideas on the "society of normalization" are obviously relevant, as are Bauman's insights about Jewish identity as the prototype of negativity during the modern era. This idea is also supported by Mayer and Traverso. As we saw in the previous chapter, before the founding of the State of Israel, the Jews "straddled" modernist conceptions of identity based primarily on citizenship of one nation-state or another.

Certainly, the Nazis' choice of the Jews as their archetypal enemies was neither inadvertent nor trivial. However, neither was it, as many have claimed, the inevitable result of centuries of anti-Semitism. Anti-Semitism cannot account for the Nazis' persecution of non-Jews and—as we will see later—has had little to do with the annihilation of populations since 1945.

In the following sections, I argue that a sociological understanding of genocide as a social practice needs to take into account three interconnected processes: the construction, destruction, and reorganization of social relations.

Accordingly, the periodization that I propose is different from that suggested by Gregory Stanton in his "Eight Stages of Genocide," which begins with the classification of groups into "us and them," and ends with the attempts of the perpetrators to block investigations of the crimes.[18]

What I present here is a six-stage process, beginning at the moment that a group of individuals with an autonomous social identity is negatively constructed as Other and continuing until its symbolic extermination in the minds of the survivors, which may happen *after* the physical acts of extermination themselves, and rob the survivors of the possibility of being subjects "for themselves."[19] Not all the stages described are strictly sequential. In practice, there is often considerable overlap between the different stages, although each of those on the path to mass murder constitutes a necessary step in the process.

The model emphasizes the negative ways in which the state brands those who think or behave differently in such diverse areas as sexuality, politics, religion, and the workplace, but also the fact that the extermination of those groups that lie outside the "norm" is a clear message to the population that no deviation from the "norm" will be tolerated. The ruthless efficiency of state punishment, reinforced by official rhetoric and allowing no exceptions, is designed to make the standardization of society seem inevitable.

Although most of the examples included below are drawn from the Nazi genocides (because they are most likely to be familiar to the reader), the model is intended as a tool for understanding many other social practices of genocide, such as those in Indonesia, Latin America under the National Security Doctrine, Cambodia, and the former Yugoslavia, to mention just a few. In other cases, like those of Rwanda or Sudan, some of the stages described may require further adjustments.

Stage One. Stigmatization: The Construction of "Negative Otherness"

The first step in destroying previously cooperative relations within or between social groups is *stigmatization*. In order to construct the "negative Other" as a distinctive social category, those in power draw on symbols in the collective imagination, build new myths, and reinforce latent prejudices. Two groups are thus created: the majority or in-group ("us"), and a minority or out-group ("them") that does not wish to be like everyone else—and therefore does not *deserve* to exist.

Various religious, ethnic, national, political, or social groups have been branded as "abnormal" or "inferior" in accordance with political needs at different periods in history. These groups have included non-Catholic Christians, such as the Cathars; Armenians, Syrians, and Greeks under the Ottoman Empire; *kulaks* in the Soviet Union; Jews and Gypsies under the Nazis; communists in Indonesia; the urban population in Cambodia; and Bosnians in the former Yugoslavia, to name just a few. In the contemporary Western world, the targets of state discrimination are sexual minorities, prostitutes, immigrants, Muslims, and the poor, among others.

Violence at this first stage is verbal and symbolic. The categories of thought and perception created will later lend legitimacy to the need for extermination, but it is too early to speak in such terms. Those in power still *tolerate* the stigmatized group, but consistently draw attention to it and problematize it. The "solution" to the problem—genocide—will come later.

The French Revolution and the nineteenth-century liberal states that grew out of it proclaimed that all men were equal, expressing the need of the bourgeoisie to wrest power from the nobility. At the same time, the notion of citizenship constructed others as equal members of society and—more generally—of humanity. This development was seen by many as dangerous, given its potential for empowering the working classes and marginal sectors of society as well. Legitimizing new nation-states on the basis of discrimination, exclusion, and genocide required a discourse different from that of liberty, equality, and fraternity. The genocidal practices of the nineteenth and twentieth centuries necessitated dividing the human race into several superior and inferior "races."

This process of redefining humanity inevitably drew on elements from the past, especially the stereotype of the Jews. Vilified for centuries by the medieval Catholic Church, by the sixteenth century European Jews were being portrayed by Christian preachers as less-than-human agents of the devil responsible for nearly every misfortune ranging from drought and the plague to street crime. From here it was a short step to the Nazis' biological, political, and psychological discourse of the Jew as the Other par excellence, accompanied by a chorus of minor Others such as gypsies, Slavs, homosexuals, political dissidents, the crazy and the lazy, the disabled, the unemployed, criminals, prostitutes, and drug addicts.

Charles Papiernik, a survivor of Auschwitz, illustrates the Nazis' need to establish a stereotypical Other:

> One day, two guys arrived at the camp from France. One of them was the typical Jew that anti-Semites liked to show off. He had a long nose and was a bit stupid, too. He must have been twelve or thirteen. He spoke loudly in French and said, "I am very well here, because at home they beat me, they beat me in school, and here they look after me." He did not understand where he was. When the SS arrived and saw that boy. . . . They had the time of their lives! They told someone to bring some chocolate to eat and they put it on the table in front of him. Then they turned to all inmates in our blockhouse and told us: "You are responsible for this boy surviving. He must survive. Because we intend to show the world what the Jews were like."[20]

Stereotyping, then, is the first step toward isolating a social group that will later be scheduled for extermination. The authorities resuscitate or reinforce prejudices existing in the collective imagination and create new symbols and myths to exclude previously assimilated (or at least tolerated) social groups. This serves a double purpose: it confirms the identity of the majority ("us") as ordinary, everyday people—and at the same time it stigmatizes those minorities ("them") who refuse to behave like everyone else and therefore *have no right to exist* at all.

Thus the Nazis revived anti-Jewish prejudices that had once been widespread in the eighteenth and nineteenth centuries and portrayed Jews in diverse and contradictory ways as usurers, capitalist exploiters, sexual miscreants and corruptors of morals, and good-for-nothings, as well as political agitators, communists, and thugs.[21] These prejudices included the stereotype of the Jews as "Christ killers" and libels about an alleged Jewish world conspiracy. The latter became prominent after the publication in Russia in 1903 of *The Protocols of the Elders of Zion*, an anti-Semitic hoax distributed in several languages throughout and beyond Europe by the tsar's secret police.[22] *The Protocols* was seen by many—including Adolf Hitler—as proof of a conspiracy among Jews, Freemasons, communists, and others to take over the world and, although exposed as a forgery in 1921 by *The [London] Times* newspaper in a series of articles reprinted in the *New York Times*, it became compulsory reading in German schools after the Nazis came to power in 1933.

Did the Nazis really believe their own anti-Semitic propaganda? Chosen as "representatives" of the unassimilated (and unassimilable) elements in German society, the Jews served the Nazis' political agenda even if many Nazi leaders—some of them men with Ph.D. degrees—must have been skeptical about official Nazi ideology. It is, however, important to note that in other historical contexts, very diverse ethnic, national, or social groups have played the role of unassimilable elements—from heretical Christian groups, such as the Albigenses and the Cathars, through "witches" from the early thirteenth to the late seventeenth centuries in Europe and America, to the Armenians, Assyrians, and Greeks in the Ottoman Empire, and Muslims in the former Yugoslavia, to mention just a few well-known instances. In today's Western societies, their place has been taken by—among others—sexual minorities, prostitutes, immigrants, Muslims, and the poor.

During this first stage, when *Otherness is being constructed*, violence is expressed through images. These images legitimize the need for extermination even though nobody is yet speaking in these terms. The authorities still tolerate those who are different, but consistently discriminate against them, branding them and constructing new identities for them. In short, this negative labeling of others is both a key process in constructing identities in the modern world and the first step toward genocide.

Despite the widespread occurrence of this process, local variations in the way others are stigmatized determine the feasibility and possible effectiveness of implementing genocide at a later date. Genocide is scarcely possible without a broad social consensus. For example, in countries like Poland, Hungary, and Romania, where prejudice and hatred against the Jews had already given rise to sporadic killings, genocide could be implemented fairly quickly after the official stigmatization process had begun. France was a special case, given the Dreyfus affair, which divided the nation in the 1890s and early 1900s, and the role of French thinkers from Count Boulainvilliers (1658–1722), whom Arendt sees as inventing the "discourse of race struggle," to Count Gobineau (1816–1882), the inventor of the notion of degenerative racism.

By contrast, in most modern, emancipated societies such as Germany, Holland, and Denmark, the process was much slower. Indeed, when Hitler ordered Danish Jews to be arrested and deported in 1943, ordinary Danish citizens helped the resistance movement to evacuate around 8,000 of them (95 percent of Denmark's Jewish population) to neighboring Sweden. Similarly, Bulgaria's civilian population played a crucial role in saving the country's 48,000-strong Jewish population by pressuring the Bulgarian government to prevent deportations even though the latter had introduced anti-Semitic legislation two years earlier clearly modeled on Germany's Nuremburg Laws.

Stage Two. Harassment

This stage marks a qualitative leap from symbolic to physical violence. In general, it advances more quickly in times of crisis, as the anxiety and latent violence resulting from current deprivations and uncertainty about the future can be directed against those who insist on maintaining a separate identity or on flouting norms others have accepted. Typically, the stigmatized group is accused of causing the crisis by corrupting public morals, undermining national unity, or conspiring with foreign agents in ways that would not normally stand the test of common sense.

Harassment is characterized by two types of simultaneous and complementary actions: bullying and disenfranchisement. First, radicals or "shock troops" carry out sporadic attacks, claiming that their "tolerance" is at an end and calling for "firm action." These attacks achieve several goals simultaneously. They deepen the process of stigmatization; they test society's readiness to buy into physical violence; and they provide an excuse to recruit and organize a repressive apparatus to "manage" the situation.[23] The authorities use the breakdown of law and order created by these "spontaneous" acts of aggression to justify authoritarian and repressive policies, and to strengthen the "legitimate" security forces. Often, the victims are so intimidated by these ongoing and seemingly indiscriminate acts of aggression that they are ready to move to the relative safety of a ghetto. Segregation is precisely what happens at stage three (see below), and generally marks the point of no return toward extermination, which is stage five.

Second, the authorities gradually deprive the stigmatized group of its civil rights. This begins with restrictions on property and marriage, as well as on practicing certain professions and customs (e.g., the Nazi prohibition on *kashrut*, or kosher slaughtering), and ends in the loss of citizenship. These measures increase support for the regime by "normal" citizens, who are able to buy the out-group's property and businesses at knock-down prices and gain access to better jobs and positions, while limiting the number of unclassifiable children of mixed marriages. At the same time, they reduce the out-group's freedom of speech, freedom of movement, and potential for development.

At this stage, policies are aimed at forcing the out-group to leave, rather than killing it outright. Those who cannot flee into exile are subject to social exclusion. This exclusion marks a much more important step toward extermination than exile, because isolating the victimized people within the "normalized" society does not resolve the dispute between same and different, but simply creates a need in the minds of the authorities to find a "final solution."

Even though extermination remains a seemingly remote possibility, this is also the point at which recruitment and training of the future perpetrators begins. Just as a regular army requires an officer corps to develop strategy and tactics, as well as to train and discipline the troops and lead them on the battlefield, a genocidal army requires an organizational structure to provide ideological indoctrination and training in kidnapping; tactics to subjugate and dehumanize the victims; torture to extract information; and finally the murder—without moral qualms or physical revulsion—of unarmed civilians.

As already mentioned, extermination at this stage is only a remote possibility and policies of physical and legal harassment are more directed toward excluding the stigmatized group. Now, exclusion can take two forms: external and internal. External exclusion involves expulsion of the group from their country or, at least, from their habitual area of residence. From the thirteenth century until Jewish emancipation in the early nineteenth century, the Jews were driven out of nearly every European country at one time or another. The Reich Central Office for Jewish Emigration, set up by Eichmann in October 1939, aimed to expel Jews from the Reich, although it is still debated whether by then genocide was not already in the cards since by February 1939 most Jews had been robbed of the means to emigrate.

However, in attempting to explain the Nazis' move from emigration to extermination policies, it is often assumed (see, for example, Christopher Browning) that emigration has proved "ineffective," as if the Nazis' only goal was to separate the out-group from the in-group. From the perspective I am trying to develop in this book, the question is whether migration effectively solves the problems created by the suppression of certain social relations linked to autonomy, solidarity, and critical thinking—solves them, that is, for the perpetrators—or whether it is just an intermediate step toward genocide.

In the case of the Jews, the question is, what would have happened if the Nazis' emigration policy had been more successful? Would the Nazis have made do with expelling the Jews from Germany, as Ferdinand and Isabella had done in 1492 in Spain? Or was death an essential ingredient of the Nazis' "technology" of power? Would it have been possible to unravel and reweave the social fabric of even the German state—not to mention the Reich or the rest of Europe—without resorting to the terror induced by mass annihilation?[24] The Nazis' insistent demands that their allies send their Jewish populations to death camps in spite of their allies' reluctance to do so—especially Italy and Bulgaria–seem to support the hypothesis that expulsion from the Reich was not enough and that the need to annihilate the Other lay at the heart of the Nazi state and its policies toward European populations.

Stage Three. Isolation

At this stage, the focus shifts to social and territorial planning. This stage has taken different forms at different moments in modern history, but the goal is always the same: to demarcate a separate social, geographical, economic, political, cultural, and even ideological space for those who are "different," and at the same time to sever their social ties with the rest of society. The ghetto, in the original sense of a restricted area within a European medieval city in which Jews were required to live, has traditionally been the most highly developed form of segregation. Other less sophisticated "ghettos" have served these same functions at different times and for different populations.

Apart from breaking all ties between the population to be exterminated and the outside world, this stage, too, achieves several objectives simultaneously. First, it makes it easier for the genocidal forces to identify the victims and, at the same time, to hide the process of harassment and extermination from the public, which would probably condemn outright murder committed in full view of the rest of society. Second, confiscated housing and property are transferred to the in-group, again strengthening support for the regime. In fact, most "ordinary" citizens in Nazi Germany felt uncomfortable witnessing the public degradation of the Jews. Although they had internalized the official discourse to the point of considering the victims to be responsible for the violence, they approved of and, in some cases, petitioned the authorities for the removal of Jews to ghettos on "humanitarian" grounds.

After a period of prolonged harassment, the victimized population often looks forward to, and even demands, relocation in a ghetto. For example, much of the Jewish community saw the Nazi ghettos as a relief from daily aggression. They did not understand that their removal from society marked a qualitative leap toward their own annihilation:[25] "The Jews began to yearn for only one thing: to escape from the world of the gentiles and shut themselves within four walls where the enemy could not get at them. It was rumored that all the Jews were soon to be enclosed in a ghetto. Some were afraid; others saw this as their salvation."[26] However, other Jews were clearer about the meaning of this stage in the overall process:

> The ghetto was not a way to achieve Jewish autonomy, as many thought, but an instrument with which to kill first our souls and then our bodies. The ghetto was destined to destroy our people, to completely erase it from the face of the earth. . . . In this way, they were killing the soul of our people, stripping them of the essential logic of common sense. With this system they corrupted the healthier impulses of an organized community. I assured them that the same thing would happen in Bialystok, because if not, the Germans would not have deployed there the ghetto, the police or the Judenrat [Jewish Council]. The Germans did not seek to help but to harm the Jews.[27]

In fact, the only "autonomy" granted to the Jewish Council was the power to draw up the lists of deportees. The Judenrat decided who would die—but not when and how—and who would survive for another month or week. By giving them this power over life and death, the Nazis not only saved themselves work but undermined solidarity within the Jewish ghettos.

To summarize: isolation, like the other stages of genocide, accomplishes several goals at once. First of all, it gives the genocidaires much more room to maneuver and identify those they wish to annihilate. Also, it removes the process of discrimination, harassment, and destruction from the public gaze, and from the eyes of those who might raise ethical and moral objections. Moreover, isolation is an important step in breaking social ties between those to be exterminated and the outside world. For this reason, one of the Jewish resistance's main objectives was precisely to stay in touch with the outside world. The chances of survival of the Jewish resistance movements depended on contacts within the non-Jewish world, but so did those of other inmates of the ghettos: the life and death of whole families as well as the success or failure of the resistance actions depended on maintaining underground networks outside the ghetto and sending children out to smuggle food and information into the ghetto.

Stage Four. Policies of Systematic Weakening

At this stage the perpetrators set priorities. They distinguish between those that *must* be exterminated, and those that *may* be exterminated, depending on the political and social circumstances and the perpetrators' capacity to kill. Once the victims have been isolated from the rest of society, the perpetrators typically implement a series of measures aimed at weakening them systematically. These consist of strategies of *physical destruction* through overcrowding, malnutrition, epidemics, lack of health care, torture, and sporadic killings; and of *psychological destruction*, manifested in humiliation, abuse, harassment or killing of family members, attempts to undermine solidarity through collective punishment, the encouraging of collaboration in categorizing and classifying prisoners, and denunciation and peer abuse.

The main goal at this stage is to select those who *must* be exterminated. Some are murdered; others die of hunger or disease; yet others *adapt* by identifying with the behavior and ideology of their victimizers. This phenomenon, similar to the Stockholm syndrome studied in hostage situations, is mentioned by many genocide survivors. It leads not only to the psychological destruction of the individual, but to that of the group, as individuals are coerced to behave aggressively toward the so-called unfit.[28]

Once the victims have been systematically weakened, and with the necessary political consensus and technical facilities in place, the process may proceed to the next stage: extermination. If not, the cycle will begin again. Subcategories of Others will be established for harassment; and the perpetrators will further degrade their prisoners (whether they still reside in a ghetto or have been transferred to a concentration camp) by making them turn against one another. Primo Levi, an Auschwitz survivor, describes how this was accomplished by the Nazis, using the *kapo* system:

> If one offers a position of privilege to a few individuals in a state of slavery, exacting in exchange the betrayal of natural solidarity with their comrades, there will certainly be someone who will accept. He will be withdrawn from the common law and will become untouchable; the more power that he is given, the more he will be consequently hateful and hated. When he is given command of a group of unfortunates, with the right of life or death over them, he will be cruel and tyrannical, because he will understand that if he is not sufficiently so, someone else, judged more suitable, will take over his post. Moreover, his capacity for hatred, unfulfilled in the direction of the oppressor, will double back, beyond all reason, on the oppressed; and he will only be satisfied when he has unloaded onto his underlings the injury received from above.[29]

In the ghettos, labor camps, and concentration camps of the Third Reich, these three stages—*physical destruction, psychological destruction*, and *selection* were repeated in a spiraling crescendo. In the Warsaw ghetto, for example, the mortality rate increased from an average of 500 deaths per month in 1939 to more than 5,000 deaths per month in 1942 as food rations were cut, living spaces became increasingly overcrowded, and infectious diseases multiplied. Starvation, illness, and constant harassment by the Nazis created a "marketplace of informers," both among the local population and among the Jews themselves: groups of people living by denouncing others, accusing them of being communists, saboteurs, and dissidents or simply having left the ghetto in search of a piece of bread. The Jewish police also sank into moral degradation, as they went from house to house looking for hidden children so as to cover the daily quota of deportees required by the Nazis.

On top of the physical and mental suffering, the Jews were forced to participate in an ongoing process of "selection" and so to construct still "others" within the Other. How successful this Nazi strategy of "divide and rule" really was is clear in Pierre Vidal-Naquet's account of the annihilation of the Jewish community in France.

The UGIF (General Union of the Israelites of France) was a Jewish organization created by the Vichy regime that brought together "noble" French Jews so "integrated" into French society that they believed themselves safe from the Nazis. After first handing over all the "foreign" Jews (Polish and Ukrainian migrant workers), the UGIF was forced to cooperate in deporting France's Jewish proletariat before themselves being deported to Drancy. In the words of Vidal-Naquet:

> The Nazis think differently: for them there is no fundamental difference between André Baur and a little Polish Jewish tailor. Whatever the stages of their plan may have been—and they were very complex—they laugh heartily at the differences between French people and foreigners, but to achieve their destructive purpose they are willing to use all existing differences, to use foreigners against the French, Leo Israelowicz—who was the head of the UGIF liaison office with the Gestapo—against André Baur, the French against foreigners. . . . This game of the rope and the hanged is terrible, tragic; the notables who ran the UGIF played it with their social and political habits, their class reflexes.[30]

The Nazis developed a whole series of clever and vicious tactics to deepen this moral confusion, establishing the number of deportees, haggling with the leaders of each Judenrat over a few thousand deportees to make them feel they have saved part of the Jewish population, but giving the responsibility for drawing up the list to the leaders of this Jewish "self-government."

And so these members of the Jewish pseudogovernments believed they had become something like demigods, capable of granting life and death, trying to rationalize their decisions by including the sick, the elderly, even children on their lists with the excuse that they must keep alive others with real chances of survival. There were also cases of corruption, leaders who changed names on the lists in exchange for money, jewelry, or anything that a family could give to "rescue" one of its members. To a greater or lesser degree, everyone in the ghettos fell into the same ethical trap. Jaika Grossman describes it with his usual wit:

> Those who believed before the war that it was possible to achieve socialism peacefully, to bring the workers to power by an indirect route,

avoiding confrontations; those who thought they could liberate the people without casualties, without mobilizations, but with a deep inner revolution; those were the same ones who brought to the people the mistaken and falsely deluded idea that Nazi conquest, murder and oppression could also be avoided. They directed their own movements and the people's to avoiding and concealing the facts in times of such desperate confrontation between two worlds. As if an entire nation could slip through the cracks in history. One or two might slip through the cracks—but an entire people? Leaders and society? We could not and did not want to understand any of them. We did not want to defuse tensions and reach a deal with them. These meetings were distressing both for us and for them. This was not a question of psychological differences between young and old, as interpreted by some.[31] Nor was it about disagreements between pessimists like us, who felt the proximity of the genocide and did not want to hide it from people, and optimists like them, who believed that humanity was about to rise up and would help them avoid misfortune. Who said that ignoring reality was being optimistic and that facing it was being pessimistic? Perhaps it was the other way round. We wanted the news about the mass slaughter of Ponar to be released on a large scale but not to generate feelings of apathy or despair in people that would lead them to say: "The SS will annihilate us anyway." That would have been criminal. We wanted to publish the truth about what awaited us, to show those terrible things that were starting to happen, show them in all their authentic crudeness, so that we could defend ourselves. We wanted to get organized, to stand in the breach, to wield our weapons while we still had time.

And our adversaries? Apparently they were still not strong enough to undertake any major projects, no grand gesture, and for that reason, were reluctant to see what was happening. Was it psychological fear? No way! A fear like that could not be attributed to "ordinary" Jews, who do not know the causes of their mistakes and do not understand their relationship with the vicissitudes of the world. That is, it was a completely private panic, with no social roots in sight. It was the fear of an ideology, a view of the world and of history that, unfortunately, managed to paralyze many. That fear also became a partaker of the historical facts.[32]

It is not easy to understand why the victims of the Nazi genocide did not refuse to get on the trains that took them to their deaths—or why the victims of other genocides, for that matter, do not resist more actively. But these populations have generally been defeated long before they reach the stage of physical annihilation. One simply has to imagine a crowd of people sitting or standing in the sun and rain for a whole week in the main square of a ghetto, undernourished, dirty, and sick, almost unable to think. Suddenly they are offered toast and jam or a cup of tea, or a change of clean clothes to get on a train. Certain newsreel images—for example, the much publicized sequence of a doctor dressed impeccably in his best suit, saying good-bye to his family as he boards the train, oblivious to his fate—have distorted our understanding of the reality of this stage. Such images simply serve to hide the "systematic weakening" these people have already been subjected to.

What is remarkable is that in such extreme circumstances, there are always individuals who do attempt to resist—often placing their own lives, along with those of their own children and other family members, at risk.[33]

Stage Five. Extermination

The extermination stage is characterized by the physical disappearance of those who once embodied certain types of social relations. The Nazi genocides mark a qualitative transformation of this stage, not only at the level of technology, but also at a political and symbolic level. Even during the death marches of the Armenian population in 1915, a personal relationship existed between the Armenians and their Turkish guards. In contrast, the industrialization of death by the Third Reich rendered the relationship between victims and perpetrators *anonymous*, as well as dissolving individual moral responsibility by breaking the process into a succession of separate stages. The production line started with the organization of trains and the deportation of the victims to the extermination camps of Auschwitz-Birkenau, Belzec, Chelmno, Majdanek, Sobibor, or Treblinka, and ended with the victims' bodies being burned and their remains ground to dust. With the gas chambers, the perpetrators did not even have to watch their victims die. This depersonalized form of murder has since been copied in other genocidal processes.

This systematic, impersonal, and tremendously efficient ability to make entire populations disappear in a relatively short period of time also marks a new stage in the exercise of power by dominant classes. The perpetrators have demonstrated to the rest of society the consequences of aspiring to autonomous control over one's own body. The new sovereign power is no longer characterized by the spectacular staging of small-scale public executions (as in earlier centuries), but by a new technology of power that, as Foucault points out, fuses the ancient sovereign right to kill with the biopolitical management of life.[34]

Stage Six. Symbolic Enactment

Just as manufacturers only realize their investments when they sell their goods, so those who practice genocide realize their investments in killing and "disappearing" people through symbolic "representations." In the case of manufacturing, physical goods must constantly be sold—in other words, exchanged for money or the abstract equivalent of money—for the manufacturing cycle to continue. Unless this happens, profit turns to loss as the unsold merchandise begins to depreciate in value. A similar logic can be found in the case of genocidal social practices. Destruction only benefits the perpetrators if it can be turned into certain forms of social narrative that re-present annihilation.[35]

In other words, genocidal social practices do not end in the physical annihilation of the victims, but rather in the symbolic ways that this trauma is represented. If the overarching purpose of genocide is to transform social relationships within a given society, it is not sufficient to kill those who think or behave differently. The types of social relationships that these people embodied (or potentially embodied) must be replaced either with traditional in-group models of relating or, more commonly, with new ways of relating. However, not all representations of the facts contribute to this transition. For example, those who hold official remembrance ceremonies, whether out of goodwill or in the belief that they can exorcise genocide merely by invoking its name, often stress the need to "remember the victims." However, the most effective form of symbolic genocide is not oblivion, which ignores the disappearance of a way of life as if it had never disappeared, but does not preclude its reappearance The most effective form of symbolic genocide is the pious pretense that genocide is somehow irrational and inexplicable.

For genocide to be effective while the perpetrators are in power it is not enough for the perpetrators to kill and materially eliminate those who stand for a particular social order the perpetrators wish to destroy. They need to spread the terror caused by genocide throughout society. Conversely, the best way to perpetuate the effects of terror in a *postgenocidal* society is by dissociating genocide from the social order in which it occurred—not in a crude and obvious way by denying the facts, as Turkey continues to do with the Armenians, but by changing the meaning, logic, and intentionality of genocide. In Foucauldian terms, we need to shift our focus from what the social practices of genocide set out to *destroy* (a culture, a national group, a political tendency), to what they were intended to *create* (usually, a new society). This supplies the key for how genocide can and should be remembered, or reappropriated. To accomplish this, we need to problematize the *assimilation structures* or levels of understanding at which various postgenocidal societies tend to narrate events, and which separate genocide from the social order that produced it. They do so not by denying the facts, but by distorting their meaning.[36]

THE DENIAL OF THE IDENTITY OF THE VICTIMS. Authors such as Hannah Arendt and Stanley Milgram have commented at length on new constructions of genocide affect and how these change our image of the perpetrators. In the past, many of these works were, as a result, struck off the list of "serious" works on the Shoah.[37]

On the other hand, the victims of genocidal social practices are deliberately and repeatedly homogenized as "innocent." The dominant discourse at the moment when genocide is implemented tends to depict victims as culpable in innumerable ways, transforming them into agents of the devil responsible for the majority of social evils. Paradoxically, however, once the genocide has been accomplished, and to the extent that the social consensus on which the perpetrators depended has been eroded, the hegemonic gaze may move toward an emphasis on the "innocence" of the victims, proceeding hand-in-hand with the demonization of the perpetrators and their relegation to the realm of "irrationality." In some societies, this process is accelerated by military defeat (as with the Nazis in Germany or the Hutu extremists in Rwanda), or by political defeat (as with the military dictatorships of Latin America). In other cases, the process occurs more slowly, as with Turkey or Indonesia. And in still other cases, when a consensus remains as to the legitimacy of the genocide in the society in which it occurred, the process of "constructing innocence" may take generations or even centuries—as with the annihilation of the indigenous populations of the modern states of the Americas.

However it occurs, this mode of constructing "innocent" victims ends up being even more effective than blaming them for their own destruction. It dilutes genocide as much as it appears to condemn it. It meshes easily with the image of mad, perverse, pathological, and evil murderers that emerges from the ways the perpetrators themselves legitimize genocide. Of course, I am not suggesting that the victims deserve their fate. Rather, I am saying that we need to look more carefully at the discourses justifying the persecution, exclusion, and extermination of different victims.

The "hegemonic gaze" may also be located outside the genocidal society itself, affecting how onlookers evaluate the genocidal process. Let us consider again the case of Nazi Germany as viewed by contemporary members of the societies that combined to defeat it. The Nazis invented the myth of Aryan superiority to differentiate themselves from other groups (ethnic, religious, political, social, national, sexual, or otherwise). Using a biological metaphor, the Nazis stigmatized people belonging to other groups as "degenerates" who had corrupted the race or the *Volk* community.[38] However, something similar has occurred in the way that Nazi Germany has been demonized in discourse since then. This relies upon a binary structure of the type described earlier—one that contrasts "irrationality" and "absolute evil" with "innocence." The metaphysical category of absolute evil distracts attention from our everyday experience, leaving us safe from the distress that we might be caused if we were to accept the genocidal potential latent in all members of every modern society.

Many writers on Nazism take it for granted that the Jews were annihilated simply because they were Jews. However, if one examines carefully the populations exterminated by the Nazis, it is clear that the Jews played a central role in this process precisely because Jewishness (from the perspective of the Central and Eastern European regimes of the 1930s) was *more* than just a question of having three Jewish grandparents. The stigmatizing of certain groups was connected (more or less accurately) with their subversive potential or inability to adapt to a given social order. It should be remembered that most Jews in the 1930s saw themselves as "international" (which does not mean that they were involved in international conspiracies, as the Nazis alleged), and so were unconvinced by nationalist ideologies.

It is surprising to note the extent to which certain political, religious, and moral tendencies of Jewish collectivities in Central and Eastern Europe in the nineteenth and early twentieth centuries—in particular, in the area the Jews called the "Pale of Settlement"—have been neglected or forgotten in scholarly analysis. A powerful symbol of this is the massive Jewish participation in numerous oppositional and contestatory movements (whether revolutionary or reformist), from the Spartacists to the communists, anarchists, Bundists (the Jewish Workers Party), and socialists, in Germany, Poland, Russia, Ukraine, and Lithuania. These include such specific cases as the "Jewish Soviet" in Hungary under the Béla Kun government, the Jewish socialist prime minister León Blum in France, and the vital Jewish participation at the leadership level of various Russian and Polish revolutionary movements.

The most important dimension, however, is not the Jews' numerically large participation in such contestatory movements, but their link with a deeper, more global element, linked to the scant support that Jewish nationalism (Zionism) and non-Jewish European nationalisms aroused among Jewish populations, until the Nazis appeared on the scene. Because of the persecutions suffered by Jews in Russia, Poland, and Lithuania, and because of their marginalization in Germany and France, Jewish communities continued to view themselves as "diasporic" in nature, founded on multiple identities, capable of transcending their Jewish cultural component; their assimilation within the national territories they inhabited, whether German, Polish, Russian, or French; their greater or lesser religious convictions (many Jewish groups were atheists, others were reformists, others Orthodox, but all considered themselves Jewish beyond their specific religious or nonreligious identification); and their political identity (which was highly varied, though in general forsaking a nationalist tendency for a diverse range of internationalist and diasporic currents of thought).

This is not to suggest that all Jews shared in this process of self-identification. In the Netherlands, for instance, Jews were much more assimilated into the national identities of their countries. But they were exceptions in the world of European Jewry during the first half of the twentieth century. In general, Jews stood apart from the wider patterns of European nationalism of the period. Only by understanding this tendency can we hope to comprehend the key elements of European Jewish identity and their role in fueling the paranoid delirium of the Nazis with respect to the supposed "risks" Jews posed to "western European identity." The Jews obviously did not represent the kind of threat depicted by the Nazis, but their general readiness to embrace multiple identities—indeed, their recognition of the multiplicity, complexity, and dynamism of identity formation—*did* pose a challenge to the narrow nationalisms prevailing in Europe at the time. This was problematic and "subversive" for a model of identity, such as the Nazis', which sought to subordinate all such identifications to those of the organic *Volk* of a well-defined national territory. In a philosophical sense, Jewish identity was constructed "in time," while modern European identities were constructed "in space."

It is this distinction that allows us to perceive Hitler not only as an alienated figure, but as an extreme expression of a hegemonic political tendency in modern Europe. This perspective also allows us to understand the complicity of diverse European regimes in the annihilation of the Jews, their failure to react, their refusal to accept Jewish refugees in their territories, among other elements that have generally remained unexplained or been relegated to a banal analysis of the greater or lesser "political will" of the various governments in question.[39]

Similarly, scattered groups of Gypsies who refused to adopt German as their mother tongue, to water down their centuries-old culture, or to accept the notion of private property were lumped together with those who refused to accept sexual norms. In fact, any group that maintained a certain level of social self-determination became a political target for the stifling heteronomy imposed by the Nazis. To recover the identity of the victims, and preserve their memory and history, it is essential for us to understand *why* they were exterminated. Far from justifying their fate, this understanding is intended to reinstate the victims as social subjects.

Bettelheim touched on this controversial issue with his questioning of the Frank family as a worldwide symbol of the Holocaust. It is not that he did not respect their suffering. Rather, he felt that choosing the Franks as a symbol made it harder to understand the genocidal process. In Bruno Bettelheim's words: "I believe that the worldwide acclaim given [Anne Frank's] story cannot be explained unless we recognize in it our wish to forget the gas chambers and our effort to do so by glorifying the ability to retreat into an extremely private world . . . that was glorified precisely because it led to their destruction. . . . What we miss is the importance of accepting the gas chambers as facts, so they can never again be allowed to exist. If all men are basically good . . . then, really, we can all continue with our daily lives and forget Auschwitz."[40] According to Bettelheim, the Frank family became a symbol of the Holocaust not just because they did not try to escape or to fight back, but because they were a "civilized family," an "assimilated" family, in this case, that was not very different from other non-Jewish families in Europe. They continued to live in their own private world until their very last day together. We might also add that the Franks were Dutch Jews, living in a Nazi-occupied territory rather than in Germany. Certainly, the Franks were victims of the Nazis; the point is that the use that has been made of their story does not help us to understand what it was that the Nazis hated about the Jews to the point of wanting to kill them all.

On the other hand, the attention given to the story of the Frank family seems to suggest that the internment in concentration camps of German antifascist Jews—Communists, Bundists, Zionists, and even Orthodox Jews—was somehow more understandable, and perhaps "almost" justifiable. After all, they were political enemies; they were not murdered simply for being Jewish. The problem is that if we condemn the Holocaust for selecting the "wrong" victims, or because the Nazis overestimated the subversive potential of Judaism and failed to understand the multiple and contradictory nature of Central European Jewish identity in the first half of the twentieth century, we perversely end up legitimizing the logic of genocide. We also miss the point that Central European Jews were murdered precisely for what they did, and not for what they failed to do.

THE TRANSFERENCE OF GUILT. A more subtle form of symbolic genocide is the transfer of guilt through scapegoating and self-scapegoating. Through a perverse psychological mechanism, those victims who actively oppose a genocidal regime—that is, those who are "less innocent"—are blamed or blame themselves for the deaths of those who are "more innocent." In this way, a chain of responsibility is forged that assigns varying degrees of guilt and innocence to the victims of genocide, while the actual perpetrators are regarded as a mere force of nature, meting out the punishment sought by the "guilty."

The Vilna ghetto established by the Nazis in the Lithuanian capital of Vilnius provides a clear example of transfer of responsibility. In 1943, the Judenrat agreed to hand over Yitzhak Wittenberg, the leader of Jewish armed resistance, to the Gestapo. In a speech delivered in the main square, Jacob Gens, the head of the ghetto, accused the resistance of provoking the Nazis into liquidating the ghetto, and turned the population against the members of the Jewish resistance. Finally, Wittenberg himself made the decision to give himself up.[41]

If there is one lesson to be learned from the Vilna ghetto, it is that appeasement does not work. Later that same year, the whole of the ghetto was liquidated, and the only people who survived were the resistance forces that fled to the surrounding forests. For the victims, appeasement was a way to buy time and avoid collective punishments; but for the perpetrators, it was simply a predictable result of the strategy of systematic weakening described earlier, allowing them time to solve the technical problems of implementing a "final solution." Appeasement brings no peace but the peace of a cemetery, where even the names of the dead have been erased.

There were many factions of the Jewish leadership of the time who accepted the notion of "collective responsibility," which turned resistance into guilt and genocide into a sort of natural force waiting to be spurred into action by "irresponsible" resistance. This logic ended up legitimizing the forces of domination, which were "peaceful" as long as they were not "provoked." And yet what some described at the time as "collaboration" was obviously just a survival strategy. To attempt to justify such behavior after the event prevents us from recovering the true identity of the victims.

HORROR AND PARALYSIS. In postgenocidal democracies, symbolic annihilation of the victims through the discourses of "innocence" and "metaphysical evil" is reinforced by the morbid fascination of the media and popular historians with the details of the crimes themselves. We are inundated with blow-by-blow accounts of suffering, descriptions of torture and execution, and other horrific testimonies, together with an abundance of spine-chilling photographs. None of these contributes much to our understanding of why the victims were killed. On the contrary, it simply perpetuates a sense of terror and paralysis throughout society. "Memory for the victims" is turned into a sort of horror show.

Similarly, the use of genocide as a political symbol in postgenocidal democracies is not linked to silence and oblivion. If the Armenian genocide continues to be a political taboo in modern Turkey, Western democracies have replaced the strategy of "taboo" with an excess of empty political declarations that avoid questions about the identity of the victims or the true beneficiaries of genocide, and so continue to make restorative justice impossible. In many postgenocidal societies, those who make a genuine effort to confront this injustice may wind up being tortured or murdered. But even when the threat of physical violence is no longer present, a network of symbolic and discursive processes continues to imprison jurists, historians, and sociologists—and even poets—within its invisible walls, limiting what can be thought and said about genocide.

Reformulating Social Relations: A Struggle for Identity

The six stages of modern genocide described above form a cycle, the central aim of which is to transform the society in which genocide takes place by destroying a way of life embodied by a particular group, and thus reorganizing social relations within the rest of society. The disappearance of the memory of the victims brought about by symbolic enactment—that is, by the enactment of genocide through discursive and other symbolic means—is an attempt to close the cycle. Not only do the victims no longer exist, but they allegedly "never existed"—or, if we know that they existed, we are no longer able to grasp how they lived or why they died. Otherwise the cycle might begin again.

What happens, then, to a society that remains silent while people are beaten in the streets and disappear? What happens to a society in which some denounce their neighbors, and others steal their jobs or businesses, their homes or other assets? All these forms of "moral participation" in genocide must inevitably lead to a blurring of moral distinctions, an inability to distinguish between right and wrong, fair and unfair. This is true not only for those who live in a time of genocide, but for subsequent generations as well.

At the same time, the trauma produced in the population by a genocidal process, and internalized as a way of relating to others mediated by terror, may manifest itself in diverse ways. One of these is survivor guilt among those who have lost relatives, friends, or colleagues. Another is the inability to assert oneself in family or social relationships or to find a group identity, found in psychotherapy patients' storylines such as these:

> "I am a Nazi, and if I express my anger, I will destroy in a most sadistic manner the lives of those who have frustrated me; in order to keep this a secret, I need to smile all the time."
>
> "I believe that my father was an SS officer, and the fact that he is my love-object has to be hidden, so I should repeat acts to deny my Germanness."[42]

The transgenerational nature of guilt and denial among members of the "in-group" is visible in the way that young ethnic German psychoanalysts, even today, are afraid to explore patients' Nazi-related family histories.[43] The attempt by the perpetrators to create a "strong" homogeneous society through terror also destroys the in-group, to a greater or lesser extent—both morally and psychologically. Moreover, postgenocidal societies that are unable to recognize and mourn the processes in which they have participated remain vulnerable to the repetition of authoritarian modes of political problemsolving. In Argentina, the expression "You don't exist" was first created by the repressors in the secret detention centers of the 1970s and filtered into in the teenage slang of the 1980s and 1990s as a colloquial form of contempt.[44]

But if genocide is not directed solely at the material victims of the annihilation process, one must ask: How could trauma affect a postgenocidal society in which most people—accomplices, informers, betrayers, or simply those who had stolen or made use of the victims' property—were silent? Can a small betrayal of human values in the course of one's work, the breaking of a strike, an act of aggression in the street, or an anonymous denunciation be viewed as moral participation in genocide, whether through active consent or tolerance of inaction? Perhaps observing the past in terms of the present, as Tzvetan Todorov has recommended, requires us to look at the present with greater mistrust.[45] Without knowing who the victims of genocide were and why they were annihilated, we hardly know who we are ourselves, and why we live as we do.

PART THREE

Toward a Historical Basis

Genocidal Social Practices in Argentina

International recognition of the importance of the Nazi genocides has given rise to a rich and complex literature attempting to explain the causes of these crimes or to choose between alternative explanations as to why they happened. As we have seen, different theories have been proposed at different times and in different parts of the world—even though some commentators reject the possibility of finding any rational explanation whatsoever. In chapters 4 and 5 I examined just a small selection of this vast literature and—because of the sociological focus of this book—the emphasis was mostly on the sociology literature and on causal models of explanation.

In contrast, there is far less literature on social genocide practices in Argentina during the military dictatorship between 1976 and 1983. This is understandable given the recent nature of the events—thirty years have gone by since the end of military rule—and the apparently less spectacular scale of the killings, not to mention Argentina's geographical location, far from the centers of world power. Nevertheless, in chapter 7 I continue to prioritize works that offer causal models of explanation, however shaky some of these may be.[1]

And that is not all. Like the previous chapter on the causes of the Nazi genocides, chapter 7 attempts to kill several birds with one stone. It suggests a tentative approach to understanding the causes of the repression carried out in Argentina by the last military government between 1976 and 1983. It examines the declarations of some of the military themselves; the report drawn up by the National

Commission on the Disappearance of Persons (Comisión Nacional sobre la Desaparición de Personas or CONADEP), set up by Raúl Alfonsín, Argentina's postdictatorial president, shortly after his inauguration on December 10, 1983; and it analyzes some academic reflections on these events written between 1980 and 2005 by authors like Guillermo O'Donnell, Luis Marín, Leon Rozitchner, Claudia Hilb, Inés Izaguirre, Eduardo Duhalde, Hugo Vezzetti, Pillar Calveiro, and Luis Romero, among others.

As chapter 7 shows, the first political attempt to bring closure to this painful period in Argentina's history applied a logic now known (pejoratively in left-wing discourse) as the "theory of the two demons." This was expressed in two decrees issued in the early days of Alfonsín's administration–Decree 157/83, which ordered the arrest of seven guerrilla leaders on charges of homicide, conspiracy, and public incitement to commit felonies, among other crimes; and Decree 158/83, which ordered the trial of the nine members of the first three military juntas on charges of homicide, kidnapping, and torture. However, because the junta trials were to be heard in a military court, a whitewash was practically guaranteed. Then came the Report of the CONADEP titled Nunca Más–"Never Again"[2]–which, to all intents and purposes, became the definitive description and causal explanation of events, and closed off other ways of thinking and acting at least until the twentieth anniversary of the coup in 1996, when new approaches emerged that spread beyond the boundaries of academia.

In chapter 8 I will try to test some of the hypotheses put forward in chapter 6 regarding genocidal social practices, in particular the periodization model and the symbolic consequences of different causal reconstructions of historical events in Argentina.

I have argued that different modes of representation are, in fact, "narrativizations" that have material effects on the symbolic ways we process the past. The focus of Part III will therefore be these stories and their material and symbolic effects in relation to the premeditated killing of population groups in Argentina during the period 1974–1983.

7

Explaining Genocidal Social Practices in Argentina

The Problem of Causation

It is difficult to find authors who provide a comprehensive meaning to the events that occurred in Argentina during the military dictatorship of 1976 to 1983. Nevertheless, both during the dictatorship and since it ended nearly thirty years ago, there have been several more or less explicit attempts by politicians, journalists, and academics to make sense of what happened through—sometimes intuitive—causal models. For the sake of brevity, these events will be treated here as genocidal social practices despite possible objections to the term "genocide," which I have already discussed in previous chapters.

Although this chapter sets out to explore these models, the lack of academic research and literature on the subject, together with the need for a case-specific approach, has led me to include works of journalism that do not necessarily come out of a formal academic research process. These explanatory models are interesting because of their potential for shaping collective memory through what I call the "symbolic enactments" of genocidal social practices.[1]

The first section of this chapter critically analyzes the notion of a "Dirty War" against "subversion." Although this way of narrating events is now largely discredited among the Argentine population, it still plays an important role in shaping some collective imagery and the way substantial sectors of the population still behave. We might describe these sectors as the "military circle" and its civilian supporters, in other words, hard-core members of the armed forces and the security forces, family, friends, and connections who, despite being a minority, continue to have a significant impact on the design of some government policies, and in some mass media.

It is worth mentioning that although this approach has been more or less discredited within Argentina, the term "Dirty War" to refer to the repression carried out by Argentina's last military government remains popular abroad, especially in academic literature written in English, which tends to use it almost exclusively. Let us begin, then, by examining the implications of the term "Dirty War."

A "Dirty War" against "Subversion," or Legitimizing One's Own Genocide

One of the first works in which the perpetrators attempted to justify the type of process they were implementing was an early work by Brigadier General Acdel Vilas, the head of Operation Independence, or Operativo Independencia as it was called in Spanish. This was a military campaign to destroy the People's Revolutionary Army (Ejército Revolucionario del Pueblo or ERP), a Trotskyist guerrilla group, which, by the end of 1974, had seized just over a third of the mountainous northwestern province of Tucumán in an attempt to copy the Cuban revolution. Operativo Independencia, which began in February 1975 under the orders of the democratically elected government of María Estela Martínez de Perón (better known as Isabel Perón), became a testing ground for the repressive methods implemented during the military dictatorship a year later.

Vilas wrote his book in 1977, only two years after carrying out the Tucumán campaign.[2] The interesting fact is that the publication of Vilas's book was forbidden by the commander in chief of the army precisely because Vilas made no attempt to hide the actions of his troops against the civilian population of Tucumán or the role played in the campaign by concentration camps and scorched earth policies. On the contrary, it described the new forms of repression in enormous detail and offered an explanatory model legitimizing such actions.

In various passages of his book, Vilas refers to the irregular nature of the war waged in Tucumán and the influence of French counterinsurgency doctrines applied in Indochina and Algeria—for example in the following paragraph:

> While I was flying, approaching, more and more, what would be for almost a year my combat trench, I thought again about the words a specialist in the glorious French army in Algeria wrote in his book—which was my bedtime reading during my spell in Tucumán. In *Subversion and Revolution* he wrote: "A slave to its traditions and training, the army is ill adapted to a war that military schools refuse to teach. In general, it insists on mounting operations against a slippery, uncatchable opponent, according to classical rules. Like a sledgehammer trying to squash a fly, it strikes, mostly at empty space, wasting considerable resources. Even a considerable increase in its resources would have no effect without first adapting its organization and tactics to a revolutionary war. The army should address the complex challenges of revolutionary war

> in a new spirit, detached from all prejudice and with the determination to solve it." The French officer's pithy considerations summarized my own ideas and concerns regarding the operations that very soon, and after a century of peace, the brigade would begin against the country's most dangerous and deadly enemy: Marxism.

In Vilas's mind, this reflection justified the need for clandestine operations in a "Dirty War" that required—in his own words—a very different army from the traditional one, and, thus, different values, different morality, another way of carrying out social practices. It meant replacing a predominantly military social practice—war—with an eminently political one—the destruction of social relations in the civilian population or, as I define it elsewhere in this book, genocide.

In his book, Vilas emphasizes the lack of political support he received from Tucumán's provincial administration, in particular from the governor of Tucumán, Amadeo Juri, and the legislature. As a result, Vilas felt the need to install a "parallel" authority to deal with the "core" of the problem: *the civilian population of the capital of Tucumán*. Not only did he aim to set up mechanisms to persecute the population and undermine solidarity, but also to "win the hearts and minds" of "civilians."

This point goes to the heart of what I am arguing in this book. Vilas's focus was not primarily the guerrillas and leftist insurgencies, or even their political fringes. The objective of Vilas's actions was to develop a series of social practices focused on *the entire population of Tucumán*. The concentration camps set up in the province, in each city, town, or village, were intended to involve the whole of society either as victims or collaborators—or sometimes in both roles one after another.

Having adopted this line of reasoning, Vilas then justified the need to dispense with an independent judiciary and with the "old" ethical rules of war in order to impose a new model of counterinsurgency warfare. In his own words, he introduced

> a Revolutionary Justice dispensed by special courts that worked on the pattern of military justice. Their characteristics were supposed to be confession as sufficient evidence of guilt; assessment of the evidence left to the individual criteria of the judges; informal court procedures to prevent cases being dismissed or overturned on technicalities; and a system of personal responsibility for military officials involved in the preliminary investigations. I decided to dispense with justice, not without a war to the death on lawyers and judges complacent or complicit with subversion.

Vilas suspected that the battle in the mountains could not be won without first changing the balance of forces in the capital city of Tucumán and the surrounding villages. This was a fundamentally *political* battle, even if it had a military outcome. And the political struggle for consensus, passive support, and collaboration—which meant, inter alia, recruiting informers—was to be won through terror.

Vilas himself recognized that the first Argentine concentration camp—the Escuelita de Famaillá, so named because it was an educational institution before being transformed into a clandestine detention center—was a theater of operations as important as the fighting in the Tucumán mountains, if not more so: "Now, if the fight in which we were involved depended on intelligence, the Meeting Place of Detainees was to be the key to the development of 'Operation Independence.'"[3]

Vilas's awareness of the *nature* of the conflict and his willingness to terrorize and/or kidnap civilians and murder them in concentration camps turns his writings into a sort of confession about the *genocidal nature* of the phenomenon, at least as Vilas and many of his fellow perpetrators perceived it. The only place in Argentina in which there was an armed left-wing militia with some operational capacity was the province of Tucumán; and yet the Argentine armed forces went on to target Argentine society as a whole, proof of which is that after the military coup on 24 March 1976, the whole of Argentina was criss-crossed with concentration camps, including territories where there had previously been no organized military forces or brigades.

Operation Independence became a testing ground for developing genocidal social practices that would later be unleashed on society at large. Concentration camps set up in the Escuelita and, soon afterward, in a dozen other locations in Tucumán together with the political measures applied by the leaders of Operation Independence in all cities and towns of the province of Tucumán—from campaigns of denunciation to decisions about the educational content to be delivered in primary and secondary schools in 1975—were a veritable field laboratory in which to test the action plan that would be implemented all over the country after the military uprising of 24 March 1976, against the government of Isabel Perón. Indeed, the military called this plan the "National Reorganization Process," a term that—in my view—proved to be impressively accurate.

As regards political responsibility, however, Operation Independence was developed entirely by the public officials of a democratically elected government. This confounds those simplistic analyses of the 1980s that contrasted democracy and dictatorship and insisted in no uncertain terms that an extremist left-wing provocation was followed by an extremist state reaction, embodied in the military coup.

The planned and systematic genocide in Argentina started under a democratically elected government. The military dictatorship systematized it to a greater or lesser degree and applied it to the rest of the country, but it was first developed at the provincial level in Tucumán. However, the persistent support given by President Isabel Perón and part of her cabinet to these genocidal social practices (against the lukewarm objections of the Tucumán provincial political authorities) was accompanied by an explicit decision to coordinate projects from the civil and military sectors.

General Ramon J. Camps, chief of police of the Province of Buenos Aires during the worst period of the repression, supported the notion of an ideological war. Though less precise than Vilas, Camps realized—somewhat belatedly, in his opinion—that "we have fought victoriously the effects of an evil, leaving intact the cause." By this he meant that the armed forces had fought against the guerrillas, but the ideologists who were the root of the problem still had to be tackled.[4]

In 1977, Camps ordered the kidnapping of Jacobo Timerman, a Ukrainian-born journalist and founder of *La Opinión* newspaper and *Primera Plana* newsmagazine. Timerman, who was Jewish, was accused of laundering money for the guerrilla organization Montoneros[5] and was personally tortured by Camps on several occasions before his release in 1980. Based on Timerman's so-called statements obtained under torture, Camps sought to demonstrate in his book *Caso Timerman: Punto Final* (The Timerman case: Full stop) that civil action—political, journalistic, and social—posed an even greater danger that military action. In Camps's opinion, the National Reorganization Process should have recognized this more clearly and should have acted more harshly against the civilian population.

In short, the Dirty War aimed at "social reengineering" to achieve its objectives in a war that could not be won by military means alone but only through kidnappings, disappearances, torture, and the systematic destruction of the civilian population—in other words, through genocidal social practices. This was seen as a successful strategy by Vilas, a "national project" by the military dictatorship's minister of planning, General Ramón Genaro Diaz Bessone,[6] and as a failure and a mistake by Camps.

Genocide Denial: The "Final Document" of the Military Junta and the Wisdom of Hindsight

After Argentina's defeat by the United Kingdom in the Falklands War on June 1982, Leopoldo Galtieri resigned as de facto president and was replaced by Reynaldo Benito Bignone on July 1, 1982. Discredited by the outcome of the war, the chiefs of staff of all three services also resigned, leaving a power vacuum. With rising inflation and the economy slipping into recession, the military began to look for what they called a "democratic way out," and Bignone was given the responsibility of winding up the dictatorship and transferring power to a freely elected government.

During Bignone's period in office, two particularly important documents appeared. The first was the Military Junta's "Final Document" of April 28, 1983, providing the Junta's official, institutional version of events from the military coup until the end of the Falklands War, especially with regard to what they called counterinsurgency. The second was Law 22,924, the Law of National Pacification, published in September of the same year. Later dubbed the Auto-amnesty Law, it pardoned members of the regime involved in human rights violations. Later, in 1985, Bignone brought out a book entitled *El último de facto* (The last de facto government), which was reprinted in 2000 in a more extended form as *El último de facto II: Quince años después. Memoria y testimonio* ("The last de facto government II: Fifteen years later. Memory and testimony).[7]

All three publications speak of the "war against subversion" but are more careful than Vilas, Camps, or Diaz Bessone not to emphasize the illegal nature of such a war. More concerned about possible prosecutions for human rights abuses than about offering a clear account of the conflict, the 1983 Final Document and Law 22,924 emphasized that the actions carried out by the armed forces were "in the line of duty." With a thinly veiled threat to those who might think otherwise, the military argued that "the armed forces have acted and will act whenever necessary pursuant to an ongoing mandate from the National Government, using the experience gathered in this painful instance of national life."[8] They recognized that "errors . . . may have been committed pursuant to the assigned mission." There was no longer any attempt to justify the illegal nature of these operations as earlier writers had done—only the "mistakes" and "excesses" committed in otherwise "legitimate" military operations.

It may seem surprising at first that the Auto-amnesty Law retrospectively absolved the military from criminal liability for their crimes right back to 25 May 1973, including the three presidencies of the democratic period between 1973 and 1976.[9] This can only be explained by the fact that the genocidal policies implemented under the military government were a continuation of those developed between 1973 and 1976, and that illegal actions had already begun during this period. This is a matter to which I will return shortly, and that calls into question the sharp separation that the discourse of the democratic transition made between democracy and dictatorship in terms of genocidal practices.

As part of his apology for the regime, Bignone's book explains at greater length the meaning of the documents that his government produced. In his view, the military had saved the country from subversion in order to introduce a new democracy. Unlike Vilas or Camps, who were fascinated by the Dirty War and the new counterinsurgency methods, Bignone was "distressed" by such actions and gave his readers to understand that any "errors" or "excesses" committed were the result of historical and political circumstances. However, the good that had resulted—the salvation of the country and the introduction of a new democracy—justified the price the country had had to pay, even if the security forces could not always be proud of the measures they had taken (although Vilas and Camps had certainly been very proud of them).

Bignone is repeatedly at pains to point out what he considers to be the "ingratitude" of those politicians who had gone along with the military government and the fight against subversion in the most unlikely places, and who were tearing out their hair—now that the battle was over—because a few mistakes had been made along the way. The list of politicians and journalists Bignone spoke with on a daily basis is interesting and suggestive of the limits—including the moral or ethical limits—placed on the Alfonsín administration. In fact, these limits were so strong that Alfonsín's government could be described as "democratist"—in other words, democratic in appearance only. Certainly, Alfonsín's government condemned the crimes committed during the dictatorship, but it did so in the abstract, placing all the responsibility on the military. It was careful not to dig deeper into the ways the military government had consolidated itself in power, including the many interrelationships it forged with political sectors of Peronism, with Alfonsín's Radical Civic Union party, and with the provincial parties, as well as with journalists and judges who since had changed sides and now supported the fledgling democracy, forgetting their words, actions, and convictions of just a few years before.

Bignone's conclusion is clear from the quotation at the beginning of his book, which echoes none other than Juan Jose Castelli, one of the country's leading rebels against Spanish rule in the years before Argentina's independence: "Were there other ways? Perhaps this was the case. We never saw them or believed that we would be able to do what we did by other means. There you have the results: enjoy them and put the blame onto us. We will be the executioners; you must be free men."[10] Castelli speaks of the country's independence in the early nineteenth century. Bignone speaks of "reorganizing the nation" through murder and torture and the creation of a "new fatherland." This fatherland would appear in all its glory in the Argentina of the 1990s, where the economic and political consequences of genocidal terror were played out in countless individual and collective practices, in both politics and business.[11]

Bignone attempts to distinguish himself and most of his peers who, he claimed, had reluctantly done their duty, from people like Camps or Vilas, who had identified with the brutal methods required for the job. Here, it is worth repeating an anecdote recounted in his book, a conversation that occurred in the early days of 1971 and which, according to Bignone, makes *all the difference* between the two factions within the military that participated in the National Reorganization Process. In 1970, Bignone had taken command of the cadet corps at the National Military Academy when, to his surprise, the director of the Academy, Jorge Rafael Videla (later president of the first military junta of 1976–1980), ordered that First Lieutenant Aldo Rico should not be allowed to have cadets under his command. Bignone asked why and Videla supposedly answered: "Because I want educators here, not people who will turn out killing machines." After the return to democracy in 1983, Aldo Rico led several mutinies requesting and in some cases achieving impunity for the perpetrators of the genocide.

Bignone's anecdote is quite astonishing. As the head of a government responsible for genocide, he quotes the man who led that government during its cruelest and bloodiest years as saying that he did not want future officers to become "killing machines." And Bignone ends his anecdote rather sententiously by stating: "This defined his [Videla's] concept of the military profession."[12] If the story is true, one cannot help remarking that both men underwent a radical change of heart in the five years leading up to the 1976 coup.

Beyond the contradictory nature of this anecdote, it is clear that neither Videla's nor Bignone's vision is that of Vilas or Camps, or Admiral Emilio Eduardo Massera, navy commander in chief at the time of the military coup and a member of the first military junta. Massera was responsible for a naval base in the city of Buenos Aires that was to become infamous as a center for torture—the Navy Petty-Officers School of Mechanics (generally referred to by its Spanish acronym ESMA), only equaled in cruelty and number of victims by the Campo de Mayo army base nineteen miles outside the city. If Vilas, Camps, and Massera believed that the nature of war excludes legal niceties (Vilas himself had intimidated lawyers and judges in the province of Tucumán), Bignone acts "against his will, with the Doctrine and the regulations in his hand."[13] Death had to be administered, distributed throughout society without mercy, and "mistakes" and "excesses" were inevitable. But these were all in the line of professional duty.

And so these men assumed the role that had been assigned to them: "We will be the executioners," Bignone states in his preface. "They will be remembered as executioners, when they were in fact the saviors. Only history can restore them to their rightful place." Bignone felt compelled to write his version of events for the history books even though he was aware (or so he suggests) of the scandal he would create when he advocated, for example, that Videla should have received the Nobel Peace Prize for the way he ended "a war he had not started."

Hannah Arendt recognized clearly that perpetrators can belong to different personality types.[14] Theodor Adorno went further and identified five types of authoritarian personality.[15] For example, Adorno would have included Ramon J. Camps within a small group of "rebel psychopaths" such as Joseph Goebbels and Julius Streicher because of the way Camps "hated" his victims and took pleasure in his work. However, Arendt was careful to point out that most perpetrators were more like Adolf Eichmann, the spineless bureaucrat who designed the so-called Final Solution to the Jewish Question.

Videla and Bignone were less apathetic than Eichmann, and closer to the manipulative type of obsessive personality identified by Adorno. They were systematic and effective in designing mass murder but never enjoyed slaughter for its own sake. On the contrary, they felt they had a duty to fulfill. It was an unpleasant obligation, but there was no other alternative than to create a new fatherland by "reorganizing" Argentinean society through genocide. In short, men like Camps and Vilas were the most despicable figures of the Argentinean genocide. But it was men like Videla and Bignone who made genocide possible and controlled the overall process

The Theory of Two Demons

The triumph of the Radical Civic Union party's candidate, Raul Alfonsín, in the national elections of 1983 led to a head-on confrontation with the military government's "self-amnesty" law and its legitimization of genocide. Having gained significant support from human rights organizations, Alfonsín had devoted part of his final election campaign to denouncing an alleged pact between the military and the Peronist trade unions aimed at guaranteeing impunity. Now, Alfonsín questioned the notion that the repression carried out by the military dictatorship could be described as a "war."

Decrees 157 and 158, drawn up by Alfonsín's Radical government, expressed a view that soon became widely accepted and that later became known as the theory of the two demons These decrees ordered the simultaneous prosecution of the leaders of the military juntas during the 1976–1983 dictatorship and the leaders of the armed left-wing organizations such as Montoneros and the ERP. Moreover, Decree 157, directed against the surviving leaders of the armed left, suggested they had started the conflict and the repression was simply a response, albeit an exaggerated one, but a response nonetheless.

These decrees were the first attempt to equate the crimes of victims and perpetrators in order to ensure "symmetrical treatment"—a discursive strategy that was undoubtedly successful and shaped the way events were perceived from the end of military dictatorship until 1996 when, on the twentieth anniversary of the coup of 1976, this version of events started to come under challenge. Certainly, the CONADEP Report "Never Again," which saw society as a victim of two simultaneous types of aggression, held sway throughout the 1980s. The prologue to the report was written by Ernesto Sabato (24 June 1911—30 April 2011), a prestigious Argentine novelist, painter, and physicist who headed the eleven-member commission. In it Sabato stated that "during the 1970s Argentina was convulsed by a terror that came from both the extreme right and the extreme left." In other words, there were two symmetrical terrors and a society caught in the middle and unable to escape from either. Sabato goes on to say that "the armed forces responded to the terrorists' crimes with a terrorism far worse than the one they were combating, and after 24 March 1976 they were able to count on the power and impunity of an absolute state, which they misused to abduct, torture, and kill thousands of human beings."

The crucial element in Sabato's account is the "victimization" of society as a whole, to which I have already alluded. Society is seen as removed from the battle between these two demonic groups—one of them, as Sabato explains, "infinitely worse" than the other, but both separate from society. Citizens are seen as *passive victims* of external aggression. "External" no longer meant from outside of the country (as when the military claimed that foreigners were responsible for the violence of the early 1970s). Instead, it meant "alienated" from ordinary society and thus relegated to the level of madness and irrationality (therefore "demonic"). By coincidence or by design, this was exactly how Nazism was viewed in the first two decades following the end of World War II.

However, this is not to say that the report of the CONADEP does not point out the systematic violation of human rights implemented by the military regime:

> From the huge amount of documentation we have gathered, it can be seen that these human rights were violated at all levels by the Argentine state during the repression carried out by its armed forces. Nor were they violated in a haphazard fashion, but systematically, according to a similar pattern, with identical kidnappings and tortures taking place throughout the country. How can this be viewed as anything but a planned campaign of terror conceived by the military high command? How could all this have been committed by a few depraved individuals acting on their own initiative, when there was an authoritarian military regime, with all the powers and control of information that this implies? How can one speak of *individual excesses*? The information we collected confirms that this diabolical technology was employed by people who may well have been sadists, but who were carrying out orders. . . . Those members of the Argentine military juntas who replied to the universal outcry at the horror by deploring "excesses in the repression which are inevitable in a dirty war," were hypocritically trying to shift the blame for this calculated terror on to the individual actions of less senior officers.[16]

Alfonsín's government later returned in its second amnesty law (Law 23.521 Due Obedience Law of 1987) to a distinction between "those who gave the orders, those who executed them, and those who exceeded them"—the so-called doctrine of the three levels first presented during the 1983 election campaign. However, the 1984 CONADEP Report clearly challenged this approach. Instead, it pointed out that kidnapping, torture, and murder had been systematically used across the country as part of a carefully designed plan. So-called excesses formed part of the overall plan.

As for the victims, Sabato began by pointing out that these had come from nearly every walk of life—social, professional, and political. He then went on to argue in one of the most revealing paragraphs of the report that "the vast majority of them were innocent not only of any acts of terrorism, but even of belonging to the fighting units of the guerrilla organizations: the latter chose to fight it out and either died in shootouts or committed suicide before they could be captured. Few of them were still alive by the time the repressive forces reached them." This paragraph introduces the idea of the innocence of the victims as opposed to the (tacitly acknowledged) guilt of the "fighting units of the guerrilla organizations." It makes the unjustified assumption that the guerrillas died fighting while the victims—that is, those people who were taken to detention centers—were all noncombatants, irrespective of their political affiliation or relationship with the armed struggle. In fact, the guerrillas were just as much victims as the people who had no relationship whatsoever to armed or political organizations—although this is not acknowledged in the report.

The hegemonic vision that emerged was one of an "innocent" society caught between two opposing types of violence: left-wing "terrorist" violence (although terrorist is clearly a misnomer),[17] and the repressive state violence carried out mostly by the armed forces.

Elsa Drucaroff has rightly pointed out that the terror described in Sabato's prologue derived from an "abstract approach to social and historical relations . . . and their replacement by non-human, demonic subjects."[18] One could argue that this alienation of society as a whole from the genocide in which it was involved and in which everybody participated one way or another—as perpetrators, accomplices, passive bystanders, or victims—was precisely why this vision achieved such a broad consensus. The notion of "collective victimization" soothed the consciences of many Argentines of the period with the thought that everybody (with the exception of left and right "terrorist groups") had been a victim and so nobody needed to question his or her own role in the genocide.

The idea of two demons jointly responsible for various genocidal social practices was defended most clearly by several intellectuals close to Alfonsín. One of the most representative of these was Pablo Giussani, whose most widely known book was *Montoneros, Armed Arrogance*.[19] Giussani saw state violence as a response to the "stupid terrorism" practiced by armed left-wing groups, of which Montoneros was the most important. According to Giussani, Montoneros believed democracy was really a covert form of fascism and that its attacks would "expose fascism" by forcing the government to resort to repression. In other words, the military had simply responded to a "provocation," but repression and annihilation had not formed part of any wider social, economic, or political process. Giussani stresses even more than Sabato the idea of a contest between two symmetrical military totalitarianisms, both alien to society. But by describing Montoneros as a "fascist" and a "Nazi" organization, Giussani confuses several very different historical, social, and political processes. Like the adjectives "delusional" and "messianic," he uses the terms "fascist" or "Nazi" less to gain understanding than to vilify armed leftist groups in Argentina, and in particular the Peronist Montoneros.

Although Giussani's work is more journalistic than academic, the denigration of this period of Argentina's history as "irrational" together with the indiscriminate application of psychoanalytic concepts to the political arena—concepts such as *dementia, delirium, messianism, arrogance, derangement, sinister, provocative, eschatological*—have been a recurrent feature of works by historians and other academics from the 1980s onward. Beyond the range of explanatory frameworks they offer, these works are characterized by their lack of respect for the victims and for the political ideas of the period they study.

Clearly, there is a need for a more careful, political analysis of the actions and defeat of Argentina's armed leftist groups. This may come from surviving members of those organizations, from people of the same generation who knew them, or from a generation too young to have participated directly in the events. But it must necessarily go beyond insults and inappropriate psychoanalytic interpretations, however harsh and unpalatable its conclusions may be.

What is striking about Giussani and his many disciples is that instead of producing a serious political review of armed leftist organizations in Argentina and Latin America, for which there was obviously a legitimate need in the 1980s,[20] they turned out a stream of propaganda that not only put those organizations on a par with the perpetrators of genocide but even made them coresponsible for their own deaths and the deaths of others by equating the victims with their murderers. In one of the most revealing paragraphs, which exemplifies the tone of his argument, Giussani says that "from the electoral rolls of the Authentic Party [the political party created by the Montoneros organization to participate in the democratic elections] emerged many of the bodies dumped in ditches and vacant lots by the Triple A, victims of a mass murder that can be only half attributed to that vigilante organization. The other half of the blame must be laid at the door of Montoneros and its cavalier disregard for safety and security."[21]

Certainly, Montoneros committed many political and tactical blunders. For example, after being expelled by Perón from his Justicialist Party in May 1974, Montoneros's leaders took the decision to go underground, waiting until after Perón's death in July 1974 to announce this measure on 6 September 1974. This led to the organization's being declared illegal just over a year later. Another example was the order for over a hundred surviving Montoneros to return from abroad for a "strategic counteroffensive" in 1979—a counteroffensive in which most of them were killed. However, it is one thing to make mistakes and another to be responsible for genocide.[22]

A more elaborate version of this approach—written in an academic style, but with similar conclusions—can be found in Claudia Hilb and Daniel Lutzky's *The New Argentine Left: 1960–1980*.[23] As the title suggests, the focus of this book is on what the authors call the "new" Argentine left, a movement that allegedly emerged in the 1960s and whose defining feature was the role these organizations gave to violence. Like Giussani, Hilb and Lutzky see violence not as a point that has been reached in a social conflict, but as the decision of one of the actors in the conflict (in this case, the "new" left). Indeed, the authors try to explain later events in terms of the climate of violence created by the "new" left—an idea developed by Hugo Vezzetti some twenty years later. Nevertheless, Hilb and Lutzky stop short of blaming the left for genocide as Giussani does. They not only keep the distinction between victims and perpetrators, but also recognize that repression was aimed at all left-wing militants and not just at innocent victims split off from this "new" left.

"Armed Actions" and the Concept of "Civil War"

In the previous section I discussed a number of classic works, all of which appeared in 1984 and were built around the "theory of two demons": Sábato's prologue to the *Nunca Más* (Never Again) CONADEP Report, and the works of Giussani and Hilb and Lutzky.[24] In contrast, Juan Carlos Marín's *Armed Actions: Argentina 1973–1976* was first published toward the end of the military dictatorship in 1982.[25] Marín's work, therefore, did not dispute these later interpretations. Instead, it used statistical analyses in an attempt to reinterpret the "armed actions" that had occurred between Perón's death in 1973 and the military coup in 1976 as part of a "civil war" that supposedly split Argentine society in two.[26]

Marín set out to understand this "civil war" by dividing "armed actions" into those that caused casualties (dead, wounded, kidnapped) and those that did not. He aimed to show that the casualties caused by the "regime" were far superior to those brought about by protest movements between 1973 and 1976, despite claims to the contrary from the armed forces and the media that supported them. In this way Marín hoped to demonstrate the different nature of the conflicting forces, their different objectives, and particularly their different achievements. As he notes quite early in his book, the armed organizations of the left had already been defeated before the coup of 1976.

It is very important to note that Marín's approach, unlike the "two demons theory" that was to predominate during the pseudodemocracy of the Alfonsín era, allows for a much better understanding of the victims and perpetrators. The victims are no longer treated as "innocent civilians" but as a social force. This was probably one reason why Marín's work was virtually ignored by subsequent writers on the subject. But it is also necessary to note that Marín's approach seriously blurs the boundaries between war and genocide by implying that all armed conflicts—including civil wars—are wars of annihilation involving genocide. Marín fails to recognize that war and genocide involve different technologies of power, and require different policies and logistics. Moreover, the fact of choosing quantitative measurements of armed events (with or without casualties) as an indicator of strength impoverishes the analysis of changes in the balance of *political* forces throughout the period in question, since these cannot be reduced to simple head counts. Nevertheless, Marín's approach is well reasoned in many respects and is one of the earliest attempts to provide a causal explanation of genocidal social practices in Argentina.

Over the last three decades, Inés Izaguirre has tried to apply some of Marín's concepts to the persecution that took place following the military coup of March 24, 1976. Just as Marx traced the origins of capitalism to earlier economic behavior, Izaguirre sees the armed actions of the 1973–1976 democratic governments as a "primitive accumulation" of capital for the genocide that followed.[27] In different works, she also set out to study the class origins and political identity of the victims of genocide and the nature of the conflicts waged during the period before the genocide.

The idea of a "primitive accumulation of genocide" is highly suggestive. However, Marín and Izaguirre do not specifically explore the concept of genocide, from either a legal or a historical-sociological viewpoint. Had they done so, the international literature published over the last thirty years would have surely provided them with a clear understanding of this "primitive accumulation."

I must confess that I am indebted to Marin and Izaguirre for an idea I have developed in previous chapters of this book—namely, that the *purpose* of a genocidal social process is to destroy the broader fabric of social relations. However, if "demonizing" approaches implicitly remove the rest of society from the conflict by treating the "two terrorisms" as a struggle between two alien forces, Marín's and—to a lesser extent—Izaguirre's approaches reduce political conflict to a series of military actions. Both writers prioritize "armed actions" over the "political actions" at a moment in the struggle when the conflict was still defined in political terms—for example, armed groups were isolated *militarily* so that they could not participate in the struggle to build a *political* consensus. As a result, both Marín and Izaguirre miss two essential and interrelated points: first, the specific role of genocidal social practices in destroying earlier social relations; and, second, the ways in which relations between various political forces were transformed between 1973 and 1983. Neither can be deduced from the number of "armed actions" and "casualties," as carried out by Marín, or from an analysis of the professional, political, or economic identity of the victims of the dictatorship, as favored by Izaguirre.

Essentially, what Marín and Izaguirre fail to understand is that whereas in a civil war one social group seeks to *defeat* another social group in order to impose its political or ideological goals, genocide goes much deeper. With genocide, there is an attempt to *reengineer* social relations as a whole. Not only are the strategy and tactics of genocide different but so, too, are its effects. Moreover, while a war involves two social forces that polarize society along military lines—no matter how unbalanced the opposing armies may be—a genocidal social practice requires only one army, that of the perpetrators.

Later, in an article published in 2001,[28] Marín attempted to understand the "reconciliation" between Argentina's genocidal society and the perpetrators of the genocide. To do so, he focused on the Catholic Church as a creator of identities for the victims, the perpetrators and society as a whole. We will return to the key role played by the Catholic Church in indoctrinating and supporting the perpetrators in a later chapter. Here, it is important to point out that in Marín's view, the Church blocked personal autonomy in the population at large not by encouraging betrayal but by treating people as children, as the medieval Church had done. Now, betrayal, as I have argued, leads to the moral destruction of the population, which, far from remaining immature, understands only too well the degradation to which it has sunk as moral accomplices in the murder and disappearance of fellow citizens. Such people are not, in my view, "childish" adults incapable of comprehending the meaning of their actions—from which they would thus be "alienated." On the contrary, Zygmunt Bauman uses the term *adiaphorization*—a term coined by Church councils in the Middle Ages—to refer to the tendency to trim and cut down the category of acts amenable to moral judgment, to obscure or deny the ethical relevance of certain categories of action, and to refuse the ethical prerogatives of certain targets of action. *Adiaphorized* adults are unable to confront the past because their moral sense is numbed through betrayal and complicity. Instead, they "disown" and block out the past with the logic of two demons.[29]

Unfortunately, Marín devotes less space in his article to the "construction of the perpetrators," a series of truly insightful suggestions that are left curtailed as a guide for future work.

The "Terrorist State"

Eduardo Luis Duhalde's book *The Terrorist Argentine State* (1983) came out at almost the same time as Marín's and so it escaped the need to pander to Alfonsín's "don't ask, don't tell" democratist policy.[30] Duhalde makes no bones about describing the events as "genocide," a term he continued to use as a member of the Argentine Commission on Human Rights (known in Argentina by its Spanish acronym CADHU), an organization of Argentine exiles living in Europe who were quick to denounce the crimes of the military dictatorship.

The commission's documents for 1977 were labeled "Argentina, Genocide on Trial," and it was from these that Duhalde took the title for his book published in Spain the same year. This is at odds with the limited use made of the concept of "genocide" during the 1980s, and it is the first use of the term to cover annihilation by the military in Argentina, at least in the documents I have been able to access.

Duhalde's book, however, privileges the notion of the terrorist state, which forms part of its title. Duhalde presents a remarkably clear analysis of the patterns of state domination and how these relate to the central role played by repression and state terrorism in shaping events during the National Reorganization Process. In this sense, his work is highly suggestive, and his ideas on the role of secrecy, the functions of terror, and the difference between "emergency measures" and a "state of emergency"—a distinction later developed by Giorgio Agamben—turn Duhalde's book into an indispensable read.

One of Duhalde's most fertile ideas is that, unlike other types of dictatorship, the terrorist state does not seek to militarize society, but to dismember it. From here it is a short step to arguing that the aim of genocide is to destroy and rebuild the social fabric. Indeed, Duhalde sometimes suggests this, as when he points out that the terrorist state encourages individualism, the breaking of solidarity, and betrayal—although he does not pursue these ideas any further.

In the 1999 edition of the *Terrorist Argentine State*, Duhalde discusses other works published during the fifteen years since the book's first edition. Some of the issues he tackles, such as the political and symbolic consequences of impunity, will be discussed in chapter 8. However, it is worth examining his discussion of whether the term "war" is appropriate to describe the events of 1976–1983. This discussion includes both the perpetrators' ideas on the subject and Marín's analysis of the term "civil war."

Duhalde points out that the concept of war is problematic in the context we are considering because of the way it equates victims with perpetrators. In his view, the fact that the guerrilla forces were incapable of beating the security forces at any moment during the conflict makes it impossible to speak of a real war, regardless of whether those who participated in the conflict did so or not. The difference is that one side was made up of a small portion of society while the other side (both under Isabel Perón's government and under the military dictatorship) controlled the state apparatus and had a virtual monopoly on violence throughout the country except very briefly in parts of Tucumán province. As Duhalde himself says: "There is no war between a fraction of society and the military apparatus of the state. On the contrary, this is what ends up making the conflict a non-war and turning it into a mere repressive policy on the part of the state."[31]

This is what distinguishes Argentina's so-called Dirty War from the Spanish Civil War and even the civil wars in Nicaragua and El Salvador, where the military situation for the insurgents was grim but not hopeless. Duhalde claims that "there can be no civil war unless both sides polarize the society militarily. In other words, this occurs when the stage of social struggle has become the theater of war."[32] Nevertheless, Duhalde points out that the facts under study form a "socio-political conflict" and not a "demonic metaphysical dispute." In other words, the term "terrorist state" does not depoliticize the conflict, but rather helps us understand the difference between social confrontation and war.

On the other hand, "terrorist state" is undoubtedly a source of confusion. The blending together of genocide and terrorism in the concept of "state terrorism" has led to countless misunderstandings and distortions. Just as the text of the 1948 Genocide Convention and much Holocaust literature ended up "depoliticizing" the concept of genocide, Duhalde's terrorist state has followed a similar path. Worse still, several reinterpretations of Duhalde's work have been based precisely on the ambiguous and versatile concept of "terrorism," especially from the late twentieth and early twenty-first centuries onward.

Although Duhalde draws attention in both editions of his book to the political nature of the conflict and the aptness of the term "genocide" to define it, the concept of the terrorist state was hijacked by the discourse of the Alfonsín era describing the surgical interventions of one demon—embodied by the military state—against another demon that challenged it. In this discourse, "state terrorism" became the counterpart of "left-wing terrorism." Duhalde does not share this approach; but because the military also described the guerrillas as terrorists, his views later came to be misinterpreted.[33]

Duhalde's work has also been misinterpreted because it contains several inconsistencies, such as when he attempts to distinguish between those people who were supposedly "primary targets" of the terrorist state and those who were "innocent victims," a distinction that seems more in line with the "democratist" approach of demonization. One paragraph in which this confusion can be seen clearly is when Duhalde says that young adolescents "were not in hiding, they went about normally, maintained normal relationships in the family, at work or in the educational institutions they attended. What danger for the terrorist state could these youngsters pose? They were little more than children, just awakening to life"[34]

Pilar Calveiro, one of Duhalde's harshest critics in this respect,[35] claims that focusing on "innocent" victims in this way both depoliticizes events and indirectly justifies state terrorism against the "not so innocent." In my view, Duhalde is far from doing this. However, later uses of his term "terrorist state" make it all too obvious that either Duhalde did not express his ideas clearly enough in some places, or that the unfortunate title he gave to his book, together with the political needs of the period, triumphed over his generally profound and coherent analysis.

Marín's theory of "civil war" met with a wall of silence. In contrast, Duhalde's approach was emptied of its critical content and watered down into an analysis of the repressive techniques of the military who usurped constitutional power. Thus the concept of terrorist state was used to legitimize theories that focused on acts of violence rather than political struggle, replicating yet again—in one form or another—the theory of the two demons.

Whether muted or distorted and depoliticized, these early approaches could not avoid mirroring the alienation of those attempting to distance themselves from recent trauma. Disturbing events were assigned to the category of the irrational, insane, and diabolically metaphysical, as happened after the Second World War in works about the Nazi genocides until the inadequacy of such an approach was exposed by Hilberg and Arendt in the early 1960s.

This similarity in the ways the two historical processes have been depicted will be analyzed in more detail in chapter 8. Suffice it to say for now that in both cases, the predominant image during the fifteen years after both genocides was one of a break in the historical continuity of the societies in which they occurred. Genocide was removed from the society in which it had taken place, thus avoiding the unpleasant question of where everyone was while it was happening.

The Bureaucratic-Authoritarian State and the Concept of "Micro-Despotism"

Like Marín and Duhalde, the Argentine political scientist Guillermo O'Donnell was also writing during the years of military dictatorship and in the two years or so between the return to democracy and the "Trial of the Juntas," in which General Videla, the first military president, and Admiral Massera, the naval commander mentioned earlier, were found guilty of murder and other crimes by a civilian court and sentenced to life imprisonment. O'Donnell later published several of his articles in his book *Counterpoints*.[36] They synthesize the two broad perspectives that O'Donnell uses to understand the phenomenon: the macro view—mainly linked to the specific characteristics of the bureaucratic authoritarian state in the period under review—and the micro view (more suggestive to my mind), which emphasizes what he calls "the unleashing of micro-despotism."

Although O'Donnell's basic macro view concept is that of the bureaucratic authoritarian state, the specific forms that this state took and the peculiar way in which class alliances were formed are analyzed with extraordinary insight. O'Donnell believes that in the months immediately after the military coup of 1976, the bureaucratic authoritarian state aimed to get rid of political interlocutors who were loosening the grip of transnational capital and the landed bourgeoisie in power in Argentina—interlocutors primarily embodied in the Peronist movement.

This macro-level need was matched at the micro level by a complementary need to destroy the principle of egalitarianism—more symbolic than real—which Peronism had instilled into society. O'Donnell explores this development in great depth in his article "And Why the Fuck Should I Care? Notes on

Sociability and Politics in Argentina and Brazil,"[37] whose title begins with a popular provocation challenging class rule in Argentina. According to O'Donnell, the political establishment tried to dislodge the notion of egalitarianism by spreading terror throughout society and installing tacit approval for "micro-despotism" by getting all those would-be Argentine authority figures in schools and factories, in the public administration, in the street and in the home to vent their latent tyranny on their subordinates—students, workers, employees, passers-by, or children—as a way of disciplining society in myriad ways.

Both these views—the macro and the micro—are compatible with other perspectives, but they fail to coalesce into a general explanation of the events of the period. O'Donnell is respectful of the victims: he avoids the issue of naming (war or repression, social forces or guerrilla forces), but he does not resort to the Manichaean oversimplification of the two demons, or to denigrating the victims as so many others have done. He does not even confuse the roles of perpetrators and victims, as was usual in the years immediately after the events.

It is striking that Guillermo O'Donnell's work has not achieved the same recognition in Argentina as abroad, especially as he was president of the International Political Science Association from 1988 to 1991 and a member of the American Academy of Arts and Sciences from 1995 until his death in 2011. At the very least, the republishing of *Counterpoints* in English in 1999 should have led scholars in his home country to question the hegemonic explanation of the "demonic groups" that supposedly attacked a defenseless society.

Representation and Subjectivity

León Rozitchner wrote several articles before, during, and after Argentina's 1976–1983 dictatorship on the subject of what to call such annihilation processes, and the consequences of naming on the way we subjectively interpret events. However, Rozitchner's approach is indirect and he makes hardly any categorical statements.[38]

Nevertheless, while he does not set out to consider events from a broader perspective—events he describes as genocide in his various writings—Rozitchner does suggest ideas that are relevant to both this and the next two chapters. On the one hand, he reformulates the categories of conflict. Reinterpreting Carl von Clausewitz's theory of war, Rozitchner suggests that, from early on, guerrilla forces in Argentina neglected the importance of subjective interpretations of events and forgot that the true strength of counterhegemonic groups lies in defensive actions, where they can score propaganda points with public opinion, not in military actions, where they are always overwhelmed by the forces of the state.[39]

Rozitchner's very sound and detailed work demystified the conditions surrounding the "new politics" of the 1980s. This was a politics legitimized and at the same time held in check (like all political power) by the military. More to the point, Rozitchner refused to use the term "war" to describe the genocidal actions of the Argentine military in the 1970s, stating that one cannot "call that type of violence" war. With impunity, they called it a "Dirty War." This was quite simply a terror campaign against an unarmed "enemy within."[40]

Examining in depth the political and military establishment's strategic objective of "reorganizing" society, Rozitchner interprets institutionalized terror as a sort of "final solution" for rebellion. Like Roberto Jacoby, Rozitchner notes that killing gives those in power a kind of added value, terrorizing everybody else into seeing themselves and those around them as powerless.[41]

Finally, another important factor that Rozitchner analyzes is the discourses of intellectuals during and after the genocide. In particular, he shows how "democratist" discourse apparently attempts to deceive the political and military establishment in a manner similar to that employed by Scheherazade, the storyteller in the Thousand and One Nights, who kept death at bay by telling the king a different story each night. In this profound questioning of the role of the new "democracy," which we saw in Giussani as well as Hilb and Lutzky and which we will find again in Vezzetti and also in Palermo and Novaro, Rozitchner suggests that

> [h]ere, in this lower world, where God is not an Argentine and we are not immortal, not even goodwill is enough. And they know it. It is dangerous for the left to think like Scheherazade and try to seduce the despot by telling him a never-ending story: that of our own impotence. Could it be that we have supplanted the trembling stories of our thousand and one nights with our "scientific" and "theoretical" inventions? Scheherazade's only power was her woman's body, her seductive hysteria, and her tongue. Will we continue telling each other stories to postpone the inevitable arrival of death?[42]

The Version of the Survivors

Apart from the authors already discussed, attempts to go beyond the theory of the two demons were confined to very small groups, and their advocates were ridiculed or ignored in public debates until the mid-1990s. Significantly, one of the voices most systematically denied was that of the survivors. As in the case of the Nazi genocides, the reflections of the survivors were carried out in private. In public, their testimony and interpretations were questioned—if not ignored outright—and a campaign was mounted to discredit them by branding them as informers, traitors, or accomplices, a campaign that exploited the confusion of perpetrators with victims, already discussed in chapter 6 in connection with transference of guilt.

Like the survivors of the Nazi concentration camps, survivors of Argentine detention centers were also blamed for having "come out alive from hell." If the families of the victims were able to tell their stories publicly, the ex-detainees were denied this possibility. Instead, their accounts were discredited as being "highly subjective." The testimony of their sufferings was heard in court to achieve the conviction of the perpetrators and then, aggressively if need be, it was switched off again like a tape recording.[43] Only the testimony of what the authorities had done to their bodies could be heard. Any reference to their identity, their past, any questioning of the accepted truths of the period, and, of course, any comment that could question the victims' status as "angels" was disqualified on the grounds that the "survivors" did not have the same moral authority to judge as the "victims" who had not survived—not even to reflect on what had happened to them and its consequences.

Despite all this, the survivors tried to construct their own understanding of events: at first alone, then in small groups which would come to the fore when the hegemonic version of events started to come under fire. The more organized collective attempts to express alternative conceptions of the past were two seminars held in 1996 and 1997 by the Human Rights Freedom Chair at the Faculty of Arts of the University of Buenos Aires and led by the founder of the department, Osvaldo Bayer. There, the survivors were able to challenge society in a public arena—the University of Buenos Aires—with their own reflections on the period in question. Some of the issues that were raised at these seminars have profoundly influenced my own thinking and will be discussed in later chapters.

Among the writings of the survivors, those of Pilar Calveiro are especially interesting. Her most significant book was published in 1998, and it is the only work written by a survivor to have sold relatively well before the beginning of the twenty-first century.[44] Following in the footsteps of Holocaust survivors like Bruno Bettelheim and Primo Levi, Calveiro sets out to investigate, through the eyes of a former detainee and missing person, the nature of concentration camp power in Argentina, an issue that had been absent from previous works except for some brief passages in the final chapters of Duhalde's *The Terrorist Argentine State.*

Although the thrust of Calveiro's work is not to provide a comprehensive analysis of the policies developed during the dictatorship, she does in fact carry out a preliminary exploratory analysis. In her work, the concentration camp system plays a key role not because of her own suffering but because, as she says, "concentration camps were the operating theaters where surgery took place [meaning the surgery needed to produce another country] —it is no coincidence that operating theater was the name given to torture chambers. They were also, no doubt, the testing ground for a new society: orderly, controlled, and terrified."[45]

According to Calveiro, a key factor operating during the 1970s is what she calls binary logic. Binary logic explains how the military and also most of their opponents, particularly the armed left-wing organizations, perceived conflict and the path they chose to resolve it: polarizing the conflict into a "war" in which there could be only "friends" and "enemies." Here is what Calveiro has to say about this:

> In the military's view, Argentina was at war, a war against subversion being waged inside and outside national borders. The military were quick to declare it and the guerrillas took up the gauntlet. Both groups spoke of war. For the military, thinking about matters in terms of war put them in a "professional" situation, removing them from the purely repressive functions historically reserved for the police, while feeding this binary view of friends and enemies. . . . For their part, the guerrillas preferred to be represented as a guerrilla army that defied another army to being seen as a small force of insurrection, with some ability to commit violence. . . . They chose to show themselves as an army at war to increase their importance and apparent dangerousness. In this sense, they incited the military to think as they did and consciously helped to spread the fiction of a popular war against an imperialist army.[46]

Later she adds:

> Concentration camps were the apparatus designed to carry out the policy of extermination, the product of this binary conception of the political and social. . . . The concentration-extermination camps were set up to disappear a whole spectrum of political, social and trade union militants that prevented the hegemonic consolidation of power. The main target of this method of repression was the guerrillas, but also included the vast spectrum of so-called subversion which has already been discussed. Although the notion of subversive was sufficiently broad to include almost anyone, its use was intended to facilitate a well-defined persecution: that of radical militants and all their points of support.[47]

The importance of Calveiro's work is that, unlike the "democratist" approaches, she does not lose sight of the political nature of the conflict and the victims. At the same time, she does not make the mistake—as the armed organizations that participated in the conflict tend to do—of categorizing it in binary terms as a civil war or revolutionary war.

Although she never uses the concept of genocide in her work, Calveiro's emphasis on concentration camps as a metaphor for the broader process of social repression of which they were a part suggests that what the military called the "National Reorganization Process" was indeed an ambitious plan in which concentration camps were only a starting point for much deeper social transformations. The book concludes with a paragraph inviting the reader to think about the sort of society terror produces: "An interesting exercise would be to understand how the power to disappear people is recycled. What are its break-ups and amnesias in this postmodern era? How does it repress and totalize, even when it manifests itself in the most radical individualism? What are its schizophrenias, and how does it feed on the false separation between the individual and the social? How can we preserve memory, find the loopholes in the system and survive it?"[48]

Written along similar lines Carlos Flaskamp's retrospective account of the period also critically examines the concept of war.[49] Recognizing that he himself had thought in terms of "war" while he was a senior commander of the leftist Revolutionary Armed Forces, Flaskamp now believes that "the subjective convictions of the actors are not decisive to settle this issue [the existence of a war]."[50] Flaskamp questions his earlier use of the term "war" on three different grounds.

First, there was no revolutionary army: "To speak of war, I must recognize the existence of two armies confronting each other. Both the ERP and Montoneros formed armed groups, but never became true armies."[51]

Second, the revolutionaries controlled no territory: The single and very temporary exception was the ERP Mountain Company. The ERP operated in the province of Tucumán. The armed revolutionary organizations did not control land areas, they were not part of military units, and they did not disperse after every action.[52]

Finally, Flaskamp suggests that, aside the perceptions of soldiers and revolutionary militants, the vast majority of the Argentine people was not at war. It suffered the consequences of Argentina's oligarchic economic policies as well as the political repression of the trade unions. The public did not at all take part in military actions nor did they feel represented by the military.[53]

Luis Mattini asks similar questions although the answers he gives are more nuanced.[54] Unlike Calveiro, Flaskamp, or the members of the Association of Ex-Detained Disappeared (AEDD), Mattini was not a survivor of a secret detention center; and, as a senior officer of the ERP, he played a leading role in the events. Nevertheless, his ideas have a lot in common with those of Calveiro or Flaskamp. Unlike the "democratist" writers mentioned earlier, Mattini does not exclude the term "war" from the very beginning. Instead, he uses the concept of war to explore the distinctiveness of the actions carried out by the terrorist state in Argentina. In his article "Was There a War in Argentina?" (1999), Mattini argues that the conflict was unlike any other war—national, civil, or revolutionary—until then and also unlike any sort of classical political repression. But the main objective in this article is to make visible the political nature of the confrontation in Argentina. As Mattini states halfway through the article, "if this is not war, let us seek the right word, but it is not simple repression, however cruel, nor simple repressive excesses. It is a category of domination characteristic of this century and which corresponds to a certain type of civilization, to the extreme variant of anonymous bureaucratic domination."[55]

Despite some confusion about the nature of Nazism (which he equates, mistakenly, with Franco's dictatorship and the repression of the Communards in Paris), Mattini seeks to draw a distinction between previous acts of war or repression and Argentina's genocidal war with its clandestine operations controlled by the government's intelligence apparatus. Without giving a definitive answer, the article characterizes the period 1956–1976 as one of "latent civil war," clarifying that in late 1974 Operation Independence initiated a new form of action, which would be extended to the rest of the country in the second half of 1975. Mattini could not find a precise name for this phenomenon. I believe that the concept of genocidal social practice, which differs both from various forms of war and from classical models of political repression, is the best suited to describing the specific nature of the conflict that Mattini recognized so clearly.

Using the Concept of Genocide to Write History

As mentioned earlier, it was not until the mid-1990s that academic works started to question the democratist approach. Gradually, scholarly publications began to promote a more complex and nuanced approach, one that drew on the silenced visions of Marín, Duhalde, O'Donnell, and Rozitchner and the hitherto disparaged voices of the survivors. The two short chapters Luis Alberto Romero devotes to the subject in his *Brief Contemporary History of Argentina* (1994) are now recognized as a turning point in historical thinking on the Argentine genocide.[56]

Although this work covers a period of more than a century, Romero takes remarkable care in narrating the events that occurred during the dictatorship, dispensing with adjectives that might suggest madness or the demonic, so common in previous works. He is also the first published writer to apply the concept of genocide to the period in question—and it is precisely this aspect of his work that has been most criticized by other historians. (I have outlined this debate in chapter 1 of this book, so there is no need to expand on it here.) Unfortunately, their criticisms have been so persistent that in his later works Romero recants on his use of the term genocide and "corrects" his "mistake" by explaining it as a "legacy of the period."[57]

In *A Brief Contemporary History* Romero turned away from the logic of the two extremisms, noting that "the proposal of the military . . . was to root out the problem which, according to their diagnosis, lay in society itself and the unresolved nature of its conflicts. The nature of the solution could be guessed from the metaphors used—disease, tumor removal, major surgery."[58]

He also rightly points out that genocide begins with Operation Independence in Tucumán in December 1974—and not with the 1976 coup—and that this political use of the concept of genocide, far from seeking to place the victims outside the political arena, restores the political content to the whole genocidal process and moves away from visions of both angelic innocence and war between rival groups. As Romero remarks,

> Beyond errors and accidents the victims were the intended ones. Arguing the need to confront and destroy armed organizations on their own ground, the operation sought to eliminate all activism, all social protest—even a modest complaint about a school report card—any expression of critical thinking, any possible political leadership of the popular movement that had developed since the middle of the previous decade and was then destroyed In that sense the results were exactly the ones intended.[59]

It is remarkable that few historians have developed Romero's brief but well-founded and interesting account even though it was published nearly twenty years ago. On the contrary, the few academic works that have appeared since then revive the model generally accepted in the 1980s, which condemns "irrational terrorism" on both sides and also condemns the trivialization of the repression as an (at most, exaggerated) extension of the struggle between two forms of terrorism. It is also worth noting that Romero himself later subscribed to this perspective, abandoning many of his own perceptions about the phenomenon in favor of a supposed "historical knowledge" that would make his own personal memory appear to be too "subjective" and shaped by the "spirit of the time."[60]

However, not all historians share the same approach. The most significant exception, in my view, is Gabriela Aguila, who has documented and analyzed the genocidal process in the city of Rosario. Aguila is also interested in the links between history and memory and the feasibility of working with recent history as "genocide," particularly as regards the roles of perpetrators and victims. Her incisive questioning of the part played by certain political figures and the media in the city of Rosario has been a constant theme of her work, and suggests promising lines of research at the national level. Her painstaking approach avoids facile statements about the "collective responsibility" of society and concentrates instead on the difficult but necessary task of defining individual criminal, political, and/or moral responsibility for genocide.[61]

The "Counterinsurgency War"

In 1999 Ariel Armony wrote a book about the role of the Argentine repressors in what he calls the "anti-Communist crusade in Central America" between 1977 and 1984.[62] Armony's focus is different from mine, but his book contains a number of ideas that are relevant to this critical survey.

Armony interprets the events of 1976–1983 as part of a "counterinsurgency war," thus linking them to the national liberation struggles in Algeria and

Vietnam and a hitherto little-explored line of thought. In Armony's view, counterinsurgency warfare cannot be equated with either a classic "civil war" or a struggle between rival groups. Nor is it state repression in the usual sense of the term. Rather, it is a new way of dealing with social conflicts that draws on colonial experiences of repressing national liberation movements in different parts of the underdeveloped world.

Armony's approach emphasizes two new elements, although one of these was already mentioned by Duhalde. The first is the importance of intelligence in planning and executing the process of repression and extermination. Duhalde had already drawn attention to this point, but Armony is much more specific, taking advantage of research done in the intervening decade and a half since Duhalde's book appeared, and the opening of various archives, especially those located outside Argentina.

The second is the role that "terror" played in transforming the fabric of social relations, an idea already suggested by O'Donnell and Juan Corradi. Armony takes Duhalde's concept of the terrorist state to analyze the role of the intelligence agencies in perpetrating terror. Although he provides little more than an introduction to a little-treated subject, his bold and original hypotheses about the role played by Argentina's intelligence services in Central America open up new avenues for research.

Nevertheless, we should be careful not to exaggerate the analogy between counterinsurgency war in the context of a struggle for national liberation and events in Argentina. As I have already pointed out in earlier chapters, postcolonial genocide and reorganizing genocide pursue very different social goals.

The similarity between the tactics developed in Algeria and Vietnam and those employed in Argentina is obvious and worth mentioning. However, here the similarities end. Treating these cases as equivalent may increase the risk of confusing a war of liberation against a foreign army of occupation with a conflict taking place at the national level, where the military behave like an "army of occupation" in their own country. In the case of Argentina, the armed forces formed part of a larger social force made up of what O'Donnell identified as the most concentrated sector of the national bourgeoisie in alliance with sectors of the transnational bourgeoisie, a far cry from military occupation by a colonial power.

Finally, Armony continues the debate about whether the nature of the conflict (in which there were almost no battles) warrants the use of the term "war," even with a qualifying term such as "counterinsurgency."

Toward a New "Reification of Violence"?

The term "reification of violence" can refer to a way of thinking that sees violence either in terms of its effects (e.g., number of "armed actions," casualties, etc.) as in Marín, or as an almost supernatural force that overwhelms both victims and perpetrators, as in the theory of the two demons. As Fernando Coronil and Julie Skurski have pointed out, "in this metamorphosis of effect into cause, violence is transfigured into an entity, an autonomous agent that disrupts order and stands against society, an asocial force beyond the normal and the normative."[63]

Shortly after the turn of the millennium, a fresh outpouring of publications appeared analyzing the experience of the dictatorship in Argentina. Hugo Vezzetti, who had published articles on the subject during the 1990s, was one of the clearest exponents of the new line of analysis proposed by these authors.[64] Nevertheless, although he offers some penetrating insights, Vezzetti's idea of state terrorism excludes not only the notion of war but also that of genocide in defining events.[65]

Although Vezzetti's intention is to distance himself from the "two demons" approach, his descriptions of rival social forces in fact have the contrary effect. The victims are disparaged with adjectives such as *scatological, grotesque, sinister, deranged, messianic,* among others, which Vezzetti not only applies to Montoneros, as Giussani did, but also to the armed left as a whole. Similarly, Vezzetti's persistent use of terms such as "terrorists" and "extremists" is linked to the idea of a feud between two opposing terrorist groups who, in Vezzetti's view, had "reciprocal extermination purposes." In this sense, he makes the worst possible use of the concept of the terrorist state.[66]

At the heart of Vezzetti's work lies a conception of "social violence" as the root of all evil—a conception that blurs (even more powerfully than Sabato does in his preface to the CONADEP Report) the difference between victims and perpetrators. This can be seen, for example, when he argues that

> even admitting that the responsibilities are not equivalent, what place was left for the role played by guerrilla terrorism that undoubtedly contributed to creating conditions favorable to the [military's] criminal enterprise and that for most of the years of dictatorship even helped it to gain widespread acceptance in society? Here, a different way of considering this figure of "two demons" emerges that must be considered in light of what has been said about representations of war in society. No exercise of memory can fail to consider the role of radical groups on the stage of indiscriminate violence and institutional chaos that provided the best excuse for the emergence of the dictatorship.[67]

However, despite its limitations, Vezzetti's book also provides a number of important insights. One of these is his approach to the problem of guilt using the perspective of Karl Jaspers—an approach to which I will return in chapter 10. Other insights include his repeated warnings about the depoliticized discourse of the Alfonsín era with regard to state repression, and his incisive criticisms of

Inés Dussel's and Silvia Finocchio's attempts to normalize and depoliticize a generation of young people by lumping together the different organizations in which they were militants.[68]

A similar perspective to that of Vezzetti is to be found in Marcos Novaro and Vicente Palermo's lengthy volume, *The Military Dictatorship 1976–1983*.[69] Again, the adjectives used to describe the armed leftist organizations stereotype their members as insane ("delusional," "exalted," and "immersed in a world of illusions") and terrorists. Not only that: they also claim that "depoliticization" was not a consequence but a cause of the killing. In a new interpretation of events, Novaro and Palermo speak—just as the perpetrators had done—of a "war against subversion" that supposedly targeted society as a whole as a way to dismember the guerrilla organizations. Unlike most of the authors mentioned so far, Novaro and Palermo see the military's operations against society as a derivative of their aim to dismantle the guerrillas. Similarly, those employers and politicians who joined the fight against subversion did so because they were "terrified" by the attacks of Montoneros rather than because they themselves played a fundamental part in the repression.[70]

The concept of genocide is also dismissed in a footnote recalling the classic distinction between "being" and "doing"—a distinction between "completely innocent" victims such as the Jews, who were supposedly murdered by the Nazis for what they were, and those "guilty" (or at least "not so innocent") victims who are murdered for what they do or think. Of course, this distinction glosses over the features of Central European Jewry mentioned earlier, as well as the fact that the other victims of Nazism, such as political dissidents, do not fit neatly into this categorization. By adding the category of innocence to an already questionable distinction between existence, consciousness, and social practice, Novaro and Palermo stake out an unusual territory in the field of human rights by accepting the perpetrators' way of characterizing events (perhaps influenced by the sources they analyze).

Nevertheless, apart from the unusual and highly questionable approach I have just mentioned, the book has some notable successes, such as its analysis of the ambiguity intrinsic in the concept of "subversive crime," which will be discussed in the next chapter, or the way it distinguishes two symbolic territories, one where people can sleep safely in their beds and another where people cringe in terror. Especially interesting is the way Novaro and Palermo identify the role of the press and other print media in monitoring and denouncing "subversion." To this end, they conducted a comprehensive and revealing survey of industry publications, popular magazines like *Gente* (People) or *Para Ti* (For You), and circulars from the Argentine Ministry of Education. These points, however, seem strangely out of place in an overall approach that is closer to the democratist position and even to the documents published by the perpetrators in 1983, discussed earlier in this chapter.

Connecting Loose Ends: Dangers and Opportunities

I wish to close this chapter with some reflections on the many different approaches analyzed here. Classifications and descriptions of events have undergone significant changes over the past two decades that need to be identified. The question is not so much whether certain characterizations are true or false, but the way in which they are accepted and their effects on the construction of a collective memory.

On the one hand, opinions are strongly divided over the existence—or otherwise—of a war, although supporters of both positions disagree among themselves over details. What the perpetrators called a "Dirty War" or "war against subversion" (a term also adopted, surprisingly, by Novaro and Palermo), Marín and Izaguirre describe as a "civil war," Mattini as a "latent civil war," and Armony as "counterinsurgency warfare." Conversely, the democratists (Sabato, Giussani, Hilb and Lutzky, and even Vezzetti) as well as Duhalde, Calveiro, O'Donnell, Rozitchner, Flaskamp, and Romero, all distance themselves, more or less convincingly, from the concept of war.

Clearly, then, the debate involves not only the question of whether or not the conflict of 1974–1983 amounted to a war, but the role played by the concept of war in describing the conflict and the conflicting forces. And this brings us to a second question which, I believe, is more important from the conceptual point of view: the extent to which the conflicting forces were really balanced determines the extent to which both sides can be considered victims and perpetrators.

In the eyes of the perpetrators, the concept of victim was inappropriate since both sides were fighting a war. There were victims and perpetrators on both sides. Thus, approaches that promote the concept of war risk endorsing a similar logic by characterizing the victims as part of a social group "at war" with another social group. In contrast, the democratists sought to split the left-wing social group into one set of innocent victims (society) and another set of "guilty victims," in some cases, along the lines of the perpetrators' own version of events.

O'Donnell, Romero, Calveiro, and, to some extent, Duhalde draw a clearer distinction between victims and perpetrators, without depoliticizing the former. Labor union activists, together with student militants and armed militants of leftist organizations, form an indivisible whole in terms of politics and as victims. Their status as victims does not depend on their greater or lesser involvement in armed struggle. That is why this group should not be confused with an army or a side in a war but should be seen as a group of people scheduled by the perpetrators for extermination, whether or not they already belonged to a real social group.

It is here that the richness of the concept of genocide opens up the greatest possibilities for understanding. Because, whether or not there was a war, the concept of genocide makes a clear distinction between the victim group and the perpetrator group—a distinction that we should not lose sight of if we are to confront the "symbolic enactment" of genocidal social practices that follows physical annihilation of the victims.

8

Toward a Periodization of Genocide in Argentina

One day there came a wind, a sweeping wind. It took our people and left us without love.

—Eight-year-old Argentinean girl, 1982[1]

One of the central arguments of this book is that genocidal social practices have underpinned the exercise of power in the modern period. This chapter suggests how the periodization of genocidal social practices developed in previous chapters can be applied in the case of Argentina, as well as pointing out the main similarities and differences between Argentina's military repression and genocidal processes elsewhere.[2]

Building a Negative Otherness in Argentina: The Figure of the "Subversive Criminal"

If we remember that the first stage of genocide is constructing a "negative Other," the central question in each case must be: What exactly was the model of Otherness, and how did it function? In the case of the Nazi genocides, any answer to these questions is necessarily complex since it must account for a wide range of groups with different identities. However, a tentative hypothesis is that the Nazis began by persecuting *anyone* who showed autonomy in any field whatsoever, and only later (about 1938) turned the figure of the Jewish-Bolshevik into a symbiotic union of ethnic and political Otherness, increasingly linked to an ethnicization of politics in which Jewish "racial degeneration" was essentialized as "irreversible."

In Argentina, both the media in the years before the 1976 coup and the political sectors that supported the dictatorship as well as the members of the military juntas themselves focused on a figure that—while not exactly the same in every instance—was clearly defined as a "subversive criminal." At first, "subversion" alone was enough (sometimes related to Peronism, other times to

Marxism, or to any form of rebelliousness). Redefining the problem as one of criminal behavior was the stratagem used to turn a political conflict into one of law and order and was in line with the French counterinsurgency doctrine in Indochina and Algeria.

Interestingly, contemporary news stories and official statements always defined this Otherness in political and moral terms—despite later attempts from different perspectives to understand and/or explain the Argentine genocide in military terms. Thus, the moral dimension transferred the conflict to the field of ethical standards, generally accepted morality, or the family. "Subversion" or "subversive crime" ended up becoming a *clear* definition (any questioning or criticism of the existing order, at whatever level, was criminalized) and also an *ambiguous* one (practically any thought, social practice, or way of relating with peers could potentially be seen as critical or rebellious).[3]

Let us look at some examples of these definitions. Roberto Eduardo Viola, de facto president between 29 March and 11 December 1981, and previously commander in chief of the army under the military junta led by General Jorge Rafael Videla, said that "subversion is any open or secret action, insidious or violent, seeking to alter or destroy moral standards and the way of life of a people, in order to take power and impose a new way of life based on a different scale of values. It is essentially a form of political-ideological reaction directed at undermining the existing political and administrative order and is based on exploiting dissatisfaction, real or imaginary, with the political, social or economic order."[4]

In another much quoted phrase, Videla, the de facto president from 1976 to 1981, also defined the enemy: "A terrorist is not just someone with a gun or a bomb, but anyone who spreads ideas that are contrary to Western Christian civilization."[5] That is, both in perpetrators' statements and in practice, repression in Argentina was a political struggle that went beyond ideological disagreement and sought to impose a particular model of society through terror and death. Thus, any attempt at self-reliance and self-sufficiency—whether promoted by a political party or by ordinary people with no political awareness at all—was repressed, and the population was homogenized into a hierarchically organized society with an authoritarian ideology, religion, and culture that the perpetrators called "Western Christianity."

This discourse with its religious overtones was fervently supported from the Catholic pulpits in Argentina, with sermons calling on the military to engage in a "holy war," as can be seen in the following homily delivered before General Viola by the military vicar and general provicar of the Argentine Armed Forces, Vitorio Bonamin, on 23 September 1975: "I salute all the men of the Armed Forces who have come here to the Jordan of Blood to cleanse themselves and take the lead of the entire country. The army is expiating the impurities of our country. Wouldn't Christ want the Armed Forces to go beyond their function one day?"[6] In subsequent statements, justifying the repressive events, the archbishop of the city of Bahía Blanca, Jorge Mayer, on 27 June 1976, said, "The subversive guerrilla wants to steal the cross, the symbol of all Christians, to crush and to divide all the Argentine people by means of the hammer and the sickle." And again Bonamín, on 10 October 1976, preached before General Bussi in Tucumán, one of the chief areas of horror: "This fight [referring to the actions of the task forces] is a fight for Argentina, for its integrity, but also for its altars. . . . This struggle is a struggle in defense of morality, of human dignity. It is ultimately a struggle in defense of God. I therefore ask for divine protection in this dirty war in which we are engaged."

Much of the media also shared the military's point of view. Mariana Heredia has painstakingly traced these attitudes in publications such as *La Nación, La Prensa*, and the magazine *Criterio*, all of them targeted at different audiences, and has shown similarities and differences in these messages.[7] In 1970, articles in the conservative broadsheet *La Nación* were already constructing political activists as the "operational support" of the guerrillas while during the same period, the tabloid *La Prensa* focused its campaign on the danger for the country of labor disputes. However, Heredia observes that even before Héctor Cámpora became president in 1973, a unified discourse was already present in both newspapers—one defining the *enemy* in two ways: "With the passing of time, a new antagonist was catching the attention of contributors to the publications . . . they identified a persistent group of 'young Jacobins' entrenched in universities and cultural life and, with the same arsenal they used inveterately to combat right-wing nationalists, they now directed their arguments against radicalized sectors of the Peronist Party."[8] When *La Prensa* spoke of "subversives," it was clearly referring not only to members of the armed revolutionary left, but to a wider group of people, as when it mentioned "groups of demonstrators engaged in street rioting, employees or workers who occupy official or private establishments, students who take over high schools, whether financed by the State or privately" (*La Prensa*, 16 June 1973). According to Heredia, the Argentine media of the period was characterized by anti-Peronist sentiment (unrelenting in *La Prensa*, and more inconsistent in *La Nación* and *Criterio*) together with concern about the left's constant questioning of the social order. The broad and ambiguous definition of "subversive criminality" was to be decisive in the creation of the "negative Otherness" that led to genocide. Thus it became possible to construct an unambiguously political enemy without a throwback to the racism of earlier genocides.

From Racial to Political Metaphors: Argentina's "Leap Forward"

In analyzing the Nazi genocides, I stressed the peculiar ethnic and political synthesis in the stereotype of the Jewish-Bolshevik. The political element was a Nazi innovation. Whereas previous genocides had been linked to colonial rule or to the founding of a new nation-state,[9] it was the attempt to destroy certain types of social relationships that turned the Nazi genocides into reorganizing genocides. Ethnicity also played a central role in the Nazi state and was anchored in earlier racism. However, both evolutionary racism and French degenerative racism were renewed by Nazi theorists like Alfred Rosenberg and Gerhard Wagner, and racism becomes a fundamental way to achieve widespread consensus for genocidal policies serving *political* ends.

Of course, the repression in Argentina was able to build on the experiences of the Nazi genocides and the counterinsurgency wars in Indochina, Algeria, and Vietnam as well as the National Security Doctrine in Latin America. Accordingly, it showed a qualitative leap in the technology of power in terms of its ability to separate political behaviors and social practices from ethnoracial connotations. Unlike Guatemala, where political conflicts were difficult to disentangle from centuries of racial prejudice and subjugation of the indigenous population—an ethnopolitical conflict expressed in the figure of the "communist Indian"[10]—Argentina invented a "negative Otherness" defined wholly in political terms. The figure of "subversive criminal" had all the degenerative features of the Nazi stereotype with none of the references to ethnicity or race.

The concept of "subversive crime" refers to a form of social practice which, as defined by the perpetrators themselves, focuses on a way of confronting reality and establishing relationships with others. This is obvious from the policies of the dictatorship in the field of education materials published at the time. For example, in 1977, the Ministry of Education of the dictatorship distributed a pamphlet entitled "Subversion within the Educational System." This considered as part of the enemy's action "the evident offensive in the area of children's literature, the aim of which is to send a type of message starting from the child and which may enable him or her to become self-educated on the basis of liberty and choice." The same official pamphlet states that "the intention of Marxist publishers is to offer books to accompany children in their struggle to delve into the world of things and the world of adults, to help them not to be afraid of freedom, to help them to have their own wishes, to fight, to assert themselves, to defend their ego against the ego which in many cases parents and institutions try to impose upon them, consciously or unconsciously victims of a system which has tried to make them in its own image and likeness."[11] The military government introduced a course titled "Moral and Civic Education," mandatory in the first three years of middle school. Together with persistent recommendations to betray others as a way of resolving social conflicts, this course not only outlined the old model of social relationships that genocide aimed to destroy but suggested a new model that would make relationships based on "equality" or "reciprocity" impossible. This new model, a key feature of genocidal social practices, can be traced back to the Inquisition.

Nevertheless, this ability to "isolate" the political and persecute only political practices prevented the purpose of genocide from being "contaminated" by the racial metaphor,[12] thus making it more efficient. Although the number of victims in Argentina was relatively small in comparison to earlier and even later systematic annihilation processes, the disappearance of certain social relations is obvious when we consider how easily neoliberal economic policies were imposed during and after the dictatorship. And yet these same policies had made little headway in Argentine society during the thirty years or so prior to the military coup of 1976.[13]

Herein, in my view, lies one of the possible continuities between the two genocidal processes analyzed in this book. Nazism made it possible to implement a genocidal social practice with a political content, even if that content was included within a racist paradigm (the ethnopolitical figure of the Jewish-Bolshevik and "Jewish degeneration" as a stereotype of "negative Otherness"). The Argentine perpetrators and their supporters went a step further, dispensing with racism and creating a highly political but, at the same time, broad and functional stereotype. "Subversive crime" no longer linked politics to an under-race but to an underworld of crime.[14]

However, although this absence of racial or ethnic elements made persecution more efficient in some ways, it also proved to be a headache for Argentina's genocidal apprentices. One of the Argentine perpetrators explains this clearly when called on to analyze the similarities and differences between the Argentine case and the lessons learned by the most important counterinsurgency experts in French Indochina and Algeria. As Argentina's interior minister during the military dictatorship, Albano Harguindeguy, told Marie Monique Robin, "The most terrible thing is how the subversives blend in with the population, making it very difficult to say who the enemy is and who is one of us. That was another difference with Algeria and Indochina, where distinctions were racial as well."[15]

In some ethnopolitical implementations of genocide, inherited physical traits (in particular, skin color) made it relatively easy to select one's victims. In other cases, like the Jewish genocide, physical traits are less easy to distinguish. For this reason, the Nazis described the Jews in ambiguous terms as being *psychologically* rather than *physically* degenerate. However, once genocide is placed on a purely political footing, the identification of potential victims becomes much more arduous. In Argentina, personal appearance (long hair, beards, and shabby clothes) was often taken as an indicator of political beliefs, but only for the purposes of random police checks. In contrast, Ariel Armony highlights the essential role played by the intelligence services in "victim selection."[16]

From the 1960s onward, Argentine military intelligence and the intelligence services attached to the national and provincial police forces spied on political and social activists, trade unionists, leaders of neighborhood groups, and students, classifying them according to the threat they ostensibly posed to society. When the coup of 24 March 1976 was launched, most of the victims had already been carefully selected through systematic surveillance. This method of targeting victims was fundamentally different from that used in racially motivated persecutions where the victims are easy to identify, although the Nazi genocides often combined both procedures—careful intelligence work and indiscriminate mass roundups.[17]

Harassment: The Logic of Triple A

In chapter 6 I defined harassment as a transitional stage from symbolic violence (negative stereotyping) to physical violence, particularly, in one of its two forms: harassment by quasi-governmental forces. It is striking that quasi-governmental forces played very similar roles in Argentina and in Nazi Germany.

In Germany, the Nazis' paramilitary *Sturmabteilung* (SA, Stormtroopers Division), had several million members and was used to attack synagogues and Jewish property throughout Germany on *Kristallnacht*, the Night of Broken Glass, in November 1938; yet it was separate from the national government. In Argentina, the main quasi-governmental organization was the Argentine Anti-Communist Alliance (known as Triple A), a death squad that functioned between July 1973 and March 1976 under the democratically elected governments of Raúl Alberto Lastiri, Juàn Perón, and Isabel Perón and which was responsible for murdering around 1,500 people. The relationship of Triple A with Isabel Perón's minister of social welfare, José López Rega, was well known but never admitted officially.

At the same time, other smaller institutions were set up to support the Triple A or carry out similar operations. This was the case of Comando Libertadores de América (Freedom Fighters of America Commando), headed by Captain Héctor Vergez, who later ran a concentration camp at La Perla, Córdoba, together with his men. It was also the case of Comando Nacionalista del Norte (Nationalist Northern Commando), operating in Tucumán under Inspector Roberto "One Eye" Albornoz. Both units were (clandestinely) attached to the Third Army Corps.

Although some of these men, like Captain Vergez, had been torturers or repressors during previous dictatorships, quasi-governmental groups first appeared with Perón's return from exile on June 20, 1973. From Perón's platform at Ezeiza Airport, snipers fired on the left-wing Peronist Youth and the Montoneros that Perón himself had encouraged during his exile and who had come to welcome their aging leader. At least 13 people were killed and 365 were injured during what became known as the Ezeiza massacre.[18]

From then on, harassment was aimed at weakening and cracking the solidarity between the labor movement, the student movement, neighborhood movements, and armed leftist organizations. The Triple A combined the selective assassination of real or potential intermediaries between various political and social movements with intimidation through sporadic attacks, death threats, and blacklists. This type of harassment was particularly successful in driving a rift between popular movements and armed political organizations, especially in the case of left-wing political organizations unsure about whether to embrace violence. Thus stage two (harassment) and stage three (isolation) of the model presented in chapter 6 were combined in Argentina.[19]

Although accounts of the Argentine genocide tend to start with the coup that institutionalized genocide, it is impossible to understand the historical context and development in which these murders took place without considering the threats, kidnappings, and killings carried out by death squads between 20 June 1973, the day of the Ezeiza massacre, and 24 March 1976, the day of the coup almost three years later. Juan Carlos Marín and Inés Izaguirre have pointed to the importance of these earlier murders as well as the type of victims targeted, usually "social coordinators" who acted as liaisons between senior members of armed leftist movements and ordinary workers or students, connecting the popular grassroots movement with its would-be political or military leaders.

This combined policy of harassment and isolation not only dismantled the connections that already existed, but made it relatively easy to annihilate both groups systematically after the coup Those annihilated after the coup included the leadership of the armed leftist organizations (which by then had already been defeated, both militarily and politically, even though they were still able to carry out sporadic armed attacks) and militants from the popular grassroots movement (trade union leaders, neighborhood committee members, student activists, etc.).

In turn, harassment by paramilitary forces accomplished all the functions mentioned in my analysis of Nazism in chapter 6. First, it created a social force of perpetrators that would later join the institutional framework of the armed forces and the police (or rather rejoin it since the clandestine units that carried out the harassment were drawn from the army and the security forces). Second, it isolated the victims and encouraged leftist militants with economic resources and political contacts abroad to flee the country. In fact, a large number of Argentine militants (in the broadest sense of the term) chose exile. Third, it generated a "state of chaos" that led to calls from politicians and the media for a force to restore law and order, especially in view of the disarray into which the Peronist government sank after Perón died and his third wife, Isabel Perón, came to power.

As in the case of Nazi Germany, law and order would only be restored by the institutional provision of genocidal social practices. This is explained in

Videla's first speech on assuming the presidency after the military coup: "Only the State, for which we do not accept the role of a mere spectator of the process, will monopolize the use of force, and only its institutions will carry out actions related to internal security. We will use force as often as needed to ensure social peace: with that goal we will fight relentlessly against subversive crime in all its manifestations, to its total annihilation."[20] Chaos "disappeared" when the various quasi-governmental groups were reincorporated into the institutional structure. However, despite Videla's statement, some units now nominally under state control continued to operate more or less autonomously. This was the case with Task Force 3.3.2, which occupied a three-story building including the officers' mess at the Navy Mechanics School (ESMA), or the criminal gang led by Aníbal Gordon, which not only carried out genocidal practices on behalf of the state but used its infrastructure for conducting personal business, kidnappings for the purposes of extortion, random kidnappings, and settling of personal scores, even if these activities were not the main focus of Argentina's genocidal forces. These actions increased from 1978 onward, when leaders of the armed forces were sure that their genocidal objectives—the dismantling and "reorganization" of society—had been met.[21]

In the case of Argentine genocide, stage two (harassment) and stage three (isolation) were thus performed simultaneously, leaving the way open for extermination. But before continuing to this next stage, it is worth considering in more detail how isolation was achieved.

Isolation, from Mapping to Policy: Material Ghettos, Symbolic Ghettos, and Political Ghettos

In chapter 6 I defined isolation as a time whose main objective was "to demarcate a separate social, geographical, economic, political, cultural, and even ideological space for those who are 'different,' and at the same time to sever their social ties with the rest of society." The Nazis isolated the Jews first through restrictions and exclusionary laws and decrees and later by physically enclosing them in ghettos. However, as I said in chapter 6, other less sophisticated "ghettos" have served these same functions at different times and for different populations.

In Argentina, isolation was mostly political. In particular, Juan Domingo Perón's government succeeded in isolating its rivals politically, so there was no need for a physical ghetto. On 25 September 1973, the left-wing Peronist urban guerrilla group Montoneros assassinated José Ignacio Rucci, who was general secretary of the right-wing CGT (General Confederation of Labor) and a close friend of Perón's, in an attempt to force the democratically elected President Perón to negotiate with them. Enraged, Perón asked López Rega to step up the operations of the Triple-A against left-wing opponents. Eventually, Perón expelled Montoneros from his Justicialist movement during a mass rally in Plaza de Mayo in May 1974.

The expulsion of Montoneros from the Peronist movement together with the murder of those who acted as intermediaries between various left-wing movements was not the only factor that isolated Peronist armed organizations. They were also isolated by their own shortsightedness. By kidnapping and murdering businessmen and Peronist labor leaders, as well as soldiers and policemen, they only alienated themselves even more from their grassroots social movements and the society they intended to lead, while reducing their access to information, commonsense perceptions of Argentine society, and particularly perceptions of their own legitimacy as political actors.

Regarding the targeting of liaisons and intermediaries by quasi-governmental forces, Teresa Meschiatti (a survivor of La Perla concentration camp in Córdoba)[22] speaks of a "selective policy of kidnapping," an appealing name in terms of theory development for the way isolation was achieved in Argentina. As mentioned earlier, these "selective kidnappings" had the clear goal of eliminating anyone able to mediate between labor, social neighborhood or student movements, and leftist organizations, particularly but not exclusively *armed* organizations. The aim was primarily to ensure that these movements did not "make the leap." However, the mistakes these organizations made during this period prevented them from recognizing their urgent and strategic need to protect their political base. The inability of the militant left to organize a "strategic retreat" played a key role in the ease with which they were isolated and then wiped out once the extermination process was unleashed.

As terror became more widespread, the government's policy of isolating militant groups was reinforced by appeals to the population to report suspects for questioning. Gabriela Roffinelli has identified the importance of such appeals in Tucumán, the quintessential Argentinean genocide laboratory. Throughout 1976, Bussi's de facto government published the following booklet in the newspaper *La Gaceta*:

> Attention People of Tucumán
> Pay attention and cooperate if you find:
>
> - That in your neighborhood, village or area young people without children or with young children have recently moved in;
> - That these couples have no relationship with the neighborhood;
> - That they have no known family;
> - That it is not clear what they are doing here or what they work at.
>
> Because these people may be a threat to your safety, to that of your family and your country. . . . Your information will be valuable.
>
> Argentine Army[23]

As the authorities called upon the population to inform on their neighbors—and suggesting through terror that this would be the only way to survive—leftist organizations were isolated from the popular movement that had nurtured them. In a clear miscalculation, some of these movements encouraged their militants to abandon their middle-class jobs and lives and move to poor neighborhoods to live like "proletarians." There, despite their willingness and enthusiasm, they found themselves hampered by their lack of contacts or skills, by living among people with whom they had no shared history of militancy and who were socially and culturally alien to them.

Although in the late 1960s and early 1970s leftist organizations had penetrated deeply into various sectors of the popular movement—especially sectors that had chosen armed struggle or were discussing this possibility—the links between these organizations and the social movements had been dismembered by the mid-1970s, well before the coup. There was little sympathy, cooperation, or even information shared among them. This was not only a result of government repression; it was also a consequence of serious errors committed by the organizations themselves.

These were the conditions that facilitated the coup, after which systematic extermination began. According to some of the repressors, the annihilation was intended to eliminate political organizations, political protests, and solidarity or simply critical thinking in Argentina for at least twenty years.[24] Sadly, this prediction proved to be extremely accurate. It was not until twenty to thirty years later that public discussion (for example, in the context of a university course rather than behind closed doors) began to focus on this specific process of destruction rather than a so-called terrorist attack on society as a whole. Of course, there is no guarantee that such discussions can play a role in developing social relations beyond the hegemonic individualism, solipsism, and commercialism of our times.

Differences between the Logic of Terror and the Industrial Production of Death

The two genocidal practices analyzed in this book differ most notably in the scope of their objectives and the methods and scale of the killing. The project of total extermination did not become a key area of Nazi state policy until mid-1942, and its scale was to exceed all expectations. The Nazis' increasing insistence during World War II on a systematic "final solution to the Jewish question" led to a metamorphosis from the concentration camp policy used to persecute non-Jewish victims, such as political opponents and "asocials"—a policy typical of modern genocides—to the industrialized murder of Europe's Jewish and Gypsy populations in death camps, or purpose-built installations where victims were gassed on arrival, although some of these were also used as concentration camps. [25]

There has been no similar decision in any other genocidal process, including the case of Argentina. Although prisoners were murdered or "transferred" to their deaths in many of the Argentine concentration camps, Argentina's genocidal policy envisaged wiping out only a small part of Argentina's population, and the numbers were not large enough to warrant a production line. In fact, no other genocide in history—including the large-scale genocides of Rwanda and Cambodia—has used an industrial production line for killing human beings.

While both processes shared the symbolic need to get rid of the bodies, the Nazi factories of annihilation with their crematoria and their mass graves were a consequence of a decision to murder *millions* of human beings. It was the sheer scale of the Nazis operation aimed at killing a whole people across a whole continent that led to the invention of the extermination camp as a "political artifact"—a technology created expressly for resolving a specific social problem.[26] In contrast, Argentina's "disappeared" were buried in unmarked graves or thrown from planes into the sea or rivers.[27]

Although I have so far developed several analogies between the Nazi and Argentine genocides, such analogies refer to concentration camps, the ways of representing the "negative Other," and the Nazis' use of what Christopher Browning, Robert Gelatelly, and Eric Johnson call "ordinary men" to destroy a specific structure of social relations. However, the Nazi genocide was more than that. Beyond the actual weight we may give to the Nazis' decision to totally annihilate the Jewish population (and I do not consider this factor to be the main explanation for Nazi genocidal policies), that decision obviously existed and it claimed many more victims than "necessary" to transform social relations. Nevertheless, Nazi overkill was not irrational even though it went beyond the bounds of political usefulness. The death camps were an innovation, making the concentration camp one of the possible stages of genocide, but not the only one.

Accordingly, those who argue that the death camps were the defining feature of the Nazi genocide and that the term "genocide" cannot be applied to other historical events are just as wrong, in my opinion, as those who argue that the Nazi genocide was simply another reorganizing genocide in which concentration camps were used. The Nazis' industrialization of death, due to the decision to annihilate an entire ethnic group, should not be ignored. But it does not, in my view, explain either the function or the true nature of the Nazi genocides, although it gives them a special historical particularity.

Genocide requires terror. In order to eliminate the negative Other, at least a significant number of victims must be physically annihilated. The more terrible their deaths, the more effectively social relations among the surviving members of society will be destroyed. But death is simply a means to bring about social change—not an end in itself. In my view, this was also true even of the Nazi genocides despite the fact that these were accompanied by what Browning calls a policy of "European racial redesign." In other words, the Nazi genocides were both a means and an end: although social reorganization gave the Nazi genocide its meaning and functionality, the fact that it was an eminently racist genocide cannot be ignored.

Stage four of the model presented in chapter 6 is called "systematic weakening." Policies of systematic weakening are to be found at all stages of various genocidal processes, including the Argentine genocide. Both *physical destruction* and *psychological destruction* (see chapter 6) were central in breaking prisoners' will to resist in Argentina's detention centers and concentration camps. But the need to split up large-scale social groups for industrial annihilation did not exist. Annihilation had a clearly political goal: "disappearing" the bodies of those who *embodied* political organization, protest, and solidarity was a way to achieve, through terror and annihilation, the closure of these social relations in the rest of society.

The "Symbolic Enactment" of Genocidal Social Practices in Argentina: Always "Never Again"

As mentioned in chapter 6, destruction only benefits the perpetrators if it can be turned into certain forms of social narrative that re-present annihilation. Having compared the material elements of genocide in both the Nazi and Argentine genocides, we will now examine social narratives associated with the two genocides—in particular, the socially divisive narratives I call the "symbolic enactment" of genocide. We will see that there are remarkable similarities between the Nazi and Argentine genocides—similarities not found, for example, in the Armenian genocide, where a persistent denial of the basic facts by the Turkish state has been the main form of "symbolic enactment" for nearly a century.

Modes of Identity Denial and Guilt Transfer

In the case of the Nazi genocides, the true identity of the victims has been denied by overemphasizing their ethnicity at the expense of their political significance. Nazi ideology made a clear link between the ethnic and the political. To claim, as many have done, that the victims "were killed simply because they were Jews" erases the political nature of extermination and treats ethnicity as if it were singular and set in stone. It is ethnic essentialism of this sort that makes the Nazis appear "irrational."

In Argentina, where an "ethnic metaphor" was lacking, this sort of denial was more difficult. Nevertheless, it was the dominant discourse between 1984 and 1996. The position of the CONADEP Report, repeated in a variety of books, articles, and films, was to replace "they must have done something [to deserve their fate]"—an expression used to justify the disappearance of people during the dictatorship—with "they had done nothing," an expression that depoliticized the victims, as noted in the previous chapter.

In time, the predominant explanation was that the victims had been mainly "innocent" people represented by the readers of certain books, students seeking to obtain a concessionary bus fare, or neighbors and relatives who just happened to be in the address books of God knows whom.[28] Very few cases—such as the leading cadres of armed groups from the left—did not fit this category.

The Nazi genocide appeared to be irrational because the annihilation of an entire ethnic group was apparently lacking in political meaning. However, the Argentine perpetrators behavior seemed even more irrational since—leaving aside the political dimension—the victims apparently had nothing in common except that they had been murdered. Certainly, they were not killed because of their ethnicity in a society where most of the population think of themselves as being part of the "same ethnic group." Because the victims did not fit into any unifying category, the perpetrators seemed to have gone completely mad, a widespread perception being that they simply "killed anybody." They were seen as psychopathic serial killers: anyone who got in their way could have been their next victim.

In this way, large parts of the population came to deny their recent past. It was as if social rebellion, solidarity, and a collective critical attitude had never existed in Argentina. In this new version of events, only a few deluded groups detached from society took up arms while sections of the armed forces implemented a system of repression that could kill just about anybody on the grounds that they were defending society from a bunch of deranged fanatics. With "normality" once more restored and those deranged fanatics now safely "disappeared," the armed forces could return to their barracks, and society was cured of the madness of the "two demons."

The meaninglessness that resulted from this denial of identity found expression in the discourses of "transference of guilt," an emblematic case being Pablo Giussani's work, although the basic elements were present in previous as well as later texts, as outlined in chapter 7. Both Giussani and Sabato, in their foreword to the CONADEP Report, unwittingly reveal the link between the denial of identity and the transfer of guilt. Their attempt to rationalize events could be paraphrased more or less as follows: "The mayhem caused by the 'demonic left' *provoked* the military into *overreacting* and, rather than fight mayhem with the rule of law, the military initiated a bloodbath in which most of the victims were *innocent*." The main difference between the two writers was their choice of adjectives.

Let us spell out the implications of this rationalization of the past:

1. The left-wing armed organizations were not a product of the national and continental social struggle of the time but deluded minority groups, fascinated by the violence of the Cuban revolutionary experience.
2. Their delirium (and not an attempt to destroy certain social relationships and impose a new system of power) was the main cause of the repression in Argentina.
3. The annihilation of the left-wing armed organizations might therefore have been legitimate. What is considered illegitimate is the "spillover," which led to the victimization of the "innocent." (President Alfonsín spoke of "excesses," the term used by Reynaldo Benito Bignone, the last de facto president of the military dictatorship.)
4. There, victims were to be "investigated" to establish their "degree" of innocence (the less involved in politics they were, the greater their innocence). During the 1980s there were even attempts to give such categories a legal footing. Ultimately, this was a way of sanctioning and legitimizing the values imposed by the genocidal process.
5. What made the whole process seem so irrational was that far more victims fitted the "innocent" category than the "guilty" one (if the latter is restricted to the *leaders* of the armed left-wing organizations). This is what morally condemns the military dictatorship in most people's minds.
6. One step that not everyone dared to take, but which the more radical supporters of this model did take, was to transform the "guilty victims" into a group of "perpetrators," making them directly responsible for the annihilation of the other members of their organizations, if not for all the victims of genocide.

Denial of the past and the transference of guilt were achieved more effectively in Argentina than after the Nazi genocides. Although the historical situation was more complex in the case of Argentina, the hegemonic redefinition of events—what I have called their "symbolic enactment"—successfully prevented the reappearance of social relations that had been extinguished. This was done by branding the left as foolhardy and responsible for the massacre.

I believe that this redefinition of events played an important role in the speed with which individualistic, neoliberal policies took root in Argentina during the twenty years after the dictatorship. As I have already suggested, its success lay in the peculiar way it avoided questioning the role of contemporary generations in the genocide. As with any denial mechanism, the extreme simplicity and incoherence of the denial did not diminish its success.

However, its rapid success was, ironically, its main weakness when a new generation burst onto the political scene: the offspring of those who had lived through the terror. A discourse of this kind was not credible for those who did not need to explain their own part in the events (either to themselves or to others)—that is, for those born around 1970, and who grew up during or after the dictatorship.

This new generation was tormented by a different set of questions: Why were the victims always spoken of in the abstract? Why was there no information about the political organizations of the period, except for disparaging accounts of their armed factions? Where were the parents of these children who grew up during or after the dictatorship when people in our country were being kidnapped, tortured, and annihilated? Why was there no information about opposition or resistance to the military dictatorship? Why had so many contemporary political leaders been involved in the military governments? Where were the thousands of accomplices needed to run a genocide? Why had the majority not raised its voices in defense of the "innocent majority" until 1983? Why had the same media and—with a few honorable exceptions—the same groups of politicians and intellectuals endorsed or at least kept quiet about the genocide, participating in meetings with the perpetrators and thus legitimizing the repression? Why was it necessary to defend the impunity of the perpetrators and their accomplices if they were no more than serial murderers and rapists who, in any other circumstances, would be hounded by courts, politicians, and the media? Why was impunity so necessary to close this "irrational, demonic, and pathological" period in Argentina's history?

These questions erupted in full force on the twentieth anniversary of the coup in March 1996 and the emergence of a new political group, Hijos por la Identidad y la Justicia contra el Olvido y el Silencio (Sons and Daughters for Identity and Justice against Oblivion and Silence), known simply by its acronym, HIJOS, which is also the Spanish word for "children." Despite the Mothers and Grandmothers of Plaza de Mayo and Family Members of the Disappeared and Imprisoned for Political Reasons (Familiares de Desaparecidos y Detenidos por Razones Políticas), this was a family link that had been missing in the human rights organizations. But, in fact, HIJOS did not represent only the children of the disappeared but all the children in society who could not understand or decode the messages of their parents.[29]

One factor that may be seen as triggering widespread disbelief in the hitherto accepted version of events was the collapse of Argentina's economy in December 2001. There was a state of siege in the Plaza de Mayo on 20 and 21 December as young people—most of them born after 1970—clashed with police. These young demonstrators repeatedly mentioned in front of the television cameras and radio microphones the legacy of "the 30,000 disappeared." Although still an abstraction, "the 30,000" was a very different kind of abstraction from that of the hegemonic discourse. Without necessarily understanding how or why, these young people connected the "30,000" with a dynamic struggle, a confrontation loaded with content.

Of course, the way a young person might interpret this struggle at the beginning of this new century was not necessarily the way the "30,000"—the young people of the 1970s—had done so. But those 30,000 were clearly *not* the 30,000 innocents who did nothing, the victims of an overwhelming, irrational force. This new abstraction of "30,000" did not restore historical truth, but it was enough to deepen the cracks that had appeared since 1996 in the symbolic enactments of genocide and that were already becoming visible before the societal breakdown of 2001.

Argentina's 2001 crisis turned out to be less revolutionary than some leftist movements hoped or believed. It did not establish a new model for understanding the genocide or allow for a return to solidarity and political give-and-take. Encouraging attempts were made in this direction by the *asamblea* (neighborhood assembly) movement that sprang up in 2002. In the *asambleas*, residents tried to solve everyday issues, such as problems of infrastructure, price increases, etc. Sadly, many traditional leftist groups denied, pursued, and ended these initiatives, seeing in them a threat to their own traditional forms of social leadership and pressure.

Nevertheless, since the beginning of the twenty-first century the hegemonic explanation of the Argentine genocide has broken down, opening up a still unresolved and highly contested debate on how best to represent Argentina's reorganizing genocide. This debate has played a key role in political youth movements, including the 30,000-strong La Cámpora, founded by Máximo Kirchner, former president Néstor and current president Cristina Kirchner's son, whose members call themselves "soldiers of Cristina."

Apart from that, a debate is pending about the nature and role of "museums of memory"—museums dedicated to remembering the darker side of the human condition. Also overdue is an attempt to understand the failure of the neoliberal policies of the 1990s without scapegoating particular politicians and officials. Rather, the conventional scapegoats (such as former president Carlos Saúl Menem) should be seen as representing certain practices common to Argentine society as a whole. Both these tasks are more feasible than they had been before 2001 as the social relations blocked by genocide are slowly revived.[30]

The Logic of Demonization and the Role of Horror

I have already analyzed at length how the demonization of the Nazi genocides (which pathologized either the Nazis in particular or Germans in general) played a crucial role in blocking historical analysis and led to alienation from personal experience. In Argentina, both perpetrators and victims were treated as pathological in the "theory of the two demons." The adjectives "hellish" and "demonic" are found in Sabato's own preface to the CONADEP Report. But the cleavage between genocidal social practices, on the one hand, and victims and perpetrators, on the other, was even greater than it had been following the Nazi genocides.

As in the case of postwar Europe, the period immediately following Argentina's last dictatorship is characterized by an excessive profusion of images of horror. Indeed, the process had already begun in 1983, the last year of the military government. The same publications that had been accomplices of the dictatorship for seven long years—*Gente, Siete Días, Para Ti*, to name only the best known—began to include interviews with relatives of victims or survivors, pictures of mass graves being unearthed, testimonies of repentance, full of banal or distasteful images highlighting the most gruesome and sickening features of horror. This so-called exposure of the dictatorship flooded public opinion with a series of lurid narratives, with particular emphasis being placed on stories of treachery and betrayal, romance between perpetrators and victims, rape, robbery, humiliation, and the details of the repressors' sadistic inventiveness.

This profusion of morbid but unexplained horror plunged readers—and the rest of society—into a state of moral paralysis. If human beings were capable of such horrors, surely it was better to stay at home and not ask too many questions. In this sense, Roberto Jacoby's research during the 1980s illustrated the shifting nature of ordinary people's fears. Jacoby discovered that, after the dictatorship, the place that felt safest was home—even though most victims of genocide had, in fact, been snatched from their homes. This finding illustrates how people's fears and perceptions of their possibilities for political action are neither rational nor coherent; rather, they are shaped by re-presentations of the recent past, the very thing we are trying to think about in these pages.[31]

At the two seminars organized by the Association of Ex-Disappeared Detainees during the years 1996 and 1997 under the auspices of the Human Rights Freedom Chair of the Faculty of Arts at the University of Buenos Aires (see chapter 7), survivors highlighted a dual psychological mandate from the genocidaires to the camp survivors. The first part of the mandate was to narrate the horror, but not in memory of the victims. After years of trying to understand why they had been allowed to survive, the ex-detainees expressed their conclusions with unflinching clarity and concision: go and tell the whole world what has happened to your bodies, what we have done to them, so that nobody ever again dares to do what you have done.[32]

The second part of the mandate discussed in the seminars was also addressed to society as a whole: *trust no one*. And Argentineans unquestionably began to distrust one another, first as an attempt at self-protection, then as part of a culture of individualism. This mandate also seemed to tell us: Beware of the camp survivors, of course, because "there must be a reason why they were allowed to live." But also beware of new friends—who knows why they have come along now—and old friends who cannot explain why they left or did not leave. Beware of those who never wanted to be friends with you and always keep their distance, because they surely have something to hide. Beware of acquaintances, because they were surely secret accomplices. And beware of strangers who come to steal property or information. Finally, beware of yourselves, of your own outrage at poverty, of your desire to change the world, of the utopia of a fairer society or compassion for anyone who is weaker. Go to therapy and, with the help of new methodologies for rapid healing and self-help, "help yourselves" and only yourselves.

Mistrust was one of the most effective ways to end relations of reciprocity and solidarity. One cannot found an oppositional or critical political struggle on a basis of mutual suspicion. This fact explains the disarray existing among the surviving leftist forces during the 1980s and 1990s. If it is impossible for me to trust anyone, then all I can do is look out for myself and take care of number one, a form of politics that ends up being antipolitical if by politics we mean the negotiation of power among *social groups*.

It was no coincidence that this distrust appeared at a time when the political system was widely discredited. Indeed, the best way to discredit any struggle in the postdictatorship era was to describe it as *political*. Even elected politicians played on this fear. "You have political objectives" was the first accusation thrown at any rival by the democratic governments of Raúl Alfonsín, Carlos Menem, Fernando De La Rua, or Eduardo Duhalde. And indeed, the whole political spectrum represented in parliament and in the hegemonic media thought in this way: "They are not defending their own interests," meaning that each person should look after his or her individual or, at best, corporate interests.

The logic of this approach suggested that if a person devoted time and energy to politics, if they cared about others more than about themselves, this should not be seen as an altruistic action worthy of emulation, a generosity that puts a concern for others above one's self-interest. Rather, such a person lacked legitimacy and was not to be trusted. From this point of view, a political struggle that could not be explained in terms of self-interest had to be a swindle or a con. Thus, horror led to paralysis, then to suspicion and distrust, and finally to individualism. And these consequences of genocide affected economic, social, and cultural policies for almost twenty years. The 2001 crisis was just a glimpse of the cracks in a social and political model that still remains dominant in its ability to discourage certain ways of relating while promoting others.

Repoliticizing the Seventies through the Discourse of War: Possibilities and Limits

Hegemonic models of representation do not develop unopposed or operate within a vacuum. Throughout this period, one of the discourses that sought to confront the depoliticizing of the Argentine genocide was that of civil war. As mentioned in chapter 7, the clearest exponents of this position were Marín and Izaguirre.

The discourse of civil war acknowledged the political nature of the struggle—or at least attempted to do so. Marín traces the conflict back farther than 1976 or even 1973, to the military coup that ousted Perón in September 1955 and especially to the bombing of civilians in the Plaza de Mayo in June 1955, the shooting of Peronist rebels in 1956 and the military's refusal to include popular sectors in the government. Persecution left the defeated sectors of the Peronist movement with few options, one of which was armed confrontation.

Seeing these historical moments and the different social forces and meanings as part of a shifting balance of power restored to both victims and perpetrators a sense of identity. Therefore, it amounted to a clear attempt at repoliticizing Argentina's recent history, an attempt that was ignored and quickly silenced by the academics and journalists of the period.

I also noted in the previous chapter, however, the limits of this approach. Treating social forces as armies—albeit engaged in a highly unequal civil war—and focusing on the military-political conflict and the number of "casualties" simply reproduced the way the perpetrators presented the conflict (the military always claimed to be carrying out a "dirty war"). At the same time, this approach made it difficult to understand how a rebellious social force had appeared which, despite the enthusiasm and triumphal perceptions of its young members, was not at all in a position to fight a civil war. More importantly, it hid the fact that the perpetrators had created a stereotype of their victims (which I call their "negative Otherness" in this book) that did not necessarily require them to be members of an army or participants in a civil war or warlike situation.

On the contrary, the Dirty War had been unleashed against the social whole to "reorganize" it. As in all reorganizing genocides, the murder of the direct victims was a message to the wider population—the indirect victims. The process did not aim to produce a specific number or type of "casualties"; rather, its purpose lay in the conclusions society would draw about the dead, the survivors, the wounded, and the exiled. In particular, the gruesome way in which the disappeared met their deaths was meant to destroy the social fabric and create a new social, cultural, and political climate—in short, a new form of governance.

There is a risk of "reifying" the Argentine genocide in terms of armed actions, casualties, and so forth if we compare it to the civil wars in Central America. In Nicaragua and El Salvador, the size of the military forces was decisive and—in each case—both sides in the military conflict were clearly defined politically. But the Argentine genocide is clearly different from these two cases, and comparisons tend to miss indentifying the specific nature of the Argentine conflict that is crucial for understanding subsequent political events.[33]

The Human Rights Organizations: Material and Symbolic Struggles

For over twenty years, the Argentine human rights organizations—with all their nuances and differences—have worked hard to undo some of the consequences of genocide, in particular through their uneven fight against impunity. First, these organizations took part in the debate on how the National Commission on the Disappearance of Persons (CONADEP) should be composed, insisting on the desirability of including a Bicameral Commission of Inquiry made up of national deputies and senators. Then they were constant and tireless in presenting testimonies and documents at the court trials of various perpetrators. Afterward, they struggled bravely at the end of the 1980s and during the following decade to overturn the impunity laws and pardons. In this way, the Argentine human rights organizations became a moral reserve of society, many of them going beyond their original agendas to denounce "trigger-happy" police, the intimidation of popular, neighborhood, or student activists, and the use of torture in prisons during the democratic period.

Here, the role played by these groups in attempting to develop an alternative view of events cannot be emphasized too strongly. And yet, despite all this, they consciously, or nearly consciously, left the fight in the hands of lawyers (who, in positivist terms, are the only ones who know) and prioritized the legal battle (the real possibility that perpetrators might be sent to prison) over the symbolic struggle (law as a producer of truth, and a socially sanctioned way of understanding the past).

Because their priority was to send the perpetrators to jail, these groups saw the symbolic aspects of the struggle as being of secondary importance. In the 1980s the need for effective action prevailed over strategic analysis—and it is hard to see how it could have been otherwise. I, too, endorsed the need to put "trial and punishment" before symbolic or political analysis. Back then, what to *call* the crimes committed, for example, seemed like a trivial language game. For this reason, trials were the result of adding together individual offenses—unlawful deprivation of liberty, murder, torture, rape, robbery, abduction of minors, kidnapping—committed against individual subjects. This was a mistake.

It is true that Eduardo Barcesat, and some other truly visionary jurists for their time, had suggested bringing charges of genocide—a crime committed not against individuals but against a social group—but the idea was rejected by the human rights organizations' lawyers because of the clearly political nature of the killings and the fact that the Convention on the Prevention and Punishment of the Crime of Genocide (1948) does not cover political groups.

In the event, however, the 1986 Full Stop Law and the 1987 Due Obedience Law proved to be stronger than any activist and/or professional legal work—except where the kidnapping of children or theft of private property was involved.[34] Because these crimes had been excluded from Alfonsín's amnesty laws, it was later possible to condemn some of the repressors to a comfortable house arrest—but impunity remained rife until the impunity laws were overturned by the Argentine Supreme Court in June 2005 with the blessing of Néstor Kirchner.

In short, prioritizing the material effects of law over its symbolic effects led to defeat on both fronts. The perpetrators remained unpunished for decades, and society's understanding of events remained trapped in a summation of individual crimes, a form of understanding that fitted perfectly with other symbolic embodiments of genocide. If it was the sum of individual violations of human rights, the perpetrators could be thought of as insane serial killers or as part of a regime that disregarded individual rights. The ideas of "excess" or "misunderstanding" were consistent with an individualistic way of understanding events.

Durkheim points out that a "social fact"—a social phenomenon like language, law, morality, or public opinion that shapes and constrains individual behavior—is total and qualitatively different from the sum of individual facts.[35] A genocide, in this sense, is a total social practice and qualitatively different from the sum of tens of thousands of homicides or unlawful deprivations of liberty, or tens of thousands of cases of torture, or hundreds of rapes. Viewing them as individual crimes meant trying those responsible for individual crimes.

Spanish law allows for an *acusación popular*, whereby an action may be brought in the public interest by any Spanish citizen, necessarily an injured party. It was not until fifteen years after the end of the dictatorship that Carlos Slepoy, an Argentine human-rights lawyer practicing in Madrid, brought an *acusación popular* in Spain against members of the Argentine military for genocide and terrorism. In doing so, he was helped by various human rights organizations that had refused to compromise their principles in all this time.

In Spain, lawyers first bring the lawsuit to an investigating judge, who examines the evidence, interviews witnesses, and determines whether the case should be brought to trial. In this case the investigating judge was Baltasar Garzón. In November 1999, Garzón charged Argentine naval officer Adolfo Scilingo—who had confessed to participating in so-called death flights—with genocide. Finally, Scilingo was convicted in 2005 of crimes against humanity. However, the action itself and Garzon's argument that genocide committed against "part of a national group" can equally well refer to the perpetrator's national group reopened the debate about how to define events in Argentina.

This debate was revived with the reopening of trials in Argentina. One highlight of these trials was the sentencing of a former senior police officer in Buenos Aires, Miguel Etchecolatz, by the Oral Procedure Court for Federal Crimes No. 1 of La Plata, Buenos Aires, in 2006. The tribunal found that Etchecolatz, who served during the early years of the military dictatorship, could not be accused of genocide because this crime had not been included in the original indictment. Instead, he was sentenced to life imprisonment for "crimes against humanity in the context of the genocide that took place in Argentina." Thus, the sentence not only emphasized that genocide had indeed been committed in Argentina, but suggested this charge be used in subsequent trials.

It is still too early to know the effects of these decisions, but they will certainly be important in confronting the symbolic embodiments of genocidal processes in Argentina. On 22 December 2010, General Videla was sentenced to life in a civilian prison for his part in the deaths of thirty-one prisoners. More recently, on 5 July 2012, Videla, Bignone, and seven others were found guilty of the systematic abduction of babies born to political prisoners. Videla received a fifty-year sentence, while Bignone was given fifteen years. However, justice in Argentina is slow and many perpetrators will surely escape jail for reasons of age if they are ever brought to trial at all.

A Struggle for Identity

It should be clear by now that my interest in defining the Argentine state terror of 1976–1983 as genocide is more than merely an academic attempt to create schools of understanding of what happened. Such schools could only settle their arguments before a jury. Nor am I attempting a specific legal debate, which is the province of trial lawyers. This debate has been taken up with the reopening of trials against the perpetrators.

Argentina's understanding of its own present depends largely on how it understands the events of the 1970s. If I have managed to convince you, the reader, that the primary goal of reorganizing genocide—at least, as it has been practiced in Argentina—is to destroy and rebuild social relations, it follows that this destruction and rebuilding requires a specific mode of "symbolic enactment" by which materially annihilated relations are reannihilated in the field of the symbolic: "There is no rebellious society. The young are not critical and show no solidarity. In truth such a thing has never existed. For it is impossible." Hence, skepticism that leads to solipsism and blinkered self-interest: "There was a sect of deluded terrorists. There was an innocent society. There was a power that, in trying to suppress the deluded, produced a series of individual violations of human rights which a democratic republic cannot tolerate. They should be expected to answer legally for each of these violations." Or not, depending on how radical one's approach is.

Genocide is aimed at a group, not at a collection of individuals. In Argentina, each of the victims was "guilty" of what the perpetrators wanted to destroy—but so too were the survivors of the detention centers and concentration camps and those who managed to avoid being abducted. However, they did not necessarily escape the effects of terror in their ways of relating to others, in their memories, and in their consciences.

Justifications of the type "there must have been a reason [why they were killed]"—cleverly reformulated by Elsa Drucaroff as "there *was* a reason"[36]—cannot be combated by claiming "they were innocent." However, turning the victims into members of an army that most never even knew they belonged to is no solution, either. In trying to understand what members of the establishment tried to destroy, what they understood by "subversive crime," perhaps we—those who were not yet born or who, like myself, remember horror prowling the streets of our childhood—will discover the kind of society our parents strove to build in Argentina. Perhaps, too, we can force them to remember what they were like when they were not only concerned about themselves, when it was much more common to show solidarity, or be critical, or trust other people—when, in short, they attempted to rebuild not only the political but, fundamentally, the social and cultural order.

In a sense, genocide undermines classical liberal law because genocide can only be exercised against a group. It is a legal category that takes no account of people as individuals, only as members of a group, as part of a social force, as the incarnation of certain social relations. Understanding the events as genocide in Argentina means being able to start this debate. And it is perhaps vital to do so from the field of law, whatever the practical outcomes may be in terms of prison sentences. It is necessary to demonstrate the genocidal nature of the events and force the perpetrators to account for the systematic nature of their practices. It is necessary to expose the definitions embedded in their genocidal as well as their postgenocidal discourses. And it is necessary to force international law to argue philosophy, to question distinctions between human groups based on identity (what they are) and action (what they do), and to recognize that excluding political groups from the 1948 Genocide Convention provided what Donnedieu de Vabres called the ideal excuse to endorse any genocidal process since all social events have a political basis.

As I have already pointed out, the debate about whether events in Argentina can or should be described as genocide is not just an academic one. But it is that, too. This book is a scholar's search for legal, historical, philosophical—and also political—meaning. Indeed, liberal constitutionalists—a species now condemned worldwide by the hegemonic media that seek to reduce our freedoms–have been at pains to point out that the main strength of law lies not in the nature of the penalties but in the way law structures the discourses of truth. This point was also made by Foucault, even before the Argentine genocide.[37] Too bad we are beginning to realize this so late in the day! How, then, should we resume the debate from this time forward?

Appendix or Digression: Papiernik, Villani, and Analogies

On a hot day in March 2001, as I was finishing my first course on "Analysis of Genocidal Social Practices" in the Faculty of Social Sciences at the University of

Buenos Aires, we organized a public event—which turned out to be very well attended—in which survivors of concentration camps told their stories and then talked to our students and anyone else who wanted to take part. The idea was to talk to them using the concepts developed during the course, many of which are contained in this book. We were accompanied by our good friend Charles Papiernik, who was interned for almost four years in Auschwitz, together with three survivors of clandestine detention centers in Argentina—Jorge Paladino, Mario Villani, and Graciela Daleo.

After some humming and hawing, Charles Papiernik refused to be the first to speak—despite the insistence of the Argentine survivors because he was the oldest—so Mario Villani took on the difficult role. His presentation was as tough as it was enlightening. He felt obliged to return—like every survivor—to the concentration camps where he had lived for nearly four years and, from there, to tell stories of resistance, friendship, humor, and grief.

Since the mid-1990s, we had been coming under mounting criticism at home and abroad for having the courage to draw analogies and carry out comparative studies between the Nazi concentration camps and those in Argentina, treating both as instances of "genocide," which was clearly "wrong" in the view of the academic mainstream.

I could not remember ever hearing two survivors speak in public about their experiences. I had not talked with Charles about the issue, so I did not know how he would take Mario's words and, more importantly, my strange proposal for them to speak together in the same forum under the umbrella heading of "Analysis of Genocidal Social Practices," as my subject was called.

I have said that Mario's testimony was moving. Charles was absolutely shocked. Not that he did not know what had happened in Argentina. In fact, he had lived in his house in Villa Crespo during the years of the dictatorship and had even spoken to relatives of the disappeared, who had told him their stories and sufferings. But as those of us who have heard numerous testimonies from survivors know, it is not the same to read the newspaper or talk with family or friends as to be present at the *reentry* of a concentration camp survivor into society, a *reentry* without which it is impossible to be a witness, a *reentry* we know will cost the witness days or weeks of renewed pain and anguish.

Charles, who was used to being a witness, was listening to another witness like himself, but not Jack Fuchs or Eugenia Unger, not a Jewish victim from the Nazi camps in Poland. This was a non-Jewish Argentinean, Mario Villani, recounting his journey through Argentina's concentration camps, in which only very occasionally the officers said something in German "to act like Nazis."

This is why Charles's eyes filled with tears as Mario was ending his reminiscences, and why he could not wait even a second more to embrace him when he concluded, hugging him like a friend or as he might have hugged his brother who did not return from Auschwitz and whom he spoke about later that evening.

When the embrace ended, someone passed the microphone to Charles. But there was only silence. Charles could not speak. I had heard him speak hundreds of times: to high school students, to Jewish community leaders, with other survivors from the Nazi concentration camps, among friends, among ourselves. But that day Charles was at a loss for words. He stared for a long time at the nearly two hundred people gathered in the Aula Magna in Uriburu Street, in the city of Buenos Aires, and he could not utter a sound.

And then he started: "I have nothing to say," he said. "I came here to tell you about genocide but I have nothing to say. What I lived through in Auschwitz was the same, the same thing he has just told you. The same."

I had to insist quietly that he speak. He was standing next to me and I was able to hug him gently and tell him that we knew it was *the same*, but for that very reason we needed to listen to him.

And only then was he able to talk about his brother murdered in Auschwitz, about the woman he was in love with for only a day, about the false rumors of an Allied advance to give courage to the dying, about stories of friendship, humiliation, resistance, and pain of the inmates of Auschwitz.

Then it was Jorge and Graciela's turn to speak. Jorge talked about his walks to the ice cream parlor with his cellmate, measured in steps inside their bunks, about his absurd illusion—which lasted well into his stay at the camp—that they would be sent to "recovery farms" in the south, about his surprise and what Pilar Calveiro would call the "lines of flight" that had stopped him from going mad.

Graciela did not testify but she tried to think: she did not want to return to the ESMA that night, but she shared with us what the ex-disappeared detainees had been mulling over for several years at their meetings, which became a valuable contribution to our own thinking.

I am not trying to say that in objective terms Auschwitz was the same as the ESMA, the Athletic Club that was a torture center in Buenos Aires, or the Olympus concentration camp, beyond Charles's need to express it in that way. Countless historians have described the specific content of these historical events. Much less work has been done on the subjective experiences of concentration camp inmates—but we can assume that our conclusions would be similar. We know that they are not "the same," and the comparisons in this book are in no way intended to suggest otherwise.

But dealing with these events together—the ESMA and Auschwitz, the Nazi genocide and the Argentine genocide—carries a different meaning from speaking about them separately. Certainly it has for Charles, Mario, Jorge, and Graciela. And also for me. And I hope, too, for my readers. Let this digression stand, then, as another justification for this book.

9

Concentration Camp Logic

For each one we touch, a thousand paralyzed with fear. We act by irradiation.

—Eduardo Pavlovsky, *El señor Galíndez*

As we have seen in previous chapters, the Nazis not only created a new type of genocide—what I call "reorganizing genocide"; they also used various methods to kill their victims, including shootings, gassings, death marches, starvation, and disease. One of the distinctive features of the Nazi genocides was the use of concentration camps as tools of oppression and mass extermination. On the other hand, the Argentine genocide—although much smaller in scale—can be thought of as one of the most successful and cost-effective instances of "reorganizing genocide" in terms of destroying and rebuilding the social fabric. An interesting innovation is that, unlike earlier genocidal processes or even other military dictatorships in the region, this self-styled "National Reorganization Process" made no bones about its true aims.

The main purpose of this chapter is to describe and account for the distinctive features of "reorganizing genocide." In particular, it will explore the material and symbolic effects of using concentration camps to "discipline" society and suggest ways of confronting some of their effects. The primary sources for this chapter are survivor testimonies from both genocides—especially Argentine testimonies, which have been studied much less frequently. These are the voices of ghosts—of the "reappeared" who came back from hell and who, in Juan Gelman's words, were twice-silenced: "from within, because they lived through unspeakable experiences; from without, because many ears are closed to what they have to tell."[1]

Survivors of the Nazi camps did not find a receptive audience until many years after their "reappearance." Bruno Bettelheim's writings, which recounted his experiences in the Buchenwald concentration camp, were rejected for years because they were considered "exaggerated" or "not credible"—and because they were too sad. The work of Primo Levi and other survivors did not become widely known until the 1970s. Perhaps it is not too surprising, then, that the

Argentine "reappeared" were either suspected of collaboration—and shunned like the plague—or transformed into talking machines, endlessly reciting a litany of horror but required to remain silent about their previous political activity or about their feelings after "liberation."[2] In both cases, the dead were blameless, while the survivors had to bear the shame of reappearance . . . Why were they still alive when others were dead? They had no right to speak, and their testimony was discredited.

In Argentina, the media devoted pages and hours of broadcasting time to giving a voice to the mothers, relatives, and even human rights activists—but not to the survivors. Once the dictatorship was over, survivors had to fight for another fifteen years before they could begin to "appear" and make their voices heard. And yet they were the ones who had returned from the horror and who knew *at first hand* what had happened in the camps and detention centers. Perhaps their real problem was that they were also members of a generation and a political project that had been defeated.

This chapter seeks to recover their voices, without which it would be impossible to reflect on the nature and role of Argentina's concentration camps as instruments of social oppression and social change.

The Peculiar Features of Reorganizing Genocide: Destruction and Reconstruction of the Social Fabric

I have already argued that what made reorganizing genocide new and different from previous genocidal social practices was that it was directed "inward" at an already established society. Reorganizing genocide sets out to transform social relations *within an existing nation-state* in ways that profoundly alter it. In this sense it is quite different from genocide aimed at "outsiders," whether these be indigenous populations (colonial genocide), former colonizers (postcolonial genocide), or unwanted groups within the context of building a new nation-state (foundational genocide). This was one of the considerations that led Spanish judge Baltasar Garzón and (later) Argentine judge Carlos Rozanski to describe the events in Argentina as genocide. State terror in Argentina had transformed the social fabric to such an extent that the "Argentine national group" (which is a national group and therefore protected by the 1948 Genocide Convention) had disappeared as such and had become radically different.

Beyond its legal implications, which were discussed in chapter 1, these arguments, in my view, are fundamental to understanding the specific nature of reorganizing genocide: its purpose and ability to alter, through death and horror, the dominant modes of social relations. In Argentina, there had been political opposition to the traditional agro-exporter and rentier economic model for over thirty years.[3] The purpose of genocide was to eliminate this resistance, which came mainly from unions and workers' commissions, political and armed movements, and student and neighborhood movements.

But this chapter also sets out to examine social facilitation[4] and the ability to resist. By social facilitation I mean social practices that make a particular policy possible or not—for example, regarding others as equals, being outraged at injustice, trusting others, putting solidarity first, taking responsibility for those in need, having the utopian dream of building a better world together, and valuing the primacy of collective decisions over individual sentiments, among others. For what was striking about Argentine politics in the 1960s and 1970s was not the leftist organizations' grasp of the historical situation or the clarity of their policy objectives. In fact, they made enormous mistakes in both areas and paid a heavy cost for them. Rather, it was the generous commitment shown by left-wing militants, including their conviction that a just society was possible. These qualities, in my opinion, do not deserve the contempt and ridicule with which they are often greeted nowadays, when individualism is more or less taken for granted.

In saying this, I am not attempting to whitewash the political and social developments of the period. On the contrary, an urgent critical appraisal of this period is needed—one that focuses either on the serious misconceptions that plagued Argentina's left-wing organizations or on the appropriateness and effectiveness of their political actions, or both. But, in our morally subjective times, where individual needs routinely outweigh collective decision-making processes and even oppositional and critical sectors place their right to protest above political consensus, it is salutary to note how this different way of doing politics was linked to a different style of social relations.

The aim of "national reorganization" was precisely to create the type of society in which we find ourselves today: an atomized community with countless individual grievances, with thousands of public figures unable to speak to one another, with numerous, self-enclosed identities—national, ethnic, sexual, and, of course, political—and with self-obsessed interest groups incapable of feeling indignant about the plight of others or even recognizing their needs. Let us briefly list some of these interest groups. They include Argentina's small savers, cheated out of their savings during the economic crisis of 2001;[5] college students defending free education; the beneficiaries of social plans; unionized workers; workers hired illegally; teachers with starvation salaries; overworked nurses; people in working-class and middle-class neighborhoods harassed by criminal gangs often run by the police themselves; relatives of victims of the AMIA bombing[6] or of the República Cromañón nightclub fire;[7] women denied the right to an abortion; indigenous peoples displaced from their traditional land; Afro-descendants, who are rediscovering their identity; and countless other sectors, each absorbed in its own problems. Often they look to journalists for answers and solutions. However, this method gives no guarantee of success and, seen in a wider perspective, it simply creates an ever more unjust and intolerant society of individualists increasingly pursuing their own self-interest. Solutions are not for society as a whole, but only for the interest group in question.

As Guillermo O'Donnell suggested, "And why the fuck should I care?" reflected a widespread sentiment among the Argentine working class, challenging established power relations, while responding to the question, "Do you know who you're talking to?" was an aristocratic attempt to project power by mere presence. In the postgenocidal period, however, "And why the fuck should I care?"took on quite the opposite meaning from that suggested by O'Donnell. Now, what no longer mattered was what happened to other people or the fact that *my* way of solving *my* problem may be creating problems for others who are not part of my interest group. The expression "And why the fuck should I care?" was no longer a challenge to an arrogant and aristocratic power figure but a rebellion against the notion of solidarity. Why the fuck should I care about hunger, suffering, the breakdown of law and order, in short, about other people's misfortunes?[8]

The political organizations of the 1970s went so far as to send many of their most intellectual and highly trained administrators to work as factory workers. In my view, this was a serious political mistake. But it showed a level of generosity and commitment that today would be unthinkable. In contrast, when representatives of different interest groups sit at a negotiating table nowadays with representatives of the state, the first question many of them ask is, "What's in it for me?" Not even "for us" but "for me." There is no need for government officials to co-opt or bribe these social interlocutors as was habitual in the past; many now set their own price for betraying their causes—a price that is usually affordable for Argentina's public administration in such a highly competitive market.

My assumption is that inward-looking individualism, selfishness, and betrayal on this scale are partly a consequence of reorganizing genocide—not an unintended or regrettable side-effect, but a desired outcome of this practice. Courage, heroism, and political commitment are not just individual qualities; they require a social environment in which they can flourish and then become either widespread or expected behaviors, or both. For the same reason, an analysis of corruption cannot assume that only a limited number of individuals—for example, the supporters of former President Carlos Menem—were (and are) essentially corrupt without considering the wider social context. By ignoring the social context, we run the risk of feeding racist theories about the Argentinean character, along lines similar to those of the nineteenth century, which deplored the *mestizo* and indigenous origins of the country's inhabitants.

Corruption became a widespread practice in Argentina after the disappearance of those who most obviously embodied cooperative and honest social relations. Most importantly, it resulted from the simultaneous loss of these individuals together with the terror generated by their disappearance in the surviving members of society. And the fundamental tool in this process of transformation—destruction and remaking—of social relations was the concentration camp. At the seminars held by the Association of Ex-Disappeared Detainees (AEDD) in 1996 and 1997, mentioned in previous chapters, we developed a metaphor created by the concentration camp survivors themselves and which—in my view—clearly summarizes how reorganizing genocide works. They called it "the metaphor of the bouillon cube (or stock cube) and soup."

As mentioned earlier, concentration camp survivors frequently ask why they were allowed to live while others perished. When asked to explain why they needed to discuss their experiences *in public*, members of AEDD answered that they felt they had been part of a bouillon cube—the concentration camp—that was intended to dissolve into the social broth as a whole. Consequently, it was important both for the survivors and for society at large to understand the nature and consequences of the concentration camp experience. In the words of the survivors themselves, "We believe the 'social soup' reproduced and induced, with varying degrees of dilution, relationships, reactions and individual and social behaviors similar to those within the concentration camps."[9] The seminars were extraordinary for many reasons that are not relevant to this discussion, but one of them is worth mentioning here.

One would have expected the media or other sectors of society to invite the "reappeared" to tell their stories at one time or another. But in fact these survivors were ignored for almost fifteen years until they took the step themselves of organizing a public discussion to help people understand what had happened—and what was still happening—in a society from which they had been absent, locked away in concentration camps. Even so, they did not ask their contemporaries—as they might well have done—how and why some people were able to go about their daily lives while others were branded forever in body and soul by the horror of the camps. Nor did they force them to listen to their testimonies—the complete testimonies that Argentine society had never wanted to listen to before. Instead, they eagerly questioned the public—young people who had been children during the dictatorship, and indeed anyone who was willing to take part—about how they had survived *outside* the camps, what life had been like for them in the "social stock," how much of the "cube" had dissolved, and what similarities and differences they saw between the camps and the surrounding society.

Justifying the need for those who had been inside and outside to work together, they said:

> We proposed a joint effort between those of us who were in the "cube" and those who were in the "soup." And the importance of working

> together from different but related perspectives arises from having noticed over the years a sense of alienation, a separation between those who seem to have suffered during the dictatorship and a great mass of people that seems not to have suffered. Not that we want to socialize our pain so that we will hurt less, but we believe it is important for society to recognize their own experiences. . . . Because that "alienation," that idea that "the dictatorship happened to militants, relatives and victims" sometimes makes the pursuit of justice seem like an act of solidarity with those who are listed as "direct victims," and not like a personal need.[10]

Some of the conclusions of the seminar, including attempts to spread distrust as a fundamental social practice, are discussed in other chapters. However, the way this particular insight appeared and was developed was novel and unique. It speaks reams about the many ways in which people were able to survive genocide, as well as the fissures in the Argentine military's project of national reorganization.

Concentration Camp Power as Social Discipline

Assuming, then, that the concentration camp was a two-way device, operating both on the inmates of the camp and on society as a whole, the question arises as to how it affected each of these two groups. Numerous testimonies of survivors of Nazi and Argentine concentration camps center on what Bruno Bettelheim describes as the "breaking down" of personality. The guards' systematic brutality was intended to break the inmates as *social beings*, destroying their capacity for self-determination. Bettelheim's work focuses mainly on personal autonomy in an individual sense. However, I think the breakdown Bettelheim describes was both individual and social. The stereotypical image of Nazi concentration camp survivors was that of the "living dead"[11]—human beings who had lost all control over their lives and were no longer able to decide even the simplest things for themselves.

While these powerless figures might seem to the perpetrators to be "ideal" members of society, it is clear that even authority would disappear if all citizens' autonomy were denied to this point. However, the example of *total domination* that occurred in the concentration camps demonstrated the perpetrators' ability to override individual and social autonomy on a wider scale. In this sense, the concentration camp was what Max Weber called an "ideal type"—a selective, one-sided representation of an aspect of social life.[12] As regards society at large, the aim was not to create "living dead," but to keep people frightened enough to ensure continuity, obedience, and order.

The literature on concentration camps and "total institutions" such as psychiatric hospitals emphasizes the deliberate and systematic destruction of personality that occurs in such places. The following procedures, described by

Bruno Bettelheim and Pilar Calveiro as well as by the sociologist Erving Goffman in his book *Asylums*,[13] are typical of most testimonies of most concentration camp survivors.[14]

1. *Destruction of Identity*

In both Argentina and Nazi-occupied Europe, the prisoner's name was exchanged for a number as soon as he or she entered a concentration camp. But loss of identity went beyond that. As Bettelheim observes, inmates were cut off from the references that defined their identity: everything for which they were known, recognized, or stigmatized outside the camp was erased, from their professional to their social status, and they were denied all contact with friends, family, or members of political organizations. Within the concentration camp, their identity was determined only by the way they behaved *within* the camp—their response to torture and brutality and their greater or lesser degree of collaboration. Faced with situations they could not even imagine before entering the camps and for which they were psychologically unprepared, their self-esteem collapsed. Viktor Frankl spent three years in Auschwitz and three other camps. He remarked: "The majority of prisoners suffered from a kind of inferiority complex. We all had once been or had fancied ourselves to be 'somebody.' Now we were treated like complete nonentities."[15]

2. *Annulment of Perception and Mobility*

While prisoners' previous identity was being erased, they were simultaneously prevented from recognizing their new environment. In the Nazi camps, detainees could be executed on the spot for trying to discover the camp's position and layout or for monitoring the punishments meted out to other detainees. Survivors also described how prisoners became cynical and apathetic, "looking without seeing," incapable of responding ethically or reflecting on their environment or fate.

In Argentina, sensory deprivation was taken a step further. On arrival at the camp or detention center, the "disappeared" were blindfolded or their heads were covered with hoods or bags—a treatment known as "walling up"—while their mobility was restricted by shackles or threats. Moreover, communication between detainees was prohibited, and sometimes they could not even communicate with the perpetrators, except during interrogations.

The combined effect of these procedures was social and physical disorientation followed by a breakdown of personality. Feelings of panic were common in prisoners subjected to these conditions for more than just a few hours. The victims, plunged into total darkness, silence, and immobility, tended to lose all track of time and space. Often, prisoners were stripped of all their clothing, which left the body not only in darkness, silence, and immobility, but also naked and vulnerable.

3. "Initiation": The Role of Torture

If incarceration in a concentration camp involved restrictions on perception and mobility and loss of identity, initiation into concentration camp life was via brutality and torture or both. Inmates were subjected to beatings, asphyxiation, and a variety of physical punishments during their first hours and days at the camp as a way to breaking them in and getting them used to their new condition.

In Argentina torture was used on a regular basis. Pilar Calveiro lists three main functions of torture in these cases:

a. Extraction of information
b. "Cleansing ritual"
c. Physical and psychological destruction.[16]

As already pointed out in other chapters, torture as a way of extracting information drew on lessons learned during the French counterinsurgency wars. Usually, prisoners were tortured for information for the first two or three days, and the procedure, as Calveiro puts it, was "aseptic" and "functional." The information obtained led to a growing spiral of kidnappings, torture, and information.

One of the oldest motivations for torture is purification. With the Inquisition, for example, the infliction of pain generally ended when prisoners admitted to their sins. Once they had confessed, they were usually killed quickly since their souls supposedly had been saved through repentance. In the Argentina of the 1970s, the victims were tortured until they accepted the guilt constructed for them by the perpetrators. Whether they were really guilty or not was—for the perpetrators' ends—neither here nor there. However, Calveiro claims that torture as a "cleansing ritual" existed only in some cases, such as the centers run by the air force and the federal police.

Calveiro is less precise about another use of torture that has existed in all concentration camps: torture as a way of breaking the inmates' will. To "adapt," inmates were required to deny their own identity and to adopt the values of their captors, but obviously this left room for dissembling and partial adaptation. The prisoners' bodies were therefore repeatedly subjected to pain in order to counteract attempts to keep identity alive—an identity that camp routines were also designed to erase, but which the detainees might nevertheless bury deep inside themselves.

4. Infantilization and Animalization

To the already mentioned procedures can be added what authors and survivors call infantilization (or regression) and animalization, all of which involve the destruction of agency and self-determination.

In the concentration camps, prisoners lost control of their most basic human functions. They were forced to ask permission to urinate and defecate, or to use a bucket inside the cell in which they were incarcerated. They had to request authorization to perform even the most basic tasks. Food, as well as being meager and of poor quality, was transformed into a sort of privilege for those who were considered well behaved. Any activity, even the most trivial, was regulated by the authorities. Often, detainees were forced to behave like animals, imitating the sounds of dogs or cows and crawling on all fours, or to go to the restroom blindfolded, where they would stumble into walls or doors, among other forms of humiliation.

This loss of control of bodily needs, which are regulated externally by the perpetrator, was compounded by the spatial and temporal disorientation mentioned earlier and the constant terror that torture could be resumed.

5. Unpredictability

Finally, there was the impossibility of knowing how to save oneself. The ultimate fate—death—was both suggested and hidden. The manner in which behavior was evaluated was whimsical and indecipherable. In some cases torture lasted weeks; in others, only a few days. In some cases, collaboration was rewarded with death; in others, it brought certain privileges. Sometimes, acts of solidarity or defiance were punished with death or a visit to the torture chamber; but on rare occasions, they were tolerated and even respected.

This contributed to the breakdown of personality, as various witnesses have testified, since it made it impossible to foresee the consequences of one's actions. Any action or inaction could result in death, but there was no pattern. Death was always just around the corner and, in the long term, seemingly inevitable; however, it was rationed in an arbitrary fashion like the food, and—in the Argentine camps—even suicide was prevented.

In many cases, the prisoners' loss of previous identity and stable references and disconnection from their own feelings and perceptions—even from their own bodies—led to a complete breakdown of personality. Recalling his experiences in the Buchenwald concentration camp, Bruno Bettelheim describes a figure that epitomizes the camp system even more than the living dead—namely, the "adapted" man. This was a person who had accepted some or all of the perpetrators' values. An extreme example was the prisoner functionary, or *kapo,* appointed by the Nazis to supervise forced labor or carry out administrative tasks in the camp. Most *kapos* behaved with extreme brutality toward other prisoners. In the Argentine concentration camps, the "adapted" could be asked to torture their companions or to work at detecting and identifying new victims to be brought in for interrogation.[17]

But, as Pilar Calveiro, Carlos Flaskamp, the Association of Ex-Disappeared Detainees, and dozens of other witnesses point out, such cases accounted for only a minority of those who underwent destruction. "Adaptation" was encouraged both inside and outside the concentration camps even though it did not often go as far as direct collaboration or the transformation of the victims into perpetrators. Its purpose was perhaps simpler: the erasing of the rebelliousness or solidarity among the survivors of the camps and—more fundamentally—in society at large.

The Limits of "Adaptation": The Adapted, the Dissemblers, and the "Living Dead"

Imitating the perpetrators' gestures, behaviors, topics of conversation, and value systems was a prerequisite for survival in a concentration camp. Inmates needed to avoid drawing attention, and—even more importantly—they needed to cultivate "adiaphorization," or moral indifference to everything they saw. They became indifferent not only to what happened to themselves, but also to their peers, many of whom were no longer there the next day because they had been killed, "deported," or "transferred," while the rest continued to be subjected to torture, abuse, degradation, and humiliation. And each day, new detainees arrived to undergo the terrible period of "initiation": torture, interrogation, degradation, and humiliation.

Survivors of the Nazi and Argentine camps describe three basic types of adapting:

1. *Total adaptation,* that is to say, acceptance of the perpetrators' values. Argentine survivors describe these people as "going over to the enemy camp." In the Nazi concentration camps, they became kapos, collaborators, and informants. In Argentina, they were especially good at torturing and interrogating former colleagues or at carrying out street sweeps for urban militants.[18] Often, this "adaptation" resulted from an inability to endure torture; but sometimes it was simply a product of the concentration camp situation. Terror was enough to gain acquiescence without the need for physical pain.
2. *Dissembling.* Because the main purpose of concentration camps was to destroy the inmates' personality, it was impossible to survive without accepting to some extent the values the perpetrators sought to instill. A significant difference in the Argentine case was the use of internment to extract information, but this rarely lasted beyond the first ten days. Therefore, the only way to resist and to survive was to adapt outwardly to these values, while resisting them internally. This behavior implied a huge psychological cost, because it required a high degree of schizophrenia to convince the perpetrators of a transformation that really did not exist, or at least did not exist to the extent the perpetrators expected or assumed.

It also required a very careful assessment of the *limits of collaboration*, to distinguish at what point adaptation was real and not merely a pretense.

A prototypical case of such behavior was shown by the "staff" of the ESMA Navy Mechanics School. As part of the navy's recovery scheme for detainees, Admiral Emilio Eduardo Massera, a leading participant in the 1976 coup, formed two work teams: one was to develop intelligence leading to new abductions and to guarantee the political continuity of the genocide; the other was to analyze and evaluate national and international policy information, with the aim of creating a political force capable of guaranteeing the continuity of the dictatorship in an eventual transition to democracy. Both groups—the "mini-staff" for intelligence work and the "staff" for political tasks—were made up of supposedly rehabilitated prisoners—in other words, "adapted" prisoners who had accepted the values of their victimizers.

For the mini-staff, dissembling was impossible, because prisoners were required to destroy the very people with whom they had been militants. But the job of the "staff" was to read press cuttings, write political reports, and photocopy and adulterate public or private documents, depending on their technical or professional competence. This allowed for an interplay between verifiable "rehabilitation" and prisoners' actions to the point where some victims effectively changed sides psychologically as well.

Dissembling placed prisoners in a permanent state of tension. They could pay with their lives for the slightest sign that betrayed their schizophrenia. Or they could be degraded to the lower echelons of camp life, which would mean renewed visits to the torture chamber, humiliation, and loss of privileges, such as slightly better food or a visit to the family. Moreover, the prisoners felt compelled to analyze each act of "collaboration" in minute detail in order to determine how useful it would be to the perpetrators and to what extent it made the prisoner the perpetrators' accomplice.

Mario Villani, who was interned in various concentration camps in Argentina, suffered one of many dilemmas when he was ordered to repair one of the instruments with which the perpetrators tortured their victims—the *picana* or cattle prod used to give electric shocks, a torture which Villani himself had suffered repeatedly. At first, Villani refused to carry out this task. However, instead of punishing him for his disobedience, the perpetrators simply turned to using more primitive instruments—such as metal objects plugged directly into the power supply—which inflicted much greater pain and physical harm. This persuaded Villani to repair the instrument of torture.[19]

Villani's dilemma illustrates indeed a permanent tension suffered by "dissemblers": the extent to which adaptation can be resisted by the dissembler's deeper psychic structure.

3. *"Living dead."* As mentioned earlier, total adaptation would mean surrendering all remaining autonomy, making it impossible for the victims to stay alive on their own. And indeed, unable to accept their captors' values or to endure the tension of dissembling, the living dead let themselves die. Their will to live was paralyzed by the camp situation. In this state, malnutrition, overcrowding, disease, and degradation undermined the victim's power of resistance and, although their bodies held out for a while, led to absolute subjective extinction.

Inside and Outside the Camps

As I have already argued, the real purpose of the concentration camps in Nazi Germany (and later in Nazi-occupied Europe) as well as in Argentina was to reshape society. Even if most people never set foot in one, the camps sent a message of terror to those tempted to think for themselves.

The prototype of the Nazi concentration camp was Dachau. Located on the site of an abandoned munitions factory about ten miles northwest of Munich, it was opened in March 1933, barely a month after the Nazis took office. Heinrich Himmler, then the police chief of Munich, described it as "the first concentration camp for political prisoners."[20] At first, it mainly housed political prisoners—communists, social democrats, trade unionists, and other political opponents of the Nazi regime. Over time, other groups were also interned at Dachau, such as Jews, Jehovah's Witnesses, Roma (Gypsies), and homosexuals, as well as so-called asocials and repeat criminal offenders. The camp's message, however, was addressed to the entire German population as a disciplinary warning about the consequences of defying authority or displaying the slightest sign of political, social, or cultural autonomy.

The Nazis covered Germany with these camps and, when war broke out in 1939, hundreds more were set up in the occupied territories, with many smaller subcamps attached to them.[21] It is calculated that approximately 15,000 labor, death, and concentration camps were built, although the exact figure remains uncertain.[22] The six extermination camps tend to overshadow the key role played by thousands of concentration camps scattered throughout Europe as a strategy of social discipline

In Argentina, more than 500 concentration camps and detention centers were distributed up and down the country. As in Nazi Germany, there was at least one camp within fifty miles of every major city so that the whole of society was trapped in a giant web of horror. As in Nazi Germany, it is not yet clear how many people were interned in these camps and centers. I do not mean those who died in them—most of these victims have now been identified—but we still do not know how many people were held for a day or two, maybe a week, and then returned to social life.[23] Nearly every day, a new survivor appears.

Poorer Argentines did not even realize they had been inside a concentration camp, so accustomed were they to being mistreated during police raids and interrogations.[24]

To sum up, the camps performed a number of simultaneous functions: they eliminated social and political resistance; they dehumanized inmates as a way of justifying and legitimizing genocide; they disciplined and regulated society through terror—a terror of the unknown as well as the known, based on rumors that awakened fantasies and tapped into people's innermost fears; a terror that bred suspicion toward those victims who "reappeared"—cutting them off from the social whole and spreading distrust among the population. This defensive attitude trapped the individual within the worldview of individualism, closing off the possibility of political action, solidarity, or cooperation.

At the same time, creating feelings of helplessness through terror was an essential strategy for silencing protest in Argentine society. The disparity between the two sides in terms of strength if not numbers—and, more significantly, the discourses built around the overwhelming nature of this "disparity"—brought political actions in Argentina to a halt. Why argue, why fight, why confront an opponent if every battle, every confrontation, is hopeless?[25] Feelings of indignation at injustice were expressed at a theoretical level, without any sort of practical application. Condemnation of injustice was at the level of abstract principle, rather than through attempts to change or transform reality—attempts that were considered doomed to failure.

This logic of helplessness functioned—and still functions—as an underground discourse in a society that had undergone the horror of genocide. As mentioned before, Elsa Drucaroff has explored the possible meanings of the words "Never Again." One of the implicit questions she addresses is: "What never again?" The phrase does not include a response but one of its underground, hidden meanings, never made explicit, is powerlessness: "We will never again be able to challenge the social order."

Defeat and Confusion: The Logic of Psychological Destruction

The perpetrators sought to produce "adaptive" behavior both inside and outside the camps, although the procedure was different in each case. One of the fundamental reasons why people tried to "adapt" *outside* the camps was because defeat came to be redefined in terms of failure, so future struggle seemed pointless. This subjective feeling of devastation destroyed the personality, transforming political or politico-military defeat into compliance and creating a state of mental "confusion."[26]

The "symbolic enactments" of genocide are the ways in which this confusion is expressed. Defeat is resignified as the logical and inevitable end to any confrontation with the hegemonic order. The struggle is then understood as a mistake. "It was all a mistake, a silly, crazy provocation." Hence the distinctive tone of many works written during the 1980s and 1990s. As mentioned in chapter 7, these works bristle with harsh epithets—messianic, delusional, irrational, deluded, scatological, sinister, proud, and dozens more synonyms—which are used to describe the radicalized militants of the pregenocide and genocide periods. Most of these authors had little personal involvement in the story they are trying to tell, and some show considerable "confusion" about their own identity. They do not feel part of a defeated generation but of a generation that went "wrong," and this denial prevents them from understanding history, in general, and their own personal experiences of the past, in particular.

The difference between defeat and denial is an important one. The defeated do not necessarily deny their past: they can analyze it in an attempt to understand their own limitations and circumstances and to learn from their mistakes. In this sense, defeat is a great teacher. Basically, when a defeat is understood as such, it encourages us to analyze our battle situations and causes of defeat, to improve or transform our tools and methods, and keep on fighting. Defeat is often the mother of victory, and no social reorganization is final, not even one founded on genocide.

By contrast, "confusion" paralyzes us in a similar or complementary way to terror. Individuals who are confused do not know what to do in life. They deny the meaning of their actions and the principles upon which these are based. They understand their struggle as futile and their defeat as unnecessary. Naively, they would like to turn back the clock in an attempt to recover the dead, the annihilated. They accept the genocidal guilt, a guilt that does not belong to them. The logic of this discourse is that if there had been no struggle, there would have been no deaths.

There is no way of proving this counterfactual argument. On the contrary, Argentina's so-called National Reorganization Process not only sought but *needed* to destroy preexisting social ties in order to impose a new economic and social order. Moreover, it is next to impossible to find any historical indicators that would show that *less* political conflict, *less* radical social struggles, or even *less* willingness to resort to political violence would have prevented the killing or at least modified the objectives of Argentina's genocidal perpetrators.

The fact is that terror and death played a central role in the National Reorganization Process. The idea that the decision to commit genocide was implemented only after Argentina's armed left began military actions—actions which, in any case, were not large enough to seriously challenge the power of the state or its monopoly of the use of force—ignores the genocidal consensus that had emerged after the bombing of Plaza de Mayo in June 1955. Argentina's more conservative sectors were prepared to stop at nothing in order to dissolve the social bonds created—or at least consolidated—by the emergence of Peronism as a social phenomenon. To argue that the policy of annihilation is rooted in the actions of Argentina's armed left is not only naive but, more seriously, it legitimizes genocide. Neither the operational capability of these forces nor the nature of the victims of genocide allows for such an interpretation.

But transforming "defeat" into a "mistake," denying the rebellious and critical spirit of those years, assuming that all political struggle is useless because it may end in genocide, and secretly accepting the brave "reorganized" new world as the only one possible—something which, for better or worse, must be accepted and digested—is simply to enact the multiple meanings of the phrase "never again." For "never again horror and death" also means "never fight again; never criticize or rebel again; never show solidarity again or feel moral responsibility for those who suffer." The genocidal power remains intact, so the only way to ensure "never again horror and death" is by guaranteeing we will "never again" make the mistake of believing we can challenge the status quo, of imagining that other social relations are possible, and of falling into the "naivety," "hallucinations," and "messianic delusions" of radical militancy.

With their utopias dead but not buried—their ideals tortured and destroyed in the camps and then "disappeared"—many members of the defeated generation, confused by terror and genocide, were all ready to cling to any wreckage they could find after the maelstrom had subsided. Thus they became an easy prey to individualism, selfish "careerism," and other postmodern religions.

And now I would like to point out once again that we cannot hope to understand the social divisions and the corruption that pervaded Argentine society during the neoliberal Menem era of the 1990s except within a context of attempting to explain a defeat that is not understood as such. Such attempts are usually futile, incomplete, and fail to replace the sense of activist experience. They leave a bitter taste in the mouth, forcing former militants to ask themselves day after day where the limits of "adaptation" lie. Should we accept only the futility of political struggle, or must we also welcome the new neoliberal order? Will it be accepted as part of our new "tolerant" and "open" identity if we share a round-table discussion with an unpunished genocidaire, or should we only talk to his accomplices? And how should we react to an invitation to reconciliation? With whom can we be "reconciled" in such circumstances?

In his book on mental hospitals, Erving Goffman distinguished four coping strategies used by inmates to adapt to the institutional situation. These strategies, he claimed, applied equally to other total institutions like prisons. These are (1) *withdrawal*, also known in psychiatric institutions as "regression"; (2) *intransigence*, whereby inmates confront hospital or prison staff or refuse to cooperate; (3) *colonization*, whereby inmates settle into a routine and make the best of the privileges available; and (4) *conversion*, whereby inmates come to see themselves through the eyes of the institution and take on the role of the perfect inmate.[27] Conversion was also studied by Bettelheim, who was particularly interested in the ways the inmates of concentration camps come to adopt the values of their victimizers.

But attempts at "conversion," either in society in general or within a concentration camp, are always problematic. Converts, whether religious, political, or ideological, are generally not accepted by anyone. The constant pressure to prove that their newfound faith is more profound and more radical than the next person's only increases their *state of confusion*. In addition, their old ideas cling to them like a second nature they cannot get rid of. The idea of starting a process of dialogue with their former enemies is too loathsome for words—not even if the perpetrators went down on their hands and knees.

Many would-be converts are unable to make the moral leap and remain mired in confusion. Midway in their conversion, they cannot come to terms with their own history. They cannot establish a pleasurable relationship with the past, which they now deny, but they are not accepted by their former enemies, either.

Understanding this process is essential if we are to challenge the logic of genocidal and postgenocidal social reorganization. Converts, in spite of everything, are not perpetrators. They are victims, even though it is difficult to see them as such, particularly in moral terms. Converts, however, are confused victims who cannot accept themselves as such, or who can only see themselves as victims in the past or in abstract terms. They blame their own rebellious spirit (mistakenly or futilely rebellious, from their point of view). Those victims who are occasionally able to recognize that they are *still* victims can only do so in the abstract. They continue to experience a deep need to deny their previous identity—an identity once expressed through a characteristic synthesis of being and doing. Just as society feels caught between "two demons," these victims confuse their aggressors with their victimized peers, or blame an irrational violence that supposedly took hold of both sides in the political struggle.

It is not possible for a society to work through the trauma of genocide unless it sees genocide as a profound defeat—one it must question, examine, understand, and learn from. We must try to make peace with our dead, not as heroes or martyrs, saints or angels, and certainly not as "delusional youngsters" or "youths fascinated by violence," but as a generation that believed in a more just and egalitarian society. A generation that embodied a utopian way of life and made many mistakes, but also produced some achievements. A generation that was defeated, and whose survivors have much to ask themselves, but also much to teach and pass on to future generations. Nothing more and nothing less.

Simultaneously, those of us who belong to a later generation need to help these survivors overcome their confusion—for our sake as much as theirs. Together, we need to leave behind the concentration camp experience—the bouillon cube and soup—and understand (again) that Argentina's current social structure is not the only one possible and that not every struggle needs to end in genocide. We must remember that the whole purpose of annihilation was to prevent us from speaking out and conveying our experiences. Annihilation was intended to stop us thinking, discussing, or evaluating what has happened to us.

Mass murder itself does not, of itself, impose these symbolic enactments. The two processes are connected, but separable. Deaths are necessary but never sufficient for the closure of social relations. Without us, closure is not possible; in us, closure will always find a limit. Maybe the time has come for these "symbolic enactments" to cease.

Resistance and "Lines of Flight"

Reflecting on the systems of power and domination that control even our most private activities, Foucault noted that "where there is power, there is resistance, and yet, or rather, consequently, this resistance is never in a position of exteriority in relation to power."[28] This principle proved to be true in both Argentina's concentration camps and the country's "social soup." In both cases, small and—for the most part—scattered pockets of resistance and solidarity sprang up, with the possibility of becoming poles of counterhegemony capable of challenging the notion of genocidal reorganization as normal or legitimate.

Foucault notes that

> these points of resistance are present everywhere in the power network. Hence there is no single locus of great Refusal, no soul of revolt, or pure law of the revolutionary. . . . Instead there is a plurality of resistances, each of them a special case: resistances that are possible, necessary, improbable; others that are spontaneous, savage, solitary, concerted, rampant, or violent; still others that are quick to compromise, interested, or sacrificial; by definition, they can only exist in the strategic field of power relations. But this does not mean that they are only a reaction or rebound, forming with respect to the basic domination an underside that is in the end always passive, doomed to perpetual defeat.[29]

Numerous survivors' testimonies describe gestures of solidarity. Papiernik tells how prisoners in Auschwitz tried to save those sicker or more starved than themselves from the gas chambers by wearing their companions' numbers and running outdoors for them in the cold. They had to run the same distance twice even though they barely had the strength to do so once. Then there were those who shared or gave away their bread ration even though they themselves were little more than skin and bone, and those who spread rumors of impending liberation to bolster hope.[30]

Other testimonies mention countless acts of sabotage. Sobibor extermination camp was closed after a rebellion that ended in the escape and flight of around 300 of its 600 prisoners, about 50 of whom avoided recapture. Similarly, there were occasional escapes from the Argentine detention centers. But just as important for prisoners' morale were the many small gestures of recognition and support they managed to exchange with other prisoners—for example, a wink or a pat on the arm. These little signs restored prisoners' self-esteem and their sense of being a person. Organizing conversations or rhythmic percussive hand claps to shatter the silence and overcome loneliness were other small but glorious ways of ceasing to be "walled up."

Jorge Paladino, a survivor of one of the Argentine concentration camps, tells how, with his bunk mate, "before going to sleep each night we walked 20 to 30 blocks and bought an ice cream on the corner of Tellier and Rivadavia Street. We discussed politics and religion."[31] Other testimonies narrate imaginary movie screenings, narrated by an inmate, or clandestine history classes. These innumerable, sometimes almost indistinguishable, actions, which Goffman calls "secondary adjustments"—that is, small but unauthorized ways of sidestepping assumptions about what one should do and therefore what one should be—allowed prisoners to re-find their own identity and avoid depersonalization.

Pablo Pozzi and Ricardo Falcón have also pointed out the many labor disputes under the military dictatorship despite strikes being banned. IKA-Renault, General Motors, Mercedes Benz, and Chrysler in 1976 and state-owned companies and textile mills throughout the period were the scenes of numerous confrontations and several deaths but also of small successes that undermined the policies of the dictatorship. These disputed successes are either forgotten or denied in most accounts of the period.[32]

This is not to say that the dictatorship's methods of dissuasion were not brutally effective. It is simply to point out that even in the worst conditions, certain people managed, in one way or another, to preserve their self-esteem together with a sense of solidarity, concern, and responsibility for others. Some workers *were* able to resist even though persecution was especially intense in the factories. Now, thirty years after the end of the dictatorship, with a new generation of young people entering political life for the first time, surely we should be able to throw off the yoke of terror once and for all.

And the Walls Came Tumbling Down: The Need to Remove the Social Blindfolds

Death, by definition, is irreversible. As much as we wish otherwise, those who embodied a particular way of life will never reappear. In contrast, symbolic processes are dynamic and reversible. Despite leaving deep scars, they *can* be transformed. If we remember that concentration camps and genocide were devised as political instruments to transform the social whole, a concentration camp analogy can help us understand how these scars remain with us today. For genocide has not only succeeded in creating psychological "walls" between Argentineans; it has blindfolded and hoodwinked us into believing we have no power of self-determination, no ability to dream or to imagine rebellion or a rebellious attitude. Nevertheless, the marches, demonstrations, and public debates that began in 1996 with the twentieth anniversary of the military coup suggest that some members of society have slowly begun to peek out from beneath their blindfolds.

Symbolic walls are more difficult to build than physical partitions, and they are also more difficult to remove.[33] I have already argued that a dialogue is needed between the generation that lived through the genocide and those generations that came afterward. I will go further: only a collective elaboration of Argentina's past—one that accepts both the pain of loss and the need to analyze defeat—can remove our blindfolds and make the walls come tumbling down. At a political level, this will allow us to own our past, to know where we come from, and to dream and plan for a better future without a bandage over our eyes.

10

In Conclusion

The Uses of Memory

One of the main arguments running through this book has been that genocidal social practices are not simply an irrational descent into barbarism fueled by hatred and prejudice, nor are they exceptional phenomena. On the contrary, they are a specific technology of power for destroying and reorganizing social relations that has played a crucial and well-defined role at different moments in history.

The ancient world practiced "*pre-state* genocide" to annihilate enemy populations. The modern world created a new social order known as the nation-state through "*constituent* genocides" and then used "*colonial* genocides" to annex and plunder territories overseas. Later, struggles for national liberation gave rise to "*postcolonial* genocides." Finally, in the cases that I have analyzed in detail in this book—Germany from 1933 to 1945 and Argentina from 1974 to 1983—murder and terror were used to transform the social fabric of two well-established societies in what I have called "*reorganizing* genocides."

What makes reorganizing genocide different from others is that it goes beyond physical annihilation. It does not end with the death of the enemy but attempts to capitalize on death through mechanisms of "symbolic enactment." This does not mean that genocide has been the only way of transforming social relations within modern societies. In fact, all sorts of revolutions—socialist, reactionary, and corporative alike—have brought about various types of social reorganization. However, genocidal social practices were frequently used to reorganize societies in the twentieth century—especially in Latin America. Moreover, in the different societies in which genocide has occurred, collective memory has processed state terror in remarkably similar ways, all of them accompanied by a redistribution of wealth into the hands of elites.

Throughout this book I have tried to show that the systematic destruction of a part of Argentina's population can be classified as genocide, both from an eminently legal and from a historical-sociological point of view. In legal terms, the still common refusal to apply the term "genocide" to the annihilation of political groups has no sound legal basis. The exclusion of political groups from the 1948 Convention on the Prevention and Punishment of the Crime of Genocide was on purely pragmatic grounds: it was feared that many states might not sign this first UN human rights treaty if it laid them open to prosecution for political crimes. However, this is not sufficient reason to *defend* their exclusion *as a matter of legal doctrine*. On the contrary, it violates the basic principle of equality before the law. Moreover, as I have shown in chapter 1, most definitions of genocide used by historians and sociologists since 1980s contemplate the annihilation of political groups as a form of genocide.

I have examined some philosophical questions about the alleged distinction between "voluntary" and "involuntary" victims, and I have pointed out the legal and epistemological inconsistencies inherent in such a distinction—a distinction that attempts to deny the genocidal nature of the policies implemented in Argentina simply because the victims were chosen for eminently political reasons. As noted by Robert Cribb, advances in sociology, anthropology, and history have shown that what, fifty years ago, were believed to be fixed ethnic or racial identities are in fact dynamic and flexible, and so are impossible, in practice, to distinguish from "political" identities (especially if such definitions have legal implications).[1]

Now, some would argue that applying the term "genocide" to state terror in Argentina "depoliticizes" our understanding of these events. This is because they fail to grasp the profoundly political nature of all genocides—even those that seem driven by irrational hatred and paranoia. And it is precisely the alienation produced by "depoliticizing" the Nazi genocide and treating it as a sort of collective madness that I am at pains to point out in this book, especially in chapter 4. Moreover, I have argued that describing state terror in Argentina as genocide not only facilitates the prosecution and punishment of the perpetrators (for example, by reducing the need for repeated questioning of victims and witnesses); it also allows for a more accurate and profound analysis of the impact on the rest of society of the systematic annihilation carried out by the military government. Specifically, annihilation targeted certain social relations, creating terror, distrust of others, and competition rather than cooperation among members of society, as well as skepticism about the possibility of critical or oppositional consciousness. All these practices became hegemonic during the 1980s and 1990s.

Throughout this book I have followed a comparative approach, taking the Nazi genocide as a sort of prototype in order to clarify certain key issues. These include the "reorganizing" nature of the social practices involved; the types of behaviors that tend to become accepted as "normal"; and the types of discourse through which the experience of genocide is understood. Because these effects of genocide were *intended*—at least by some of the perpetrators—I have called them forms of "symbolic enactment" and I have included them as a stage *within* the genocidal practice itself.

In chapters 4 and 5 I reviewed attempts by historians and sociologists to explain the causes of the Nazi genocide. In these chapters I critically evaluated the "symbolic enactment" of the Nazi genocide found in various types of narrative: the idea that Nazi genocide—or more exactly, its reduction to the Shoah—were a "unique" event and therefore not comparable with other atrocities; the idea that the Nazis were irrational demons–thus making the Shoah incomprehensible; the idea that such horror is untellable—thus silencing any attempt to understand its consequences; the idea of a specifically German genocide (*Sonderweg* theories), outside mainstream European history and inspired by age-old anti-Semitism; the "intentionalist" theory that the Nazi genocide followed a plan that was already in place when Hitler came to power in 1933. I also examined theories about Hitler's proposed racial restructuring of Europe; theories about the extermination of the Jews as part of a European civil war or counter-revolutionary process; theories that explain Nazism as part of "normalization" processes in modern societies; and theories that understand genocide as a "social relationship" peculiar to capitalism, among others.

After this critical review of causal theories of genocide, my attempt to understand genocide as a specific way of "reorganizing" social relations led me, in chapters 6 and 8, to examine the typical path followed by these grisly processes of social reengineering. I proposed a model consisting of six stages: stigmatization (the construction of "negative otherness"), harassment, isolation, systematic weakening, physical extermination, and symbolic enactment. I also outlined the defining features of each of these stages in the two historical cases in question—Germany between 1933 and 1945 and Argentina between 1974 and 1983—as well as the chief similarities and differences between them.

Chapter 7 also examined alternative ways of defining the Argentine "Reorganization Process"—whether as civil war, counterinsurgency war, terrorism, or state terrorism—together with concepts such as the bureaucratic-authoritarian state, military dictatorship, micro-despotisms, and the binary "friend or foe" logic of power, among others. On the basis of these ideas, I suggested that the ability to understand state terror in Argentina as a genocidal social practice whose basic aim is to "reorganize" society—whether or not it exhibited features of other processes such as war—is essential for understanding the material and symbolic processes that occurred after the physical annihilation of the direct victims. The indirect victims, it will be remembered, were the rest of society. Symbolic processes appear in full force in narratives commemorating genocide.

Finally, chapter 9 explored the purpose and functioning of concentration camps, and the ways their tentacles operated not only on the direct victims—those interned in the camps—but also on the social whole, by encouraging denouncement and betrayal, distrust toward others, and other ways of destroying or impeding reciprocal relationships between peers. I argued that the fear of torture goes deeper in its effects than torture itself. At the same time, I emphasized what I call the *state of confusion* to which a generation of survivors succumbed—survivors who never even set foot in the concentration camp circuit directly. This *state of confusion*, found in many works of the period, comes from identifying defeat with ideological error. Those who are confused regard critical or oppositional consciousness as a mistake and attempt to *convert*, or at least *adapt*, to the hegemonic values of order and peace—the peace of the graveyard—and come to terms with the disappearance of solidarity, reciprocity, and responsibility for the poor and dispossessed.

The processes that make genocide possible at all have a long history. In fact, they constitute some of the most ingrained attitudes and behaviors in modern societies. In chapters 6 and 8 these processes were categorized under the headings of stigmatization, harassment, and isolation, and I argued that their victims tend to be population groups that are growing and/or changing. In fact, racism and genocidal social practices have functioned as ways of resolving the contradictions of modernity surrounding the issues of equality, sovereignty, and autonomy. As we saw in chapter 3, there have been glaring discrepancies between these principles on paper and their effect in practice in modern societies.

Of course, a book of this length cannot answer all the questions that would result from a serious attempt to confront both the causes and the consequences of genocidal social practices. It has not even tried to develop what many contemporary scholars and even some United Nations documents define as a system of "early warning" or "prevention" of genocide. Nevertheless, it is much more than a chronicle of annihilation and atrocities. It has not only attempted to problematize banal or simplistic approaches to genocide; it has also explored what happens *before* and *after* genocide. One of its central themes is the social practices that pave the way to genocide; another is how certain types of memory and certain narratives not only tend to become hegemonic in postgenocide societies, but also serve to transmit terror to new generations. In considering genocide as a process and a technology of power, I hope to have cleared the ground for new questions, surely more complex and more useful for confronting resurgences of this particular form of social engineering.

So, having reached this point, I would like to make a few suggestions for further research. One important area for investigation is the ways in which identity and Otherness are constructed—since these constructions lie at the heart of all genocidal social practices—and the role of segregation and exclusion in genocidal processes. Another important area is the question of guilt—how to assign responsibility to the different actors. This is important not only for bringing the perpetrators to justice but also for clarifying the symbolic struggles underlying judicial processes and for constructing a new ethics, a political tool against the dehumanization and adiaphorization underpinning genocide.

The Processes of Constructing Identity and Otherness

We need to remember that genocide, like other social practices, is a process that unfolds over time. It is impossible to commit genocide without first building models of identity and Otherness, symbolic representations that suggest ways of perceiving ourselves and those whom we cast in the role of Other. Moreover, although the two develop more or less simultaneously, the Other may not be demonized until much later in the process.

The formulation of separate ethnic and national identities is a distinguishing feature of modernity even if some of its features predate the modern era. Negative typecasting has taken various forms from a simple dichotomy between civilization and barbarism to sophisticated racial theories or the racialization of class relations.[2] Whatever the case, stereotyping is a necessary step on the path toward genocide, and detecting and deconstructing negative labels while they are still being formed may help prevent genocide, or at least prevent it being repeated.

Although identity is dynamic and multiple, the construction of a negative Other forces us to limit our own identity to a narrow set of criteria. In the modern period, these criteria have mostly been nationalistic, sometimes tinged with religion (as in the case of "Western Christian" values), secularism (as in the case of French citizenship), or even agnosticism and racism (as in the case of the "new man" of the Third Reich).[3] Without this way of getting rid of the Otherness within ourselves—an Otherness that is part of both personal identity and the identity of every modern nation-state—the dehumanization of other human beings required to commit genocide would simply not be possible. It is not at all easy to kill people we think of as belonging to our own community. It is much easier to kill or help to kill those we look on as strangers or aliens. Zygmunt Bauman has coined the term "adiaphorization" to describe insensitivity and moral indifference to the suffering of strangers—an attitude that tends to merge with negative stereotyping among the direct perpetrators.[4]

As I have pointed out elsewhere, this way of constructing identity involves several interlocking processes:

- Reduction of the multiple dimensions of identity to just one (national, religious, ethnic, or another)
- Creation of a "normal" identity, including acceptable and unacceptable forms of deviance for different categories of social actors
- Alienation and dehumanization of collective identities that fall outside the accepted limits of deviance and indifference toward the possible fate of deviants

Therefore, any attempt to tackle or prevent genocidal social practices must begin with this construction of identity and Otherness. Indeed, it is precisely these constructions that the perpetrators set out to impose, not only through terror but later through the memory of genocide in postgenocide societies. Thus, genocidal social practices will be difficult to prevent unless we question the paradigm of identity by exclusion, with its accompanying processes of normalization, alienation, dehumanization, and adiaphorization.

Similarly, perpetuating binary visions of "us" and "them" after genocide has occurred simply serves to legitimize future acts of countergenocide by the "victimized group." Israel's violations of human rights in the occupied Palestinian Territory (supposedly legitimized by the suffering of European Jews under Nazism), the terrorist attacks of Palestinians living under Israeli occupation, the killings of Hutus in the Democratic Republic of Congo in revenge for the genocide against the Tutsis in Rwanda, the killings of Serbs in Kosovo in revenge for the murder of Kosovo Albanians, and the killing and expulsion of the German population by the Soviet Union from those areas of Eastern Europe in which the Nazis had committed atrocities are just a few examples where debates rage about who is "good" and who is "bad." Part of this binary way of thinking is that each group must be, intrinsically, either perpetrators or victims.

Types of Guilt: A Reflection on Karl Jaspers

In 1945 and 1946, during the immediate postwar period, the German philosopher Karl Jaspers gave a series of seminars that were published in 1946 under the title *Die Schuldfrage*. The first English translation was published the following year as *The Question of German Guilt*. In this work, Jaspers tried to accept and, at the same time, distinguish the different sorts of German guilt under the Nazis. He was thus confronting both the "demonization" of Germans as a whole and collective guilt, on the one hand, and German self-justification or genocide denial, on the other.

Jaspers distinguished four types of guilt: criminal, political, moral, and metaphysical. This distinction serves to highlight that responsibilities are diverse and not all actions can be judged in the same way. In Jaspers's view, criminal guilt referred to acts that violate the law (genocide, murder, torture, unlawful arrest, etc.), while political guilt referred to the degree of responsibility each citizen bore for the Nazis' rise to power and subsequent criminal actions. Political guilt depended both on the extent to which individuals agreed with Nazi policies and how effectively (or ineffectively) they had resisted them. Moral guilt referred to acts of commission or omission that facilitated or supported criminal actions. Finally, metaphysical guilt presupposed the existence of solidarity among human beings that made each individual co-responsible for all the rest. The mere fact that some had survived while others had perished implied that one could always have done more to prevent those deaths, even giving one's own life in exchange for the lives of others.

Jaspers's four types of guilt are particularly suggestive in that each category implies a specific response. In Jaspers's view, criminal guilt can only be met with punishment; political guilt, with defeat; and moral guilt, with repentance. However, for metaphysical guilt there is no answer: we are stuck with it for the rest of our lives even when we attempt to change the workings of society in order to prevent another similar event from shocking our own spirit and the conscience of humanity. In Jaspers's view, metaphysical guilt can be removed only by God.

It is true that Jaspers's reflections of German guilt were largely ignored in postwar Germany.[5] Nevertheless, it is remarkable that no reflections of this kind have emerged in relation to genocide in Argentina. On the contrary, Decrees 157 and 158 issued by Raúl Alfonsín's government in Argentina in 1983 had the effect of confusing criminal and political guilt, by simultaneously judging those who committed political mistakes—the left-wing politico-military organizations—together with those who had used state power to commit serious human rights violations within a framework of genocide, and who were therefore criminally guilty.[6] In the 1990s, this confusion was carried to the extreme of trying to seat the criminally and morally guilty at the same table and asking them both to repent, while taking for granted that the perpetrators of criminal acts should be granted impunity. The repentance of vast sectors of the population for complicity or connivance in genocide or for ill-conceived attempts at resistance was placed at the same level as the supposed "repentance" of those who had raped, tortured, and murdered hundreds of citizens in cold blood. Thus, against all logic and decency, the perpetrators were given an equal right to speak, and even to be elected to public office.[7]

The preciseness of Jaspers's categories may help to address these problems differently. For one thing, it is very difficult for society to construct a new version of events until the question of criminal responsibility has been at least partially resolved. The repeal and annulment of the impunity laws was and still is a major step toward establishing the relative responsibilities of militants or ordinary citizens. Criminal guilt is not canceled by repentance—only by punishment. No repentance can be genuine if it represents or offers a way to escape punishment. The reopening of the cases against Héctor Julio Simón and Miguel Osvaldo Etchecolatz, for example, showed that, far from being "reconciled," society had been waiting patiently for impunity to end. It also showed that there is no other way to resolve conflicts and arguments or lay history to rest—individually and collectively—except by starting the long journey through the criminal justice system. This is the only way to apportion blame equitably for past wrongs.

True repentance comes only after justice has been done, not as a way to avoid punishment. By contrast, the "repentant" Argentine genocidaires made their remorse known to society only as long as they were safe from punishment. As soon as they were threatened with justice, they tried to defend their crimes again, even declaring themselves willing and ready to repeat the same crimes if society insisted on bringing them to trial. On the other hand, a widespread inability to distinguish different levels of guilt and responsibility has plunged Argentine society into a "confusion" that affects our very sense of identity, both individual and collective.

Continuing with Jaspers's four categories, no one to date has admitted any *political* responsibility for genocide. On the contrary, the same members of Argentina's political parties who, at best, failed to halt the genocide—and, in many cases, were intellectual or passive accomplices thereof—have presented themselves since 1983 as the guarantors of the new "democracy." Instead of recognizing their own inadequacies, silences, or complicities—flaws which in Jaspers's view, at the very least, would disqualify them from holding political office again—these willing or unwilling collaborators in genocide entrenched themselves in the political system and, to a certain extent, in academic and intellectual circles. It has long been time for them to make way for new generations or for those who had been hounded from politics by the dictatorship,

Jaspers emphasizes primarily the moral responsibility of individual persons. Nevertheless, one cannot help noticing that most Argentineans are remarkably complacent about their own behavior during the genocide. This is true even among intellectuals and artists who are normally more self-critical.[8] Instead of exploring the question of moral responsibility, this generation regarded itself as a victim—but in an abstract sense. The victim card is the easiest one to play in a postgenocidal context because it blocks uncomfortable questions about one's own possible material and/or moral contributions to mass murder. Moreover, abstract self-victimization precludes any examination of the impact of horror on one's own perceptions of reality and ways of relating to others.

If what I have just said sounds demanding or accusatory, that is not my intention. Most Argentineans could not have done much more than they actually did. It is not part of my task to point the finger of blame or grant my own generation the right to judge the moral behavior of its predecessors. My purpose is simply to propose a new reflection about the effects of abstract and collective self-victimization on social relations. Most concentration camp survivors, however, are burdened with the guilt of having survived, and this is a guilt society reserves *for them alone.* Those who were closest to the horror—in the next bunk or in the same torture chamber—are reproached for not trading places with the victims. This reproach, however, is not made against the rest of society. Concentration camp survivors tend to be excluded from social life because "they must have done something to still be alive." But this accusation is not directed against their contemporaries who kept their heads down to escape detention.

I repeat that with this analysis of moral responsibility I do not propose to judge a generation of survivors—much less those who survived the concentration camps. But the question, as Jaspers pointed out, may allow each of us to judge him- or herself and accept the consequences of moral guilt. During the Nazi era, collaboration was often active and took the form of denouncing one's neighbors; under the dictatorship in Argentina, collaboration was more passive, with some moments of popular support for the regime during the World Cup in 1978; during the military's government's campaign "Argentinians are human and right" in 1979 (in answer to accusations of human-rights violations); during the visit of the Inter-American Commission of Human Rights (IACHR), also in 1979; or during the Malvinas/Falklands War in 1982, a war that had massive popular support.

In short, my aim here has been to expose the process whereby Argentine society freed itself of moral guilt by blaming those who had suffered most and by placing itself beyond good and evil as the abstract victim of two terrifying demons. I am convinced that unless we can raise these questions and—beyond asking who supported or helped the regime—accept moral responsibility for what we could have done and did not do, there will be no collective working through of the Argentine genocide. Only by facing these issues fairly and squarely can we lay to rest the horror that—whether we like it or not—changed the way members of a whole generation related to one another.

Politics and Ethics: Some Suggestions by Emmanuel Levinas

If reversing the consequences of a "reorganizing genocide" is a decidedly political act, so too is confronting the conditions that make genocide possible in the first place. It is also an ethical issue, for we are responsible for how we conceptualize our own identity and the identities of others, as well as for any limits we put on this responsibility. In this sense, the Jewish philosopher Emmanuel Levinas has suggested a way of looking at this ethical dimension that is eminently political.[9]

Levinas understands Otherness as a fundamental fact of human life. But unlike more philosophical interpretations of Otherness or politically correct discourses about "respect" and "tolerance" for others, Levinas is not interested in just *any* Other, and certainly not in abstractions. On the contrary, Levinas sees the Other as the foundation of ethical life. The Other is the face of the widow, the orphan, the beggar, and the stranger—figures that come straight from the Bible. Levinas repeats these figures each time he refers to Otherness. They do not speak to us simply from the fact of their existence, but from their pain, their dispossession, their need, and a responsibility that makes us—the holders of wealth, power, knowledge, health, happiness, or whatever—guilty of the Other's suffering.

Levinas poses an asymmetrical and nonallergic relationship with Otherness. This is not just any Otherness but a "deprived" Otherness in which our responsibility for others is not balanced on their part by any responsibility toward us. There is no moral quid pro quo, and we expect nothing in return for what we do. Unlike the contractual model of ethics, which in the final analysis is based on the market metaphor, Levinasian responsibility is not guided by any expectation about the Other's past or future actions. Responsibility for others derives entirely from their dispossession or need.

This radical ethical-philosophical view of the dispossessed Other as one whose life and well-being demand our *total responsibility*, a duty of service, provides a starting point—although others are possible—for designing a policy to confront the genocidal potential that resides in every modern human being, while offering a profound way of reshaping our understanding of moral responsibility and, therefore, our own identity.

In any situation where another human being is disparaged, harassed, reviled, isolated, stigmatized, kidnapped, tortured, or killed, we have absolute and total responsibility in moral terms for that person's fate. Responsibility is shared by everybody: family members, friends, and acquaintances, but also by the witnesses of the kidnappings, the victims' neighbors, and the torturers' acquaintances. Genocidal social practices cannot develop if we move toward a moral reformulation of this type, and the concept of genocide as the partial destruction of our own national group is a crucial step in that direction. Genocides need the *active consensus* of the population through shared prejudices, or at least a *passive consensus* in the form of a numbing of moral values and indifference toward the fate of persecuted minorities (what Bauman calls adiaphorization). Rethinking our moral approach in a Levinasian sense in order to save others could jeopardize our welfare (perhaps "comfort" would be a better word) and even put our own lives at risk. However, it is one of the most promising ethical and moral strategies for challenging the growing hegemony of genocidal practices as ways of reorganizing social relations across national groups by means of terror.

Without a major transformation of our processes of identity construction, without a restatement of the limits of our responsibility for others, and without understanding that each of us is an inseparable part of any social practice prevailing in our society, and therefore morally responsible for its effects, we have no chance of banishing genocide as a tool of social engineering. This new approach is both ethical and political, and its success or failure will determine the type of society in which we and our children will live.

NOTES

The following acronyms are used in the notes:

CEAL	Centro Editor de América Latina
CELS	Centro de Estudios Legales y Sociales
EDUNTREF	Editorial de la Universidad Nacional de Tres de Febrero
EUDEBA	Editorial de la Universidad de Buenos Aires
FCE	Fondo de Cultura Económica
FLACSO	Facultad Latinoamericana de Ciencias Sociales
ICC	International Criminal Court
ICTR	International Criminal Tribunal for Rwanda
PI.CA.SO.	Programa de Investigaciones sobre Cambio Social
UNSC	United Nations Security Council

INTRODUCTION

1. In fact, Raphael Lemkin had been working on the subject for nearly two decades. Lemkin was horrified by the Armenian genocide and later by genocidal social practices of the Nazis. However, he first coined the term "genocide" in his classic work *Axis Rule in Occupied Europe* (Washington, DC: Carnegie Endowment for International Peace, 1944).
2. Genocide has been a crime under international law since the UN General Assembly adopted the Convention on the Prevention and Punishment of the Crime of Genocide (CPPCG) in December 1948. In fact, drafting of the Convention began in 1946 and lasted for over two years. There were many disagreements, including whether political groups should be protected. Finally, political groups were excluded in order to ensure ratification by as many states as possible. Since the CPPCG came into effect in January 1951, it has been ratified by most countries in the world. The issues surrounding the exclusion of political groups from the Convention are of fundamental importance and will be discussed in detail in chapter 1 of this work.
3. It should be noted that little was written about Nazism until the 1960s and 1970s. Since the early 1980s, the number and range of studies have increased almost exponentially. Until the 1960s, however, very few people considered the Nazi genocide as a key development in contemporary European history or a fundamental problem for philosophy and the social sciences.
4. See, in particular, Hayden White, *Metahistory: The Historical Imagination in Nineteenth-Century Europe* (Baltimore: Johns Hopkins University Press, 1973).

5. See Vahakn N. Dadrian, "The Common Features of the Armenian and Jewish Cases of Genocide: A Comparative Victimological Approach," in *Victimology: A New Focus: Violence and Its Victims*, ed. Israel Drabkin and Emilio Viano (Lexington, MA: Lexington Books, 1974; Vahakn N. Dadrian, "The Comparative Aspects of the Armenian and Jewish Cases of Genocide: A Sociohistorical Perspective," in *Is the Holocaust Unique?* 3rd ed., ed. Alan S. Rosenbaum (Boulder, CO: Westview Press, 2009), 139–174; and Vahakn N. Dadrian, "The Historical and Legal Interconnections between the Armenian Genocide and the Jewish Holocaust: From Impunity to Retributive Justice," *Yale Journal of International Law* 23, no. 2 (1998): 504–559. For an account of the Rwandan genocide, see Vahakn N. Dadrian, "Patterns of Twentieth-Century Genocides: The Armenian, Jewish, and Rwandan Cases," *Journal of Genocide Research* 6, no. 4 (2004): 487–522.
6. This point was made by the International Criminal Tribunal that tried the crimes in Rwanda and has been conceded by Dadrian himself. It has also been well received by Eric Markusen and Alison Des Forges, among others.
7. For Kiernan's most complete work on Cambodia, see Ben Kiernan, *The Pol Pot Regime: Race, Power, and Genocide in Cambodia under the Khmer Rouge, 1975–1979* (New Haven: Yale University Press, 1996). For a comparative analysis, see Ben Kiernan, "Twentieth-Century Genocide: Underlying Ideological Themes from Armenia to East Timor," in *The Specter of Genocide: Mass Murder in Historical Perspective*, ed. Robert Gelatelly and Ben Kiernan (Cambridge: Cambridge University Press, 2003).
8. See Kiernan, "Twentieth-Century Genocide," 51.
9. See Enzo Traverso, *The Origins of Nazi Violence*, trans. Janet Lloyd (New York: New Press, 2003). For the work of Huttenbach, see Henry Huttenbach, "The Fatal Links in the Genocide Chain: From Armenia (1915) to the Final Solution (1942)," First International Meeting on Genocidal Social Practices, Buenos Aires, 2003.
10. See Enzo Traverso, *Le Totalitarisme: Le XXe siècle en débat* (Totalitarianism: The twentieth century in debate)(Paris: Seuil, 2001). For a discussion of comparative studies, see: "Totalitarianism: Use and Abuse of a Concept," in *Genocidio: La administración de la muerte en la modernidad*, ed. Daniel Feierstein (Buenos Aires: EDUNTREF, 2005).
11. Among those I have omitted because of their questionable theories and politics are Ernst Nolte and Andreas Hillgruber. Nolte portrays Nazism as a "European reaction" to "Bolshevik terror," comparing the repressive methods of Nazism and Stalinism in order to establish causal connections between the two and minimize the role played by Germany's—and Europe's—ruling classes in implementing genocide. Thus, the Nazi genocide—in Nolte's view—was simply a "defensive" response by civilized Europe, shocked at the "barbarism" of the "Slavic" Russian Revolution. In other words, it was communism that unleashed total war in Europe. Andreas Hillgruber shocked German and European scholars with his analysis of the "end" of European Jewry and the "tragedy" of the German army on the Eastern Front at the end of World War II. Hayden White has insightfully pointed out that Hillgruber pushes discourse to its limit by describing the sufferings of the German army as a "tragedy" while referring to the sufferings of European Jews with the neutral and impersonal term "end." Answering calls for a ban on Hillgruber's work, Hayden White argued that Hillgruber's was just one more way of emplotting a historical discourse. The real question was how to account for the ideological implications of different discourses. For Hayden White's approach to the Holocaust, see "Historical Emplotment and the Problem of Truth," in *Probing the Limits of Representation: Nazism and the "Final Solution,"* ed. Saul Friedlander

(Cambridge, MA: Harvard University Press, 1992). A more acceptable but clearly conservative approach is found in the work of Eric Weitz, who attempts to link Nazism, Stalinism, and genocide in Cambodia. Weitz suggests revolutionary upheaval as the main explanation for the appearance of genocidal social practices in these three political and social experiments. As can be seen very clearly from these examples, the ideological implications of any given approach may be more or less obvious, more or less explicit, but they cannot be eliminated and are always implicit in the historical examples chosen for comparison. See Weitz's "The Modernity of Genocide: War, Race, and Revolution in the Twentieth Century," in *The Specter of Genocide: Mass Murder in Historical Perspective*, ed. Robert Gelatelly and Ben Kiernan (Cambridge: Cambridge University Press, 2003).

12. Barbara Harff, "The Etiology of Genocides," in *Genocide and the Modern Age: Etiology and Case Studies of Mass Death*, ed. Isidor Walliman and Michael Dobkowski (Syracuse, NY: Syracuse University Press, 2000).

13. I follow Michel Foucault in my use of the terms "diagram of power," "technology of power," and "devices of power." These concepts will be dealt with at length in chapter 3.

14. A possible example is Arno Mayer in *Why Did the Heavens Not Darken? The "Final Solution" in History* (New York: Pantheon Books, 1990). Mayer provoked enormous disapproval for suggesting—perhaps somewhat sketchily—that the key to understanding both Nazism and the Nazi genocide was anticommunism. Mayer's theory will be examined in this book, particularly in chapter 5. For a critique of Mayer, see Christopher Browning, "The Holocaust as By-product? A Critique of Arno Mayer," in *The Path to Genocide: Essays on Launching the Final Solution* (Cambridge: Cambridge University Press, 1998).

15. The six extermination camps—Auschwitz, Treblinka, Belzec, Sobibor, Chelmno, and Majdanek—were all located in occupied Poland. Extermination camps (*Vernichtungslager*) or death camps (*Todeslager*) were built specifically for industrial-scale murder in gas chambers and remained in operation between 1942 and 1945. In contrast, concentration camps (*Konzentrationslager*) were primarily intended as places of incarceration, forced labor, and torture of detainees. The first camp in Germany was opened on 22 March 1933 at Dachau near the city of Munich. It is estimated that the German Reich was crisscrossed by between 2,000 and 5,000 camps (including labor camps, transit and collection camps, prisons, ghettos, and other means of enclosure), whose purpose was different from that of the extermination camps. For a survey of the Nazi concentration camp sites and an attempt to classify them, see Aharon Weiss, "Categories of Camps, Their Character and Role in the Execution of the Final Solution of the Jewish Question," in David Bankier, ed., *The Holocaust: Perpetrators, Witnesses, and Bystanders* (Jerusalem: Magnes Press, 1986). For some suggestions on ways to analyze the "reorganization" of German society, see Robert Gellately, *Backing Hitler: Consent and Coercion in Nazi Germany* (Oxford: Oxford University Press, 2001); and *The Gestapo and German Society: Enforcing Racial Policy, 1933–1945* (Oxford: Oxford University Press, 1990).

16. Although Argentina's military dictatorship seized power in a coup on 24 March 1976, the extensive and systematic destruction of population groups began almost immediately after the death of President Juan Domingo Perón on 1 July 1974. At first, executions were carried out exclusively by state paramilitary organizations like the Argentine Anticommunist Alliance and the Commando for the Liberation of America,

until the Argentine army launched "Operation Independence" in the province of Tucumán in December 1974.

17. See Eugenio Raúl Zaffaroni, *Criminología: Aproximación desde un margen* [Criminology: An approach from the periphery] (Bogotá: Temis, 1998).

CHAPTER 1 DEFINING THE CONCEPT OF GENOCIDE

1. Cited at the beginning of the Revised and Updated Report on the Question of the Prevention and Punishment of the Crime of Genocide, UN Doc. E/CN.4/Sub.2/1985/6—also known as "The Whitaker Report."
2. The Kingdom of Spain, founded by Ferdinand and Isabella in 1492, was Europe's first modern proto-state. Its Catholic confessionality excluded Jews and Muslims both physically and symbolically despite centuries of social integration. In the same year, 1492, Columbus reached the Americas, and soon afterward debates began about whether the newly discovered peoples of the Americas were human or not. Perhaps an earlier starting point for our model is *Malleus Maleficarum* (The hammer of witches) published in Germany in 1487. Originally applied to women freethinkers, the methods outlined in this handbook for witch-hunters and inquisitors were used by the Inquisition over the centuries in the protomodern stigmatization, harassment, and destruction of people and social relations.
3. M. Bjørnlund, E. Markusen, and M. Mennecke, "What Is Genocide? A Search for Common Ground between the Legal and Non-Legal Definitions," in *El genocidio: Problemas teóricos y metodológicos* (Genocide: Theoretical problems and methodologies), ed. Daniel Feierstein (Buenos Aires: EDUNTREF, 2005). Work submitted in English at the First International Conference on the Analysis of the Social Practices of Genocide, Faculty of Law, University of Buenos Aires, 11–15 November 2003.
4. M. Shaw, "War and Genocide: A Sociological Approach" (2007). *Online Encyclopedia of Mass Violence*, www.massviolence.org/Article?id_article=45.
5. Although I have used the term "genocidal social practices" more or less intuitively in earlier writings (e.g., *Cinco estudios sobre genocidio* [Five studies about genocide] [Buenos Aires: Acervo Cultural Editores, 1997]), I first became aware of its potential for systematic explanation after speaking to survivors of the Argentine genocide. As Marx says about social relations and Piaget says about awareness: *"He doesn't know it but he does it."* It was these survivors who made me *know it*.
6. Political groups were protected in both the Secretariat Draft of May 1947 and the Ad Hoc Committee Draft of April 1948.
7. The United States did not ratify the Genocide Convention until 1986 on the grounds that it challenged "national sovereignty by subjecting individuals to an international rather than national tribunal." William Pfaff, "Judging War Crimes," *Survival* 42, no. 1 (2000): 50.
8. Ward Churchill, *A Little Matter of Genocide: Holocaust and Denial in the Americas, 1492 to the Present* (San Francisco: City Lights Books, 1997), 410.
9. A catch-22, coined by Joseph Heller in his novel *Catch-22*, is a logical paradox wherein an individual finds him or herself in need of something which can only be had by not being in need of it. It refers also to a difficult situation from which there is no escape because it involves mutually conflicting or dependent conditions.
10. Raphael Lemkin, *Axis Rule in Occupied Europe: Laws of Occupation—Analysis of Government—Proposals for Redress* (Washington, DC: Carnegie Endowment for International Peace, 1944), 79.

11. "Each society has its regime of truth, its 'general politics' of truth—that is, the types of discourse it accepts and makes function as true." Michel Foucault, "Truth and Power," in *Essential Works of Foucault 1954–1984*, vol. 3: *Power*, ed. J. B. Faubion, 201–222 (New York: New Press, 2000).

12. Another important point is that political groups (and more inclusive terms such as "any group," "any community" as well as sexual groups, health groups, and others) have been included in definitions of genocide contained in the penal codes of a number of states, such as Bangladesh, Colombia, Costa Rica, Ethiopia, France, Finland, Ivory Coast, Lithuania, Panama. Peru, Portugal, Romania, and Uruguay, among others. This trend has increased in recent years. Argentina has not yet included genocide in its penal code, but all the bills presented—including one currently under discussion in Parliament—protect political and other groups.

13. Special Rapporteur is a title given to individuals who bear a specific mandate from the UN Human Rights Council (or the former UN Commission on Human Rights), to investigate, monitor, and recommend solutions to human rights problems.

14. There have been two major United Nations documents on genocide, the Ruhashyankiko Report of 1978 and the Whitaker Report of 1985. Ruhashyankiko recognized that the Convention was only a "point of departure" for preventing and punishing genocide but advised against modifying the Convention. Instead, he suggested preparing new instruments where appropriate.

15. In his report, Whitaker cites Donnedieu de Vabres's criticism of the Convention: "Whereas in the past crimes of genocide had been committed on racial or religious grounds, it was clear that in the future they would be committed mainly on political grounds" (Whitaker Report, para. 36).

16. *Ethnocide* is the destruction of the culture of a people, as opposed to the people themselves. *Ecocide* is a large-scale destruction of the natural environment.

17. Unfortunately, this article of the Spanish Penal Code was suppressed in 2010.

18. Case No. IT-95–10-T, para. 82. Emphasis in the original.

19. Acdel Vilas, Nuncamás.org (ed.): "Tucumán, enero a diciembre de 1975" (Tucumán: January to December 1975) (Bahía Blanca: Inédito, 1977).

20. R. D. Lewontin, "The Apportionment of Human Diversity," *Evolutionary Biology* 6 (1973): 381–397.

21. S. Wallman, "Ethnicity Research in Britain," *Current Anthropology* 18, no. 3 (1977): 531–532.

22. According to the court, the new Article 607, which follows the terms of the Genocide Convention of 1948, did not allow for the inclusion of the victims within the category of a "national group."

23. Timothy Longman, "Christian Churches and Genocide in Rwanda," revision of a paper originally prepared for the Conference on Genocide, Religion, and Modernity United States Holocaust Memorial Museum, Washington, DC, 11–13 May 1997. http://faculty. vassar.edu/tilongma/Church&Genocide.html.

24. Ibid.

25. See, for example, Alison Des Forges, *"Leave None to Tell the Story": Genocide in Rwanda* (New York: Human Rights Watch, 1999). In fact, this was also noted by the ICTR judges.

26. Bjornlund, Markusen, and Mennecke, "What Is Genocide?"

27. *Prosecutor v. Rutaganda* (Case No. ICTR-96–3), Judgment and Sentence, 6 December 1999, paras. 56–58, 373. The mixed approach, case by case, is also found in *Prosecutor*

v. Musema (Case No. ICTR-96–13), Judgment and Sentence, 27 January 2000, paras. 162–163. The idea of the subjective definition of victims by the perpetrator had been previously developed in *Prosecutor v. Musema* and by Frank Chalk and Kurt Jonassohn, *The History and Sociology of Genocide: Analysis and Case Studies* (New Haven: Yale University Press, 1990), a line taken before and after such a work by many researchers in the field of genocide studies.

28. See Ralph J. Henham, *Punishment and Process in International Criminal Trials* (Aldershot, UK: Ashgate, 2005), 117.

29. The countries are the Democratic Republic of Congo, Uganda, and the Central African Republic. In the fourth case, Sudan, ICC intervention followed a reference by the Security Council of the UN (UNSC Resolution 1593).

30. For recent work on the situation in Colombia, see Andrei Gomez, "Perpetrator Blocs, Genocidal Mentalities, and Geographies: The Destruction of the Unión Patriótica In Colombia and Its Lessons for Genocide Studies," *Journal of Genocide Research* 9 (2007): 1–24; and Marcelo Ferreira, "Genocidio reorganizador en Colombia: A propósito de una sentencia del Tribunal Permanente de los Pueblos" (Reorganizing genocide in Colombia: Apropos a sentence from the People's Permanent Tribunal), in *Terrorismo de Estado y Genocidio en América Latina* (State terrorism and genocide in Latin America), ed. Daniel Feierstein (Buenos Aires: Prometeo, 2009).

31. William Schabas, *Genocide in International Law*, 2nd ed. (Cambridge: Cambridge University Press, 2009).

32. This was clearly the case in Latin America, Indonesia, and several other countries during the 1960s, 1970s, and 1980s, and even Rwanda during the 1990s.

33. See the Introduction to this book.

34. Vahakn N. Dadrian, "A Typology of Genocide," *International Review of Modern Sociology* 15 (1975): 204.

35. Irving Horowitz; *Taking Lives: Genocide and State Power* (New Brunswick, NJ: Transaction Books, 1980), 17.

36. Leo Kuper; *Genocide: Its Political Use in the Twentieth Century* (New Haven: Yale University Press, 1981), 39.

37. Ibid.

38. Frank Chalk and Kurt Jonassohn, *The History and Sociology of Genocide: Analysis and Case Studies* (New Haven: Yale University Press, 1990), 23.

39. Helen Fein, "Genocide: A Sociological Perspective," *Current Sociology* 38 (1990): 24.

40. Barbara Harff and Ted Gurr, "Toward Empirical Theory of Genocides and Politicides," *International Studies Quarterly* 37:3 (1988): 359–371.

41. Steven T. Katz, *The Holocaust in Historical Context*, vol. 1: *The Holocaust and Mass Death before the Modern Age* (New York: Oxford University Press, 1994), viii.

42. Cited in *The Nanking Atrocity, 1937–38: Complicating the Picture*, ed. Bob Tadashi Wakabayashi, Asia Pacific Studies Series (New York: Berghahn Books, 2007), 277.

43. Henry Huttenbach, "Locating the Holocaust on the Genocide Spectrum: Towards a Methodology of Definition and Categorization," *Holocaust and Genocide Studies* 3, no. 3 (1988): 389–403.

44. Mark Levene, *Genocide in the Age of the Nation State*, vol. 2: *The Rise of the West and the Coming of Genocide* (London: I. B. Tauris, 2005), 35.

45. Jacques Semelin, *Purify and Destroy: The Political Uses of Massacre and Genocide* (New York: Columbia University Press, 2007).

46. See Israel Charny, "Toward a Generic Definition of Genocide," in *Genocide: Conceptual and Historical Dimensions*, ed. George Andreopoulos (Philadelphia: University of Pennsylvania Press, 1994), and Helen Fein, *Genocide: A Sociological Perspective* (London: Sage Publications, 1993).

47. See Harff and Gurr, "Toward Empirical Theory of Genocides and Politicides," and Semelin, *Purify and Destroy*.

48. However, when I first spoke with Henry Huttenbach and Frank Chalk about applying their definitions to the Argentine case, it was not evident to them at all that the concept of genocide was appropriate. This section is partly based on conversations I have held with them, as well as with Eric Markusen, Enzo Traverso, Bruno Groppo, Barbara Harff, and Ted Gurr, among others.

49. Harff and Gurr, "Toward Empirical Theory of Genocides and Politicides," 362.

50. This section was inspired by conversations with three Argentine philosophers, Héctor Schmucler, Gregorio Kaminsky, and Pablo Dreizik, and an Italian researcher, Enzo Traverso, each with different ideas on this matter. Obviously, the conclusions I present here are my own.

51. "Lectures on the History of Philosophy," cited in *Reading Hegel: The Introductions* (Melbourne: re.press, 2008), 225. "In order to comprehend what development is, what may be called two different states must be distinguished. The first is what is known as capacity, power, what I call being-in-itself (*potentia*); the second principle is that of being-for-itself, actuality (*actus*). If we say, for example, that man is by nature rational, we would mean that he has reason only inherently or in embryo: in this sense, reason, understanding, imagination, will, are possessed from birth or even from the mother's womb. But while the child only has capacities or the actual possibility of reason, it is just the same as if he had no reason; reason does not yet exist in him since he cannot yet do anything rational, and has no rational consciousness."

52. Karl Marx, "Economic and Philosophical Writings," in *Selected Writings*, ed. David McLean (New York: Oxford University Press, 2000), 84.

53. The identity of the victims in a genocidal process is defined by the perpetrators, not by the victims. An extreme case is Günther Fleischel, an enthusiastic Nazi and SA man in Hanover, who discovered he was a Jew after his father died in 1937. Imprisoned and later deported to the Riga ghetto, Fleischel remained loyal to Hitler until his death in the ghetto in 1943.

54. See my comment on Gobineau below.

55. See especially Oswald Spengler, *The Decline of the West*, abridged from the 1926 original, ed. Helmut Werner (New York: Oxford University Press, 1991), 348–351.

56. In contrast, the Nazis and many criminologists of the 1930s believed that criminal and asocial behavior was genetically transmitted.

57. In December 1977, Sisters Alice and Léonie were kidnapped along with ten other people connected with Mothers of the Plaza de Mayo after requesting the government to divulge the names and whereabouts of the "disappeared." The two nuns were repeatedly tortured before being thrown out of a plane while still alive into the sea.

58. Argentina's Military Code of Justice, which included the death penalty, was not abolished until 2008.

59. The General Jewish Labor Bund was a Jewish socialist party in Poland that promoted the political, cultural, and social autonomy of Jewish workers.

60. As mentioned in the Introduction to this book, Goldhagen later essentialized Germans as being anti-Semitic.

61. When the Nazis adopted Gobineau's theories, they were forced to edit his work extensively, much as they did with Nietzsche's writings.
62. Interestingly, the Nazis also applied the term of "criminal" to describe their victims, including Jews. This is brilliantly examined in two books that have not received the attention they deserve, despite their original and provocative approach. The works in question are Philip W. Blood, *Hitler's Bandit Hunters: The SS and the Nazi Occupation of Europe* (Dulles, VA: Potomac Books, 2008); and Eric A. Johnson, *Nazi Terror* (New York: Basic Books, 2000).
63. Nevertheless, the Nazi heritage was not limited to the use of concentration camps, torture, and mental breakdown. The Argentine perpetrators also treated certain victims with unusual cruelty, particularly Jewish prisoners.
64. This process operates in conjunction with the attempted "conversion" of society through terror. These practices—the effect of the concentration camp "outside" the concentration camp—will be discussed in detail in chapter 9.

CHAPTER 2 TOWARD A TYPOLOGY OF GENOCIDAL SOCIAL PRACTICES

1. Raphael Lemkin, *Axis Rule in Occupied Europe: Laws of Occupation—Analysis of Government—Proposals for Redress* (Washington, DC: Carnegie Endowment for International Peace, 1944), 79.
2. See Frank Chalk and Kurt Jonassohn, *History and Sociology of Genocide: Analyses and Case Studies* (New Haven: Yale University Press, 1990). For a discussion of alternative typologies, see "A Typology of Genocide and Some Implications for the Human Rights Agenda," in *Genocide and the Modern Age: Etiology and Case Studies of Mass Death*, ed. Isidor Wallimann and Michael Dobkowski (Syracuse, NY: Syracuse University Press, 2000).
3. Lemkin, *Axis Rule in Occupied Europe.*
4. For Charny's typology, see: "Toward a Generic Definition of Genocide," in *Genocide: Conceptual and Historical Dimensions*, ed. George Andreopoulos (Philadelphia: University of Pennsylvania Press, 1994).
5. See Helen Fein, *Accounting for Genocide* (New York: Free Press, 1979).
6. See Leo Kuper, *Genocide: Its Political Use in the Twentieth Century* (New Haven: Yale University Press, 1982).
7. For an account of Mao's "killing quotas" in the early 1950s, see Changyu Li, "Mao's "Killing Quotas," Human Rights in China (HRIC), 26 September 2005, at Shandong University: http://hrichina.org/sites/default/files/oldsite/PDFs/CRF.4.2005/CRF-2005–4_Quota.pdf.
8. See Roger Smith, "Human Destructiveness and Politics: The Twentieth Century as an Age of Genocide," in *Genocide and the Modern Age*, ed. Walliman and Dobkowski. However, I disagree with Smith's arguments about the delegitimization of ideologies or end of "grand narratives," which are so typical of postmodern discourse.
9. Barbara Harff, "The Etiology of Genocide," in *Genocide and the Modern Age*, ed. Walliman and Dobkowski.
10. In the case of constituent genocide, "us" and "them" components of the stigmatization process are still under construction. In the case of postcolonial genocide, the "outsider" was formerly one of "us," and with reorganizing genocide—what Kuper and Smith call "domestic genocide"—they are still one of "us" and so need to be subtyped,

or mentally segregated from the rest of society. In my view, the Nazis were the first to segregate others in this way through stigmatization or "construction of negative otherness." For the modes of construction of the notions symbolic of "self" and "outsider" see in Noufouri Hammurabi, *Del Islam y los árabes: Acerca de la percepción argentina de lo propio y lo ajeno* (Islam and the Arabs: On the Argentine perception of self and other) (Buenos Aires: Cálamo de Sumer, 2001).

11. I would like to acknowledge Barbara Harff's work for the concept of postcolonial genocide. In my earlier work, I confused this type of annihilation with colonial genocide and reorganizing genocide. But it has its own distinctive nature and—in the twentieth century—has served as a bridge between constituent (foundational) and/or colonial genocide and the more specific form of reorganizing genocide.

12. The "concentration camp" aspects of Nazism and the Argentine genocide of this fourth type will be examined in detail in chapter 9.

13. Zygmunt Bauman has already provided a thorough and insightful account of this issue in *Modernity and the Holocaust* (Cambridge, UK: Polity Press, 1989).

14. For a discussion of the topic and the role of the notion of "frontier" in this process, see Esteban de Gori and Marina Gutiérrez, "Fronteras y genocidio: Violencia y represión como política de Estado en Argentina a fines del siglo XIX" (Borders and genocide: Violence and repression as a state policy in Argentina in the late nineteenth century), mimeo, 2005.

15. With respect to the Amazon, see Andres Ruggeri, "Un caso de genocidio y conquista en la Amazonia: los Waimiri Atroari y la dictadura militar brasileña" (A case of genocide and conquest in the Amazon: The Waimiri Atroari and the Brazilian military dictatorship). This paper was first presented at the First International Meeting on Analysis of Social Practices of Genocide, Buenos Aires, November 2003, and is published on the CD of the meeting.

16. For more on Algeria, see María Eugenia Jeria and Rosario Figari Layús, "La construcción de otredad en Algeria: El tratamiento político del otro en la colonización y en la guerra contrarrevolucionaria en el marco de la liberación nacional" (Construction of otherness in Algeria: The political treatment of the other during colonization and the counterrevolutionary war in the context of national liberation), a paper presented in the framework of the graduate course "Analysis of Genocidal Social Practices," Faculty of Social Sciences, University of Buenos Aires, December 2004.

17. See Lucrecia Molinari, "Análisis de las prácticas sociales genocidas: El caso de El Salvador" (Analysis of the social practices of genocide: The case of El Salvador), a paper presented in the framework of the graduate course "Analysis of Genocidal Social Practices," Faculty of Social Sciences, University of Buenos Aires, July 2005, and published in *Terrorismo de estado y genocidio en América Latina* (State terrorism and genocide in Latin America), ed. Daniel Feierstein (Buenos Aires: Prometeo, 2009).

18. Carlos Figueroa Ibarra, "Cultura del terror y Guerra Fría en Guatemala" (Culture of terror and Cold War in Guatemala), in *Hasta que la muerte nos separe: Poder y prácticas sociales genocidas en América Latina* (Till death do us part: Power and genocidal social practices in Latin America), ed. Daniel Feierstein and Guillermo Levy (La Plata: Ediciones al Margen, 2004).

19. Giorgio Agamben, *State of Exception*, trans. Kevin Attell (Chicago: University of Chicago Press, 2005), 2.

20. "Apuntes sobre novedad y articulación: El nazismo y el genocidio nazi" (Notes on novelty and articulation: Nazism and the Holocaust), in *Genocidio: La administración de*

la muerte en la modernidad (Genocide: The management of death in modernity), ed. Daniel Feierstein (Buenos Aires: EDUNTREF, 2005).

21. Martin Edwin Andersen, *Dossier Secreto: Argentina's Desaparecidos and the Myth of the "Dirty War"* (Boulder, CO: Westview Press, 1993).

CHAPTER 3 RECONCILING THE CONTRADICTIONS OF MODERNITY

1. Foucault has explored several aspects of technologies of power, and this discussion builds on his analyses. A technology of power typically affects a range of human behaviors. In *Discipline and Punish* (1975), Foucault focuses on modes of control and management of the physical body. He expands on this approach in his *History of Sexuality* (1976–1983), where he includes the role of moral regulation. He analyzes moral regulation from another perspective in *Technologies of the Self* (1982). Moreover, in lectures published under the title *Society Must Be Defended: Lectures at the Collège De France, 1975–76*, Foucault analyzes the consequences of these technologies of power at what he calls the "bio-political" level for mass population control and how technologies of power might contribute to hegemonic ways of understanding and representing the world.
2. See Zygmunt Bauman, *Modernity and the Holocaust* (Ithaca, NY: Cornell University Press, 1989).
3. Subject of Rousseau's Book One of *The Social Contract*, p. 1.
4. Immanuel Kant, "Of National Characteristics, So Far as They Depend upon the Distinct Feeling of the Beautiful and Sublime," in *Observations on the Feeling of the Beautiful and the Sublime*, trans. John T. Goldthwait (Berkeley: University of California Press, 1991), 110–111.
5. Immanuel Kant, *Über die verschiedenen Rassen der Menschen (On the Different Races of Man)*, 1775.
6. The text of this speech was sent to Argentina by the Argentine consul in Munich, Ernesto Sarmiento, and can be found in the Testimony Archive, Centre for Social Studies, from the archives of the Ministry of Foreign Affairs, Foreign Trade and Worship of Argentina. A surprising feature is the accompanying note by Sarmiento: "In the hope that this work may be of some use to our country on the burning issue of race about which we have heard so much recently and, although at home it has not taken on the passion or proportions that it has taken on in Europe, I hope this matter can be studied by those in the know and, adapting it to our ways, could be used for a future study of the Immigration Law that will contemplate the new situations arising from new problems in which Argentine medical staff could (and why not?) study (who knows?) *[sic]* the most interesting and necessary type of race for the future of humanity."
7. Gerhard Wagner, "Rasse und Bevölkerungspolitik" (Race and population politics), Der Parteitag der Ehre vom 8. bis 14. September 1936, Offizieller Bericht über den Verlauf des Reichsparteitages mit sämtlichen Kongreßreden (Munich: Zentralverlag der NSDAP, 1936), 150–160. A speech and official report by Wagner on Nazi racial policy delivered at the 1936 Nuremberg rally.
8. For an account of both types of policies—in particular the persecution by the Gestapo of those who had sex with Polish citizens—see Robert Gellately, *Backing Hitler: Consent and Coercion in Nazi Germany, 1933–1945* (Oxford: Oxford University Press, 2001), and *The Gestapo and German Society: Enforcing Racial Policy, 1933–1945* (Oxford: Oxford University Press, 1990).

9. In the worst of the European colonies, the Belgian Congo, anywhere between two million and fifteen million are thought to have been murdered. See Adam Hochschild, *King Leopold's Ghost: A Story of Greed, Terror, and Heroism in Colonial Africa* (New York: Mariner Books, 1998), 62.
10. James D. Marshall, "Foucault and Neo-Liberalism: Biopower and Busno-Power," University of Auckland, 1995. http://www.ed.uiuc.edu/eps/PES-Yearbook/95_docs/marshall. html.
11. Michel Foucault, *Society Must Be Defended: Lectures at the Collège de France, 1975–76* (New York: Picador, 2002), 254.
12. "Instrumental reason" focuses on *how* rather than *why* things should be done. According to the Frankfurt School, instrumental reason was responsible for the rise of fascism and the reduction of human beings to objects of manipulation.
13. Note that the natural law is not an external source of authority, nor should it not be confused with the physical laws of nature, which science aims to describe.
14. See *The Moral Judgment of the Child*, by Jean Piaget, with the assistance of seven collaborators (Glencoe, IL: Free Press, 1932).
15. A protoform of reorganizing genocide emerged in late fifteenth-century Spain after the Inquisition was created to discover and punish false converts to Christianity. Spain—Europe's first modern nation-state—was a confessional state, and Jews (in 1492) and Muslims (in 1501) were given the choice of conversion or exile. With the advent of colonialism, repression of the domestic Other gives way to repression of the colonial Other (e.g., Native Americans or the inhabitants of Africa, Asia, or Oceania) before repression returns to Europe in the late nineteenth century with the suppression of the Paris Commune (1871), a wave of anti-Semitic pogroms in Ukraine and Poland (1881–1884), and the suppression of the Russian revolutionaries of 1905.
16. Cited in José Luis D'Andrea Mohr, *Memoria debida* (Buenos Aires: Colihue, 1999), 70.
17. Daniel Feierstein, *Seis estudios sobre genocidio: Análisis de relaciones sociales. Otredad, exclusión, exterminio* (Six studies about genocide: Análysis of social relations. Otherness, exclusion, extermination) (Buenos Aires: EUDEBA, 2000).
18. Sigmund Freud, *From the History of an Infantile Neurosis.*
19. The following case shows how this uncertainty works. A man reported a Jewish woman to the Gestapo for prostitution and having sex with German men. The man later admitted that he had also slept with the woman, but had decided to denounce her before she could denounce him. The man was sentenced to just one year in jail for his cooperation. Cited in Robert Gellately, *The Gestapo and German Society: Enforcing Racial Policy, 1933–1945* (Oxford: Oxford University Press, 1990), 686. For a version of events that gives a greater weight to the role of the authorities, see Eric A. Johnson, *Nazi Terror: The Gestapo, Jews, and Ordinary Germans* (New York: Basic Books, 1999).
20. Jeremy Noakes and Geoffrey Pridham, eds, *Nazism: A History in Documents and Eyewitness Accounts, 1919–1945* (Department of History and Archaeology at the University of Exeter, UK, 1983), 429–441.
21. Document included in the AIDA report (International Association for the Protection of Performers, Victims of Repression) and included by Prudencio Garcia in *El drama de la autonomía militar* (The drama of military autonomy) (Madrid: Alianza, 1995).
22. See, for example, Primo Levi, *If This Is a Man*, published in the United States under the title *Survival in Auschwitz*, 2013; Bruno Bettelheim, *The Informed Heart: Autonomy in a Mass Age*, 1979; and Charles Papiernik, *Unbroken: from Auschwitz to Buenos Aires*, 2004, among many others.

23. See, for example, Roberto N. Kechichian, *Formación moral y cívica: Tercer año del ciclo básico y educación técnica* (Moral and civic education: Third year of the basic cycle and technical education) (Buenos Aires: Editorial Stella, 1981). This manual contains the "minimum content" defined in the Ministerial Resolution of 8 September 1980.
24. The "picket" movement of unemployed workers that emerged in Argentina in December 2001 (although it had been building for several years) seems to be a clear attempt to break this pattern of domination. But it, too, has been hindered by fragmentation and sectarianism. In particular, leftist political parties have tended to create divisions and subdivisions within the movement.
25. For a critique of the concept of authenticity, see Charles Taylor, *The Ethics of Authenticity* (Cambridge, MA: Harvard University Press, 1991).
26. Zygmunt Bauman has described these processes with greater clarity; see, for example, *Work, Consumerism, and the New Poor* (Issues in Society) (Gedisa: Open University, 1998); *Liquid Love: On the Frailty of Human Bonds* (Cambridge: Cambridge University Press, 2003).
27. See Emmanuel Levinas, *Totality and Infinity: An Essay on Exteriority*, trans. Alphonso Lingis (Pittsburgh: Duquesne University Press, 1969).
28. Gramsci speaks of a failure to move from "economic-corporate" to "eminently political" relations, although he is here referring to the inability of the ruling classes to inspire or connect with the masses. See Antonio Gramsci, *Selections from the Prison Notebooks*, ed. and trans. Quintin Hoare and Geoffrey Nowell Smith (New York: International Publishers Co., 1971), 270.
29. Ibid.

CHAPTER 4 DISCOURSE AND POLITICS IN HOLOCAUST STUDIES

1. To understand the debate about "normalizing" Nazism, it is suggestive to address the controversy between Martin Broszat and Saul Friedländer about ways to write the history of Nazism. A summary of this debate can be found in Ian Kershaw, *The Nazi Dictatorship: Problems and Perspectives of Interpretation* (Baltimore: Edward Arnold, 1985). Some aspects of this discussion are also developed in Charles Maier, *The Unmasterable Past: History, Holocaust, and German National Identity* (Cambridge, MA: Harvard University Press, 1999).
2. I have taken the concept of "Non-Germans" from Kershaw's *Nazi Dictatorship* since German concerns about Nazism were different.
3. Because of its popularity, *Hitler's Willing Executioners* was one of the first works on Nazism to be translated into Spanish. It was published by Taurus, Madrid, in 1998. Works critical of Goldhagen have also been translated, including Omer Bartov's *Ordinary Monsters*; Christopher Browning's *Daniel Goldhagen's Willing Executioners*; and Hans Mommsen, "The Thin Patina of Civilization: Anti-Semitism Was a Necessary, but by No Means a Sufficient, Condition for the Holocaust," in the compilation by Federico Finchelstein, *Germans, the Holocaust, and Collective Guilt: The Goldhagen Debate* (Buenos Aires: EUDEBA, 1999), summarizing the discussion generated in Argentina among Holocaust historians by Goldhagen's work.
4. See, for example, Lucy Davidowicz's classic book, *The War against the Jews* (New York: Pocket Bantam Books, 1986), or Yehuda Bauer's *The Holocaust in Historical Perspective* (Seattle: University of Washington Press, 1982), as the most representative.

5. At the launch of his controversial book in Germany, Goldhagen himself explained that the "German disease" had been "cured" after the war, making this sedative attempt at interpretation ridiculous: the pathological condition of the German people was locked away at some moment in the past and simply left there, with no risk for the present.
6. Michel Foucault, *Society Must Be Defended: Lectures at the Collège de France, 1975–1976* (New York: Picador, 2003).
7. It should be noted that not all views of uniqueness are linked to demonization theories. However, because the two perspectives are complementary, they tend to become interwoven.
8. See the repeated questioning of this position by authors such as Leo Kuper, Frank Chalk, Henry Huttenbach, Vahakn Dadrian, Israel Charny, Helen Fein, Barbara Harff, Eric Markusen, among some others. In view of the fact that many Holocaust researchers did not even recognize the Armenian genocide as such, dissent with the notion of uniqueness eventually led to the creation of the International Association of Genocide Scholars (IAGS) in 1994. IAGS brings together experts from around the world—including some researchers from the field of Holocaust studies—who are concerned with comparative issues within a more open view of genocide studies. The European Network of Genocide Scholars (ENOGS) was set up with similar objectives. In 2005, it became the International Network of Genocide Scholars (INOGS). Most of the IAGS Resolutions were passed during the 1990s and concerned the Armenian case, as this was the first case to disrupt the uniqueness frame.
9. Vahakn Dadrian, "The Convergence Aspects of the Armenian and Jewish Cases of Genocide: A Reinterpretation of the Concept of Holocaust," *Holocaust & Genocide Studies* 3, no. 2 (1988), 165.
10. See Steven Katz's classic work *The Holocaust in Historical Context* (Oxford: Oxford University Press, 1990) and Deborah Lipstadt's *Denying the Holocaust: The Growing Assault on Truth and Memory* (New York: Plume, 1994). A good example of Yehuda Bauer's early position is *The Holocaust in Historical Perspective*. His later position can be found in *Rethinking the Holocaust* (New Haven: Yale University Press, 2002).
11. See the Introduction for Hayden White's notion of history as a narrative framework.
12. For the evolution from colonial genocide to the Holocaust, see Enzo Traverso, *The Origins of Nazi Violence* (New York: New Press, 2003).
13. Silvia Sigal used a similar argument to question the use of the term "genocide" to describe events in Argentina between 1974 and 1983 in a controversial speech at the Second International Meeting on the Construction of Collective Memory, organized by the Comisión Provincial de la Memoria (Memory Commission of the Province of Buenos Aires). Her speech was published in *Revista Puentes*, no. 5, Centro de Estudios por la Memoria, La Plata, 2001. Other points raised by Sigal are discussed in chapter 1 of this book, and in chapters 7 and 8 in connection with Argentina.
14. For a detailed discussion of what was and what was not new about the Holocaust, see the suggestive work of Guillermo Levy and Tomás Borovinsky: "Apuntes sobre novedad y articulación: El nazismo y el genocidio nazi" (Notes on novelty and connectedness: Nazism and the Holocaust) in *Genocidio: La administración de la muerte en la modernidad* (The management of death in modernity), ed. Daniel Feierstein (Buenos Aires: Eduntref, 2005).
15. The policies of resettlement in the East and the Madagascar Plan were developed at the highest levels of Nazi decision making.

16. Helen Fein, "Genocide, Life Integrity, and War Crimes: The Case for Discrimination," in *Genocide: Conceptual and Historical Dimensions*, ed. George Andreopoulos (Philadepia: University of Pennsylvania Press, 1997), 95.

17. For a lucid critique of Nolte, see Charles Maier, *The Unmasterable Past: History, Holocaust, and German National Identity* (Cambridge, MA: Harvard University Press, 1997), or Enzo Traverso, "The New Anti-Communism: Rereading the Twentieth Century," in *History and Revolution: Refuting Revisionism*, ed. Mike Haynes and Jim Wolfreys (Brooklyn, NY: Verso, 2007). Also Enzo Traverso, *The Origins of Nazi Violence* (New York: New Press, 2003). In fact, Nolte's comparative perspective minimizing genocide grows out of the Cold War approach to "totalitarianism" discussed in the next chapter.

18. The philosopher Jürgen Habermas responded to Nolte's book accusing Nolte and others of trying to whitewash the German past by ignoring the specifically German aspects of the Holocaust. This gave rise to an intellectual and political controversy in West Germany—the *Historikerstreit* (literally, "historians' quarrel")—which lasted from 1986 to 1989. At the heart of this dispute was the relationship between history and memory.

19. In the case of Cambodia, one of the most extensive and well documented works is Ben Kiernan, *The Pol Pot Regime: Race, Power, and Genocide in Cambodia under the Khmer Rouge, 1975–79* (New Haven: Yale University Press, 1996). Despite a long-standing debate among Asian historians, there seems to be a growing consensus—in line with Benjamin Whitaker's Report to the United Nations—on the classification of social practices such as genocide. In the case of the Soviet Union, Genocide Studies usually focuses on the famine in Ukraine in the early 1930s. An example of this position is Barbara Green, "Stalinist Terror and the Question of Genocide: The Great Famine," in *Is the Holocaust Unique?*, ed. Alan Rosenbaum (Boulder, CO: Westview Press, 1996). The debate has been revived in recent years and extended to other cases, although this has led to strong disagreements. A summary of approaches that use the concept of genocide to describe Stalin's treatment of different nationalities within the Soviet Union can be found in a special issue of the *Journal of Genocide Research* 4, no. 3 (September 2002), particularly in the articles of Brian Williams, "Hidden in the Soviet Muslims Ethnocide Borderlands: The Ethnic Cleansing of the Crimean Tatars"; Michaela Pohl, "'It Cannot Be That Our Graves Will Be Here': The Survival of Chechens and Ingush Deportees in Kazakhstan, 1944–1957"; and Curtis Richardson, "Stalinist Terror and the Kalmyks' National Revival: A Cultural and Historical Perspective." In previous issues, see also the work of François Grin, "Kalmykia, Victim of Stalinist Genocide: From Oblivion to Reassertion," *Journal of Genocide Research* 3, no. 1 (March 2001), 97–116; and J. Otto Pohl, "Stalin's Genocide against the 'Repressed Peoples,'" one of the attempts to label Stalin's political killings as genocide, in *Journal of Genocide Research* 2, no. 2 (June 2000), 267–293. Along the same lines, see the article by Nicolas Werth, "The Mechanism of a Mass Crime: The Great Terror in the Soviet Union, 1937–1938," in *The Specter of Genocide: Mass Murder in Historical Perspective*, ed. Robert Gellately and Ben Kiernan (New York: Cambridge University Press, 2003), 215–240. For contrasting views, see Enzo Traverso, "El totalitarismo. Usos y abusos de un concepto" (Totalitarianism: Uses and abuses of a concept), in *Genocidio: La administración de la muerte en la modernidad* (Genocide: The management of death in modernity), ed. Feierstein (Buenos Aires: Eduntref, 2005).

20. Cited in Hans Stoffels, ed., *Terrorlandschaften der Seele: Beiträge zur Theorie und Therapie von Extremtraumatisierungen* (Terror landscapes of the soul: Articles on the theory and therapy of extreme traumatization) (Regensburg: S. Roderer Verlag, 1994).

21. Walter Benjamin, "On the Concept of History" (1940), trans. Harry Zohn, in *Selected Writings*, vol. 4, ed. Howard Eiland and Michael W. Jennings (Cambridge, MA: Harvard University Press, 2003).

22. In his graphic novel *Maus*, Art Spiegelman narrates a young man's attempts to talk to his father, a survivor of Nazi death camps. In this narrative, Jews are depicted as mice, Germans as cats, Poles as pigs, and Americans as dogs. Appealing to the conventions of the comic book, *Maus* is written with exquisite sensitivity and depth. However, it raises the issue of whether there are legitimate and illegitimate genres for narrating an experience like the Nazi genocide. Certain classical historians see the use of a "minor" genre like the comic book as a heretical and disrespectful way to refer to such events. White's ideas are very stimulating in the context of this debate.

23. See in particular Hayden White's classic work *Metahistory: The Historical Imagination in Nineteenth-Century Europe* (Baltimore: Johns Hopkins University Press, 1973). For a reworking of some of these arguments, see the summary by Veronica Tozzi in the Spanish version of Hayden White, *The Historical Text As Literary Artifact* (Barcelona: Polity Press, 2003).

24. For White's analysis of this specific topic, see "Historical Emplotment and the Problem of Truth," in *Probing the Limits of Representation: Nazism and the "Final Solution,"* ed. Saul Friedlander. However, this is not his best work on the issue of modes of representation.

25. Roland Barthes distinguishes between "transitive" and "intransitive" writing along the lines of the older formalist distinction between "literary" and "nonliterary." Hayden White, in "Historical Emplotment and the Problem of Truth," 46, argues that "intransitive writing, in rejecting figurality and narrative emplotment altogether, effaces the subjectivity of the author by allowing the facts of the Holocaust, in their 'actuality' and 'literalness' to speak essentially for themselves."

26. White, "Historical Emplotment and the Problem of Truth," 48.

27. Nevertheless, this is not White's best work, and he rather spoils his case by claiming that the alternative to a nondistancing approach is what in Greek is traditionally called "middle voice"—a middle ground between the active and passive voice, the intentional and the involuntary—that White identifies in the writings of Primo Levi.

28. For a neuroscience approach to memory, see especially the work of Gerald Edelman, Nobel Prize in Medicine and Physiology in 1972. Edelman developed a large-scale theory of brain function known as "neural Darwinism," first published in 1978, in a book called *The Mindful Brain* (Cambridge, MA: MIT Press). From his copious bibliography, it is worth highlighting *The Remembered Present* (New York: Basic Books, 1989), *Neural Darwinism* (Oxford and New York: Oxford Paperbacks, 1990), *Bright Air, Brilliant Fire* (New York: Basic Books, 1992), *A Universe of Consciousness: How Matter Becomes Imagination* (New York: Basic Books, 2001) (co-authored with Giulio Tononi), and *Wider Than the Sky: The Phenomenal Gift of Consciousness* (New Haven: Yale University Press, 2005). Among writers on neuroscience he has influenced are such important names as Jean Pierre Changeux, Giulio Tononi, and Israel Rosenfield, among others.

29. Tzvetan Todorov, "The Uses and Abuses of Memory," in *What Happens to History: The Renewal of Ethics in Contemporary Thought*, ed. Howard Marchitello (New York and London: Routledge, 2001), 11–22.

30. Walter Benjamin, "On the Concept of History" (1940), trans. Harry Zohn, in *Selected Writings*, vol. 4, ed. Howard Eiland and Michael W. Jennings (Cambridge, MA: Harvard University Press, 2003), 391.

CHAPTER 5 THE PROBLEM OF EXPLAINING THE CAUSES OF THE NAZI GENOCIDES

1. For discussion of the work produced in Germany itself, particularly in the Federal Republic but also in the Democratic Republic, see Ian Kershaw, *The Nazi Dictatorship* (Baltimore: Edward Arnold, 1985).
2. Raul Hilberg, *The Destruction of the European Jews* (New Haven: Yale University Press, 2003).
3. Hannah Arendt, *Eichmann in Jerusalem: A Report on the Banality of Evil*, rev. ed. (New York: Penguin Classics, 1964), 276.
4. Theodor Adorno, *The Authoritarian Personality* (New York: Design, 1965).
5. Some examples of these discussions can be found in Hannah Arendt, *The Jew as Pariah: Jewish Identity and Politics in the Modern Age*, ed. Ron H. Feldman (New York: Grove Press, 1978)—in particular her exchanges of letters with Walter Laqueur and discussions with her former friend, Gershom Scholem.
6. Christopher Browning, *Ordinary Men: Reserve Police Battalion 101 and the Final Solution in Poland* (New York: HarperCollins, 1992).
7. The already cited works of Ernst Nolte portray Nazism as a "reaction" to Bolshevism, minimizing Nazi crimes by presenting them as a pale reflection of those committed in the Soviet Union. As mentioned earlier, Jürgen Habermas's criticism of Nolte's position sparked a debate known as the *Historikerstreit* among German historians. Here we are more interested in certain mythic visions of Nazism in Germany and how these allowed the work of a revisionist like Nolte to find an echo among historians and among ordinary Germans tired of being presented as evil madmen by European and American historians during the 1950s and 1960s. Nolte put into words and justified previously silenced attempts to "normalize" German history in works such as those of Martin Broszat.
8. In truth, these discussions are also associated with a political history, not only in Germany but also in Italy and France, as pointed out by Daniel Lvovich in *Historia reciente de pasados traumáticos: De los fascismos y colaboracionismos europeos a la historia de la última dictadura argentina* (Recent history of traumatic pasts: From fascism and European collaborationism to the history of Argentina's last dictatorship), an unpublished original work which the author kindly allowed me to read and which was later published in *Historia reciente: Perspectivas y desafíos para un campo en construcción* (Recent history: Prospects and challenges for a developing field), ed. Marina Franco and Florence Levin (Buenos Aires: Paidós, 2007). Lvovich's comparisons with Argentina's dictatorship are highly relevant to my own work here.
9. Zygmunt Bauman, *Modernity and the Holocaust* (Cambridge, UK: Polity Press, 1989).
10. Enzo Traverso, *The Origins of Nazi Violence* (New York and London: New Press, 2003).
11. Ibid.
12. Hannah Arendt, *The Origins of Totalitarianism* (New York: Harcourt, Brace, 1951). This book was Arendt's passport to academic prestige. The dissemination of her work on totalitarianism and the respect she earned contrast strangely with the widespread hostility toward her work on Adolf Eichmann almost ten years later, see *Eichmann in Jerusalem* (New York: Penguin Classics, 2006).
13. Slavoj Zizek, *Did Somebody Say Totalitarianism?* (London: Verso, 2001).
14. Enzo Traverso, *Le totalitarisme: Le XXème siècle en débat* (Totalitarianism: The twentieth century debate) (Paris: Points-Seuil, 2001).

15. Franz Borkenau, *The Totalitarian Enemy* (London: Faber & Faber, 1940).

16. This perspective degenerated into overt racism two decades later with Samuel Huntington's theory of a "clash of civilizations" or references to the incompatibility between the West and the "Arab world" by authors such as Giovanni Sartori. See Giovanni Sartori, *Pluralismo, multiculturalismo e estranei. Saggio sulla società multietnica* (Pluralism, multiculturalism, and strangers: Essay on multiethnic society) (Milan: Rizzoli, 2000); and Samuel Huntington, *The Clash of Civilizations* (New York: Polity Press, 2000).

17. Cited in Kershaw, *Nazi Dictatorship*, 30.

18. Leon Trotsky, "Manifesto of the Fourth International on Imperialist War and the Proletarian World Revolution. Adopted by the Emergency Conference of the Fourth International, May 19–26, 1940." http://www.marxists.org/history/etol/document/fi/1938–1949/emergconf/fi-emerg02.htm.

19. Ernest Mandel, *The Meaning of the Second World War* (London: Verso, 1986).

20. At the political level, this blindness was even more acute. During the discussions at the United Nations Convention on the Prevention and Punishment of the Crime of Genocide, the positions of the Soviet Union and the socialist bloc (with the exception of the Yugoslav delegation, under the leadership of Tito, who developed a position diametrically opposed to this view) refused to look beyond the most basic ways of understanding genocide, insisting that genocide be defined in terms of the social practices of Nazism and thus preventing it from being understood as a constituent practice of modernity (even as a constituent practice of capitalism). The exclusion of political groups from the definition of genocide (discussed in detail in chapter 1 of this book) was due largely to the stubborn opposition from the Soviet Union to its inclusion (to prevent discussion of its own processes of repression). This exclusion, however, made the Convention inapplicable in genocidal processes that suppressed national liberation struggles (Indochina, Algeria, Vietnam) and the annihilation of the communist opposition in Indonesia or East Timor (occupied by Indonesia from 1975 onwards) or genocides in Latin America inspired by the National Security Doctrine. All these events, moreover, met with a lack of response from the Soviet Union as part of its strategy of appeasement in the Cold War. For the case of East Timor after the Indonesian invasion, see John Taylor, "'Encirclement and Annihilation': The Indonesian Occupation of East Timor," in *The Specter of Genocide: Mass Murder in Historical Perspective*, ed. B. Kiernan and R. Gellately (Cambridge: Cambridge University Press, 2003), 163–185. For internal repression in Indonesia, ten years earlier, see Leslie Dwyer and Degung Santikarma, "When the World Turned to Chaos: 1965 and Its Aftermath in Bali, Indonesia," in the same volume. See, too, Robert Cribb, "Genocide in Indonesia, 1965–66," *Journal of Genocide Research* 3, no. 2 (June 2001), 219–239.

21. For a detailed discussion of these concepts and operations in modernity, see chapter 3.

22. See Tim Mason, "Intention and Explanation: A Current Controversy about the Interpretation of National Socialism," in *Nazism, Fascism, and the Working Class: Essays by Tim Mason*, ed. Jane Caplan (Cambridge: Cambridge University Press, 1995). For a critical account of this debate, see Kershaw, *The Nazi Dictatorship*.

23. Arno Mayer, *Why Did the Heavens Not Darken?: The "Final Solution" in History* (New York: Pantheon Books, 1989).

24. Christopher Browning, *The Path to Genocide: Essays on Launching the Final Solution* (Cambridge: Cambridge University Press, 1992).

25. Bauman's *Modernity and the Holocaust* has already been mentioned extensively in this book, but this approach seeks to insert it into the discussion between Mayer and Browning, trying a third approach to the question of why the Jewish people were annihilated under Nazism.
26. This issue is dealt with in another context and with other cultural groups in the highly suggestive work of Hammurabi Noufouri, *Del Islam y los árabes: Acerca de la percepción argentina de lo propio y de lo ajeno* (Of Islam and Arabs: About Argentina's perception of self and others) (Buenos Aires: Editorial Cálamo de Sumer, 2001). Hammurabi Noufouri is the Chair Professor of Islamic and Mudejar Art at the School of Architecture, Design, and Urbanism of the University of Buenos Aires. I have taken the concept of "identity based on exclusion" from various works of his.
27. This original article by Tony Barta, much cited by genocide scholars, appeared as "Relations of Genocide: Land and Lives in the Colonization of Australia," in the excellent early compilation by Isidor Wallimann and Michael N. Dobkowski, *Genocide in the Modern Age: Etiology and Case Studies of Mass Death* (Westport, CT: Greenwood Press, 1987). It is a real pity that Barta did not continue this line of analysis. Despite proving problematic and questionable, it is certainly original.

CHAPTER 6 RESHAPING SOCIAL RELATIONS THROUGH GENOCIDE

1. In writing this chapter I have drawn principally on the testimonies of Bruno Bettelheim, Viktor Frankl, Jaika Grossman, Schmerke Kaczerginsky, Primo Levi, Marek Edelman, Tzivia Lubetkin, Charles Papiernik, Jack Fuchs, Iankl Nirenberg, and Irene Birnbaum. I have also included material from my own personal interviews with Charles Papiernik, which consisted of about twenty meetings over the period of a year. A selection of these were published in Charles Papiernik, *Ser humano en Auschwitz: Conversaciones con Charles Papiernik* (To be human in Auschwitz: Conversations with Charles Papiernik) (Buenos Aires: Acervo Cultural Editores, 2000). I also had occasion to personally interview Marek Edelman in a long talk lasting about three hours when he visited Buenos Aires in 1990.
2. Jean Piaget, *The Moral Judgment of the Child* (Glencoe, IL: Free Press, 1948), 319.
3. Ibid., 324.
4. Robert Paul Wolff, *In Defense of Anarchism* (Berkeley: University of California Press, 1998), 19.
5. See Bill Ashcroft et al., *Key Concepts in Postcolonial Studies* (London: Routledge, 2003).
6. See Frantz Fanon, *Black Skin White Mask* (New York: Grove Press, 1967).
7. This obsession can be found also in other genocides, as in Argentina, Chile, and Uruguay, where dozens of testimonies from survivors of detention camps confirm that the perpetrators employed the most diverse forms of torture and mistreatment to "break" their victims psychologically.
8. Primo Levi, *Survival in Auschwitz* (New York: Touchstone, 1995), 22.
9. Michel Foucault, *Society Must Be Defended: Lectures at the Collège de France, 1975–1976* (London: Penguin, 2004), 15–16.
10. For an analysis of anatomo-politics and biopolitics in Foucault, see "Genealogy of Racism," in *Society Must Be Defended* (New York: Picador, 2003), and *Discipline and Punish: The Birth of the Prison* (London: Allen Lane, 1977).
11. Michel Foucault, *The History of Sexuality*, vol. 1: *The Will to Knowledge* (London: Penguin, 1998), 137.

12. Foucault, *Society Must Be Defended*, 256.

13. Robert Gellately, *Backing Hitler: Consent and Coercion in Nazi Germany* (Oxford: Oxford University Press, 2001).

14. Ibid., 40.

15. Ibid., 97.

16. Ibid., 142.

17. Ibid., 125.

18. Gregory Stanton, "The 8 Stages of Genocide," www.genocidewatch.org/eightstages.htm. What these two approaches do have in common, however, is that both are "nonlinear" and identify processes that are interrelated and overlapping rather than specific events.

19. This structure is derived from my earlier work, *Cinco estudios sobre genocidio* (Five studies on genocide) (Buenos Aires: Acervo Cultural Editores, 1997), and later *Seis estudios sobre genocidio: Análisis de relaciones sociales: Otredad, exclusión, exterminio* (Six studies on genocide: Analysis of social relations. Otherness, exclusion, extermination) (Buenos Aires: EUDEBA, 2000). At the time of publication, these books were only available in Spanish.

20. Charles Papiernik, interview in the context of this research, November 1997. Other elements of his testimony can be found in *Una vida* (A life) (Buenos Aires: Acervo Cultural Editores, 1997). Part of our talks are included in *Ser humano en Auschwitz*.

21. Adorno wrote a lucid analysis of the self-contradictory character of the accusations made by anti-Semitic ideology. See T. W. Adorno, Else Frenkel-Brunswik, Daniel Levinson, and R. Nevitt Sanford, *The Authoritarian Personality* (New York: Harper & Row, 1950). It is very suggestive that highly prejudiced subjects criticize Jews, in the same survey or interview, as being too closed and too invasive, labor hoarding and work-shy, hypersexual and seductive and also withdrawn, subverters of the social order and also its most conspicuous defenders.

22. There are even homegrown Argentine versions of these conspiracy theories, from the myth that Jewish soviets or councils had been set up in Buenos Aires to the "Plan Andinia," a hoax about an alleged Jewish plot to conquer Patagonia spread by a right-wing professor at the University of Buenos Aires in 1971. During the "Tragic Week" of 7–14 January 1919, many Jews were tortured and interrogated to make them "confess" to their part in setting up the Judeo-Bolshevik soviets in Buenos Aires. Similarly, the journalist Jacobo Timerman was tortured during the military dictatorship of 1976–1983 for information—among other things—about the "Plan Andinia."

23. This effect should not be overlooked. In Nazi Germany, the victims often asked to be isolated in order to escape the harassment to which they were subjected. At the same time, others demanded that the victims be removed so that they would not have to witness more unpleasant scenes of public degradation. Thus, once the Other has become a "negative Other," the victims are blamed for any discomfort or unpleasant situations that occur when they are punished for continuing to live among "normal folk." In Argentina, the actions of the AAA (Anti-Communist Alliance Argentina) and other paramilitary forces during the years 1974 and 1975 caused large sectors of the population to argue for the "need" to regulate these actions within an institutional framework. The state terrorism of the military dictatorship was implemented to meet

this "need and to organize terror, murder, and repression from the appropriate institutional bodies: the security forces" (i.e., the police and the military).

24. Discussions of why the Nazis moved from a policy of forcing Jews to emigrate to a policy of extermination often assume that the earlier policies failed, as if the Nazis' only goal was to separate the "different" from the "same." One wonders, however, if migration actually solves the problems of eradicating certain social relations (autonomy, solidarity, and critical thinking), or if it is just an intermediate step toward genocide. What would have happened if the policy of expelling Jews from Germany had succeeded? Would it have been enough to expel stigmatized groups, as the Inquisition had done in Spain? Or did death play a central role in this new technology of power in constructing power relations? Could the Nazis have broken down social relations within the German state—let alone within the Reich or across the whole of Europe—without the use of terror involving mass annihilation? See, for example, Christopher Browning, *The Path to Genocide* (Cambridge: Cambridge University Press, 1992). For the role of the term "Nazi terror" in Nazi genocidal social practices, see Eric A. Johnson's *Nazi Terror: The Gestapo, Jews and Ordinary Germans* (New York: Basic Books, 1999). For a discussion of the role of terror in Argentina, see the early work of Juan Corradi: "The Modes of Destruction: Terror in Argentina," in *Telos* 54 (1982–83); *A veinte años del golpe: Con memoria democrática* (Twenty years after the camp: With democratic memory) (Rosario, Argentina: Homo Sapiens, 1996); and Juan Corradi, Patricia Weiss Fagen, and Manuel Antonio Garretón, *Fear at the Edge: State Terror and Resistance in Latin America* (Berkeley: University of California Press, 1992).
25. In general, this is how isolation is perceived in the logic of the ghetto. The perception was similar in the first proto-Jewish ghetto in the city of Venice starting in 1515.
26. Jaika Grossman, *La resistencia clandestina* (The secret resistance) (Buenos Aires: Ed. Milá, 1990), 30.
27. Ibid., 83.
28. See Bruno Bettelheim, "Individual and Mass Behavior in Extreme Situations," *Journal of Abnormal and Social Psychology* 38 (1943), 417–452.
29. Primo Levi, *Survival in Auschwitz*, 83.
30. Pierre Vidal-Naquet, "La soga y el ahorcado," in *Los judíos, la memoria y el presente* (The Jews: The memory and the present) (Buenos Aires: FCE, 1996), 226–227.
31. This position is very clear, since it sees a "political difference." For an approach that treats the problem in terms of a "generation gap," see Israel Gutman, *Youth Movements in the Underground and the Ghetto Revolts* (Jerusalem: Yad Vashem, 1971).
32. Grossman, *La resistencia*, 105–106.
33. On this point, see Feierstein, *Seis estudios sobre genocidio*, especially chapters 4 and 5.
34. Foucault, *Society Must Be Defended*, chap. 11.
35. For a more extended account of what I understand by this concept, see my *Cinco estudios sobre genocidio* and *Seis estudios sobre genocidio*.
36. For an account of assimilation structures, see the work of Jean Piaget and Rolando García, *Psychogenesis and the History of Science*, trans. Helga Feider (New York: Columbia University Press, 1988).
37. Both the "humanity" Arendt conceded in Adolf Eichmann as an exemplary parent figure and the genocidal potential in ordinary people discovered by Milgram were too painful, and almost impossible to swallow for Jewish scholars of the time, who preferred to treat the Shoah as a metaphysical phenomenon. (See chapters 4 and 5.)

38. The Nazis also applied "reeducation" policies for "undisciplined workers" and even for some political dissidents and those accused of "crimes of opinion" (who were sent to labor or concentration camps). On the other hand, Jews, Gypsies, homosexuals, "asocials," "Bolsheviks," and Russian political prisoners were considered "racially degenerate," and thus irredeemable, with definitely no place in the new German society. Members of these groups were at first shot publicly and/or secretly, and later annihilated in mass extermination camps.

39. For a historical analysis of the political, cultural, and identity aspects of Jews in the Pale of Settlement during the interwar period, see Ezra Mendelsohn, *The Jews of East Central Europe between the World Wars* (Bloomington: Indiana University Press, 1987). For a perspective that emphasizes the political character of Jewish identity during this time, and its links to the Nazi logic of destruction, see Arno Mayer, *Why Did the Heavens Not Darken? The "Final Solution" in History* (New York: Pantheon Books, 1990). For a perspective more centered on Jewish identity as multiple identity, see Zygmunt Bauman, *Modernity and the Holocaust* (Cambridge, UK: Polity Press, 1989).

40. Bruno Bettelheim, "The Ignored Lesson of Anne Frank," in *Anne Frank: Reflections on Her Life and Legacy*, ed. Sandra Solotaroff-Enzer (Urbana: University of Illinois Press, 2000), 186–190.

41. For a detailed analysis of the Vilna ghetto, see my article, "The Dilemma of Wittenberg: Reflections on Tactics and Ethics," *Shofar: Journal of Jewish Studies* 20: 2 (Winter 2002), 61–68.

42. Vamik Volkan, Gabriele Ast, and William F. Greer Jr., *The Third Reich in the Unconscious: Transgenerational Transmission and Its Consequences* (New York: Brunner-Routledge, 2002), 40.

43. Ibid., 160.

44. For a detailed account of the effects of the Argentine genocide on language, see Marguerite Feitlowitz, *A Lexicon of Terror: Argentina and the Legacies of Torture* (New York: Oxford University Press 1998).

45. Tzvetan Todorov, "The Abuses of Memory," *Common Knowledge*, no. 5 (1996).

PART 3 TOWARD A HISTORICAL BASIS

1. In this review of different causal explanation of events, I have excluded several important texts on the period—for instance, Elizabeth Jelin's work on memory, the early works of Hugo Quiroga and César Tcach, the suggestive writings of Ludmila Catela da Silva on the ways different actors represent experience, or Beatriz Sarlo's reflections on the status of survivor testimony, among others. This is because these works are concerned with other issues, and not with providing causal models of events. Some of them will be referred to later to account for specific aspects of the phenomenon under study. I have also omitted many reflections by political militants of the 1980s and 1990s, particularly those that have not been published in academic works. Although some selection is always necessary, I recognize that my understanding of the different consequences of genocidal social practices in Argentina has undoubtedly been influenced by the writings of these very different political groups. Moreover, although they are concerned with a comprehensive description of how concentration camps functioned in Argentina rather than with a broader analysis of the period, I am indebted to Alipio Paoletti's work, *Como los nazis, como en Vietnam: Los campos de concentración en Argentina* (Like the Nazis, like Vietnam: The concentration camps in

Argentina), published by the Mothers of Plaza de Mayo, Buenos Aires, 1996. (In fact, the book was written in 1986 and first published in 1987.)

2. While this concept of closure is my own, I have since found a similar use of the term in Maria Sondereguer, "Los relatos sobre el pasado reciente en Argentina: Una política de la memoria" (The stories about the recent past in Argentina: A politics of memory), which appeared in *Iberoamericana: Ensayos sobre letras, historia y sociedad*, no. 1 (Madrid: Editorial Iberoamericana, 2001). Sondereguer, in turn, develops the concept used by Inés González Bombal in "Nunca Más: El juicio más allá de los estrados" (Never again: Judgment beyond the courtroom"), published in Carlos Acuña et al., *Juicios, castigos, memorias: Derechos Humanos y justicia en la política argentina* (Judgments, punishments, memories: Human rights and justice in Argentine politics) (Buenos Aires: New Vision, 1995).

CHAPTER 7 EXPLAINING GENOCIDAL SOCIAL PRACTICES IN ARGENTINA

1. This brings us to an ethical issue that I must address before starting this chapter. During the years I have been teaching "Analysis of Genocidal Social Practices" at the University of Buenos Aires, I have refused to include on my reading lists texts written by perpetrators of genocide. However, after discussions with the members of my chair team, and with many students, I began to doubt my initial decision, realizing that such readings are necessary despite the moral disgust they produce. I had to accept that it is not wise to ignore the words of the perpetrators, particularly when, as in the cases of Acdel Vilas, Ramón Camps, or Genaro Diaz Bessone, they are not mere manifestos "denying" the events, but are instead attempts to promote a particular way of understanding these events and that, one way or another, they recognize the nature of the practices involved—forced disappearance, torture in interrogations, harassment and murder of civilians, among others—and try to justify them within the framework of a causal explanation.
2. Vilas Acdel's book is titled *Tucumán: Enero a diciembre de 1975* (Tucumán: January to December 1975) and is reproduced in full at www.nuncamas.org. All quotes and comments in this chapter are taken from this source.
3. "Meeting place of detainees" was one of the euphemisms used by the military to refer to the concentration camps.
4. The Camps quotations are taken from *Caso Timerman: Punto final* (The Timerman case: Full stop) (Buenos Aires: Tribuna Abierta, 1982). It is noteworthy that the expression "full stop" that Camps uses to close off Argentina's genocidal experience was also the one chosen by Alfonsín's democratically elected government for its first impunity law in 1986.
5. Montoneros (Spanish: Movimiento Peronista Montonero—MPM) was a Peronist urban guerrilla group that engaged in armed struggle from 1970 to 1979. The name alludes to nineteenth-century caudillo-led armies. The definitive split between left- and right-wing Peronism came in 1973 with the Ezeiza massacre, which marked Perón's return from eighteen years of exile. Members of the Triple A (Argentine Anti-Communist Alliance), who were sworn enemies of Montoneros, opened fire on the crowd awaiting Perón's arrival at Ezeiza airport. Perón sided with the Peronist right wing and expelled Montoneros from the Justicialist party in May 1974. By 1977 Montoneros had been almost completely destroyed.
6. For Diaz Bessone, in addition to the "National Project" drafted by the military dictatorship's Ministry of Planning, see Ramón Genaro Díaz Bessone, *Guerra revolucionaria*

en la Argentina (1959–1978) (Revolutionary war in Argentina [1959–1978]) (Buenos Aires: Círculo Militar, 1996).

7. A de facto government is one that has come to power by unconstitutional means—usually by force.

8. Final Document of the military junta, in Stella Maris Ageitos, *Historia de la impunidad: De las Actas de Videla a los Indultos de Menem* (History of impunity: From Videla's Proceedings to Menem's Free Pardons) (Buenos Aires: Adriana Hidalgo Editora, 2002), 96–114. In the same work, see Law 22,924 "of National Pacification" (later known as the "amnesty law"), on 121–124.

9. Héctor J. Cámpora, 25 May 1973 to 23 September 1973; Juan Domingo Perón, 23 September 1973 to 1 July 1974, and María Estela ("Isabelita") Martínez de Perón, 1 July 1974, to 24 March 1976.

10. Reynaldo Benito Bignone, *El último de facto II: Quince años después* (The last de facto government II: Fifteen years later), published at his own expense at San Miguel Copy Center, San Miguel, Argentina, 2000.

11. Corrupt practices among both civil servants and businesspeople were the product of a worldview based on unbridled individualism and selfishness, which can be thought of as an adaptive response to a terror that had destroyed nearly every trace of solidarity.

12. Bignone, *El último de facto II*, 30.

13. Ibid., 40.

14. Hannah Arendt, *Eichmann in Jerusalem: A Report on the Banality of Evil*, rev. and enl. ed. (New York: Penguin Books, 1977).

15. Theodor Adorno et al., *The Authoritarian Personality* (New York: Harper, 1950).

16. The full text of the CONADEP Report is available in English at http://www.desaparecidos.org/nuncamas/web/english/library/nevagain/nevagain-002.htm.

17. Whether these armed leftist organizations were "terrorists" or not is an issue that—without ever being made explicit—divides many of the approaches described in this chapter. Historically, terrorism is associated with violence directed against civil society as a whole, where the random nature of the victims is precisely what spreads terror. Terrorism involves attacks on highly populated areas and places such as bars, restaurants, railway stations, and supermarkets, sending the message that no one is safe. In contrast, the armed left in Argentina in the 1960s and 1970s—however legitimate or illegitimate their attacks may have been—never indulged in "random" terrorism with the one exception of the bombing of the building of Federal Coordination, an area used by the security forces and not a "neutral" area frequented by the general public. By describing these groups as "terrorists" and comparing them with other political groups that do (or did) practice terrorism—for instance, long-standing political organizations like ETA (Euskadi Ta Askatasuna, a Basque nationalist organization) or the IRA (Irish Republican Army) and even many Palestinian armed groups and important sectors of Islamic fundamentalism in the twenty-first century—not only creates confusion but seems to endorse the new security doctrines promoted by the United States since the 9/11 Twin Towers tragedy. Although the latter most certainly was a "terrorist" attack, the doctrines to which it gave rise use "terrorism" to describe a wide range of activities, from any type of armed action to simply belonging to certain ideological or religious groups, or participating in the antiglobalization movement or indigenous organizations, among others.

18. Elsa Drucaroff, "Por algo fue: Análisis del 'Prólogo' al *Nunca Más*, de Ernesto Sabato," (There must have been a reason: Analysis of the "Preface" to *Never Again* by Ernesto Sabato), *Tres Galgos*, no. 3 (November 2002).
19. Pablo Giussani, *Montoneros, la soberbia armada* (Montoneros, armed arrogance) (Buenos Aires: Sudamericana-Planeta, 1984).
20. This need, as I have just noted, continues to exist today. For not only was the debate never settled, it was barely started.
21. Giussani, *Montoneros*, 103.
22. I am not trying to justify the armed organizations of the left, let alone their political leaders who continued to insist on a policy of "offensives"—with terrible consequences for both the members of these organizations and their relatives—when what was required was a "strategic retreat." What I am saying is that however misguided they were, we should never lose sight of the fact that these political groups were also victims of a genocidal process.
23. Claudia Hilb and Daniel Lutzky, *La nueva izquierda argentina: 1960–1980* (Política y violencia) (The new Argentine left: 1960–1980 [Politics and violence]) (Buenos Aires: CEAL, 1984).
24. In fact, Hilb and Lutzky are among the few authors who cite Marín. They criticize his work harshly, especially his description of the period as a "war."
25. Juan Carlos Marín, *Los hechos armados, Argentina, 1973–1976: La acumulación primitiva del genocidio* (Armed actions, Argentina 1973–1976: The primitive accumulation of genocide) (Buenos Aires: PI.CA.SO./La Rosa Blindada, 1996). (Although I used this edition, which is the most revised and expanded one, Marín wrote the original version during the dictatorship, and there are several editions before this one.)
26. Marín did not write a new book on the subject until 2001—a brief treatise on civil society, genocide, and the perpetrators, which will be discussed later.
27. Marín added Marx's idea of "primitive accumulation" as the subtitle to the 1996 edition.
28. This is "La conciliación de los victimarios: Una larga historia a propósito del genocidio" (The reconciliation of the perpetrators: A long history on the subject of genocide), mimeo, 2001, later published as a supplement by the Popular University of the Mothers of Plaza de Mayo in the newspaper *Página 12*.
29. I have taken the expression "adiaphorization" from Zygmunt Bauman. While it appears in several of his works, I think it acquires its deepest sense in *Postmodern Ethics* (Oxford: Blackwell, 1993). There he uses the term—taken from the ecclesiastical concept of *adiaphoron*—to account for behavior that arises from "moral indifference," from an inability to evaluate in terms of merit or sin, of good or evil—in short, from a loss of moral judgment. We could understand this adiaphorization as resulting from "subjective leveling," an idea that will be developed in chapter 9.
30. The book *The Argentine Terrorist State* was first published in Spain in October 1983 and republished in Argentina in 1984. A new edition of this work and the one I refer to here, *El Estado Terrorista Argentino: Quince años después, una mirada crítica* (The Argentine terrorist state: Fifteen years later, a critical vision), was published by EUDEBA, Buenos Aires, 1999. In fact, this new edition is really two books in one—the unrevised 1984 edition together with a new "Part One" containing 200 pages written in 1998.
31. Ibid., 174.
32. Ibid.

33. Despite the fact that Duhalde clearly defines the notion of "terrorist state" in his book, some authors have chosen the term as a way of denying the appropriateness of the term "genocide" in this context. This contrasts with the repeated use of both concepts in Duhalde's book and the priority given to the term "genocide" by the Argentine Commission on Human Rights (CADHU) in its legal complaints, which inspired Duhalde's book.

34. Duhalde, *El Estado Terrorista Argentino*, 347.

35. See Pilar Calveiro, *Poder y desaparición: Los campos de concentración en Argentina* (Power and disappearance: The concentration camps in Argentina) (Buenos Aires: Colihue, 1998), especially 135–137.

36. Guillermo O'Donnell, *Counterpoints: Selected Essays on Authoritarianism and Democratization* (Notre Dame, IN: University of Notre Dame Press, 1999).

37. Ibid., 165–193.

38. I am referring to articles such as "Psychology and Politics: The Question of Exile," "Philosophy and Terror," "Exile: War and Politics, an Exemplary Sequence," all written between 1980 and 1990. These articles were published together with some earlier ones in León Rozitchner, *Las desventuras del sujeto politico: Ensayos y errores* (The sorrows of the political subject: Trials and errors) (Buenos Aires: Ediciones el Cielo por Asalto, 1996).

39. Some of these ideas are taken up by Pilar Calveiro *in Política y/o violencia: Una aproximación a la guerrilla de los años setenta* (Policy and/or violence: An approach to the guerrillas of the seventies) (Buenos Aires: Norma, 2005). However, this is a first and somewhat hasty sketch. Unlike her other works, it slips at times into insults about the alleged dementia, madness, or irrationality of the armed left. Nevertheless, many of her ideas are incisive and merit deep and complex discussion, which, as I have said, has barely begun.

40. Rozitchner, *Las desventuras del sujeto politico*, 133.

41. For Jacoby's work, see *El asalto al cielo* (The assault on heaven), mimeo (Buenos Aires: Cuadernos del CICSO, n.d.).

42. Rozitchner, *Las desventuras del sujeto politico*, 149.

43. I am aware that this conclusion differs radically from that of Beatriz Sarlo in *Tiempo pasado: Cultura de la memoria y giro subjetivo, Una discusión* (Time past: The culture of memory and the subjective turn. A discussion) (Buenos Aires: Siglo XXI, 2005). In the Argentina of the 1980s and 1990s, Sarlo finds a wealth of evidence and ways of representing the events—a view I do not share with her. Very little of the evidence analyzed by Sarlo comes from survivors of the concentration camps; most of it comes from militants who had managed to avoid the clandestine detention centers—either by sheer good fortune or because they were able to flee the country.

44. Pilar Calveiro, *Poder y desaparición: Los campos de concentración en Argentina* (Power and disappearance: The concentration camps in Argentina) (Buenos Aires: Colihue, 1998). The author wrote the book in 1994, but it was only published—in an abridged form—four years later.

45. Ibid., 11. This metaphor can be compared with that developed by members of the Association of Ex-Disappeared Detainees about concentration camps as a "bouillon cube" or "stock cube" for a "social soup" that affected the whole population, an idea which will be developed later.

46. Ibid., 88.

47. Ibid., 92, 134.
48. Ibid., 169.
49. Carlos Flaskamp, *Organizaciones político-militares: Testimonio de la lucha armada en Argentina (1968–1976)* (Political-military organizations: Testimony of armed struggle in Argentina [1968–1976]) (Buenos Aires: Ediciones Nuevos Tiempos, 2002).
50. Ibid., 214.
51. Ibid., 212.
52. Ibid., 213.
53. Ibid., 214.
54. To my mind, his clearest work on the issue is "¿Hubo una guerra en la Argentina?" (Was there a war in Argentina?), published in *La escena contemporánea*, no. 3 (1999), 12–21.
55. Ibid., 17.
56. *Breve historia contemporánea de la Argentina* (A brief contemporary history of Argentina), 1st ed. (Buenos Aires: FCE, Buenos Aires, 1994), chap. 6: "Dependencia o liberación" (Dependence or liberation), 1966–1976, and chapter 7: "El Proceso" (The Process), 1976–1983.
57. Ibid., 207.
58. For a review of the concept by Romero himself in a contentious and controversial article about the consequences of certain uses of memory, see Luis Alberto Romero, "Recuerdos del Proceso, imágenes de la democracia: luces y sombras en las políticas de la memoria" (Memories of the process, images of democracy: Lights and shadows in the politics of memory), a paper presented at the History and Memory Colloquium, Faculty of Humanities and Education Sciences, National University of La Plata, April 2002, and published in *Clío & Asociados,* no. 7 (2003). Despite these problems, the text points out a key issue for this book: the alienation produced by democratist texts on the "process" that took place between 1976 and 1983—an exculpatory alienation of society as a whole that demonized the military and has contributed little to the understanding of the Argentine genocide. These points are analyzed later in this book. I am indebted to Daniel Lvovich for pointing out to me some of the features of Romero's article as well as the discussion that this triggered.
59. Romero, *Breve historia contemporánea*, 210.
60. One wonders whether there was also the "spirit" of a "new era" that produced these "new" approaches on the issue. That is, if one can ever get rid of the "spirit of time." On this topic, see the review article of Romero by Luciano Alonso and María Laura Tornay, "Políticas de la memoria y actores sociales (a propósito de un ensayo de Luis Alberto Romero)" (Politics of memory and social actors [à propos an essay by Luis Alberto Romero]), *Clío & Asociados*, no. 8 (2004).
61. For the work of Gabriela Aguila, see "El terrorismo de Estado sobre Rosario (1976/83)" (State terrorism on Rosario (1976/83]), in *Rosario en la historia: De 1930 a nuestros días* (Rosario in history: From 1930 to the present day), ed. Alberto PLA (Rosario: Editora UNR, 2000), vol. 2. A shorter and updated version can be found in "Dictadura, sociedad y genocidio en la Argentina: La represión en Rosario, 1976–1983" (Dictatorship, society, and genocide in Argentina: Repression in Rosario, 1976–1983), in *Hasta que la muerte nos separe: Poder y prácticas sociales genocidas en América Latina* (Till death do us part: Power and genocidal social practices in Latin America), ed. Daniel Feierstein and Guillermo Levy (Buenos Aires: Ediciones al Margen, 2004).

62. Ariel Armony, *Argentina, the United States, and the Anti-Communist Crusade in Central America, 1977–1984* (Athens: Ohio University Press, 1997).

63. Fernando Coronil and Julie Skurski, eds., *States of Violence* (Ann Arbor: University of Michigan Press, 2006), 1–2.

64. Hugo Vezzetti, *Pasado y presente: Guerra, dictadura y sociedad en la Argentina* (Past and present: War, dictatorship, and society in Argentina) (Buenos Aires: Siglo XXI, 2002).

65. Vezzetti rules out the concept of war for much the same reasons as Duhalde. This leads to a dilemma: how to deny the concept of war without depoliticizing the conflict. This dilemma is posed very clearly by Mattini, who stresses that the answer to this question does not necessarily constitute the focus of the debate, namely, whether or not there was a war and how to affirm the political nature of the victims while recognizing that they were not necessarily militarized or at least not armed, even though they clearly politicized and opposed the regime. Vezzetti rules out the concept of genocide on the basis of the distinction between "being" and "doing" (already analyzed and criticized in chapter 1 of this book) and the political nature of the events in Argentina, which he tries to differentiate from the "apolitical" nature of the Nazi genocides, a problem I have already discussed in previous chapters. It is worth noting that most of these views are based on a partial or superficial knowledge of other genocidal processes, including the genocide carried out by the Nazis and their concentration camps, but also other important and problematic cases such as the genocide in Rwanda (Vezzetti cited this as a paradigmatic example of "ethnic" genocide) in which, however, the political factor was central in the choice of the victims of the massacre and where, paradoxically, the ethnic character was called into question. Indeed, the very complexity of the issue led to interesting developments in the proceedings of the International Criminal Tribunals, which tried those cases, and in case law about genocide. For a discussion of the legal ramifications of this discussion on genocide and politics, see, for example, the work of Matthias Bjørnlund, Eric Markusen, and Martin Mennecke, "¿Qué es el genocidio? En la búsqueda de un denominador común entre definiciones jurídicas y no jurídicas" (What is genocide? In search of a common denominator between legal and nonlegal definitions), in *Genocidio: La administración de la muerte en la modernidad* (Genocide: The management of death in modernity), ed. Daniel Feierstein (Buenos Aires: EDUNTREF, 2005).

66. The question of whether to characterize armed leftist groups in Argentina as "terrorists" not only implies a reasonably symmetrical balance of forces between victims and perpetrators, but has complex and troubling political consequences because of the way the term "terrorist" is currently used in the new "doctrines of international security."

67. Vezzetti, *Pasado y presente*, 123.

68. Inés Dussel, Silvia Finocchio and Silvia Gojman, *Haciendo memoria en el país del Nunca Más* (Looking back on the country of Never Again) (Buenos Aires: EUDEBA, 1997).

69. Marcos Novaro and Vicente Palermo, *La dictadura militar 1976/1983: Del golpe de estado a la restauración democrática* (The military dictatorship 1976/1983: From the coup to the restoration of democracy) (Buenos Aires: Paidós, 2003).

70. See, in particular, ibid., 70–71.

CHAPTER 8 TOWARD A PERIODIZATION OF GENOCIDE IN ARGENTINA

1. The child was the daughter of an assistant to the seminar held by the Association of Ex-Disappeared Detainees at the Human Rights Free Chair, Faculty of Arts, University of Buenos Aires, in 1997.
2. The reflections on this problem contained in this chapter have been greatly enriched by the contributions of successive generations of students to the course "Analysis of Genocidal Social Practices" that I teach at the University of Buenos Aires. In particular, I would like to highlight the work of Mercedes Aramburu, Eva Camelli, Verónica Daián, Rosario Figari Layús, María Eugenia Jeria, Jimena Juárez, Bettina Presman, Ana Lía Rodríguez, Gabriela Roffinelli, María Cristina Scarsi, and Lior Zylberman, from whom I have taken several suggestions.
3. This is what allows us to observe the spirit of the times that surrounded negativized figures in Argentina, a mixture of militancy, youth, and critical rebelliousness well illustrated by Alejandro Cattaruzza in "El mundo por hacer: Una propuesta para el análisis de la cultura juvenil en la Argentina de los años setenta" (A world in the making: A proposal for the analysis of Argentine youth culture in the 1970s), *Entrepasados. Revista de Historia* 6, no. 13 (1997). However, Cattaruzza fails to realize that the greater or lesser degree of coordination between the cultural climate and armed left-wing organizations was not a "misunderstanding" but precisely the kind of social relations and practices that the perpetrators set out to eliminate, and which constituted their definition of "subversive crime."
4. Statement by General Roberto Viola, *La Nación*, 20 April 1977, quoted in Inés Izaguirre, *Los desaparecidos: recuperación de una identidad expropiada* (The disappeared: The recuperation of a stolen identity) (Buenos Aires: Cuadernos del IIGG, Journal of the Faculty of Social Sciences, 1992), 36.
5. Declarations of Jorge Rafael Videla at a press conference with British journalists in January 1978, quoted in Eduardo Duhalde, *El Estado terrorista argentino: Quince años después, una mirada crítica* (The Argentine terrorist state: Fifteen years later, a critical look) (Buenos Aires: Argos Vergara 1999), 67.
6. This and the following quotes are taken from Judge Baltasar Garzón's indictment in November 1999 of Adolfo Scilingo and other Argentine perpetrators for terrorism and genocide. For a detailed analysis of the role of the Catholic Church during the genocide in Argentina, see Emilio Mignone, *Iglesia y Dictadura* (Church and dictatorship) (Buenos Aires: Universidad Nacional de Quilmes and Página/12, 1999) (first edition by CELS, 1986); Horacio Verbitsky, *El silencio: De Paulo VI a Bergoglio: Las relaciones secretas de la Iglesia con la ESMA* (The silence: from Paul VI to Bergoglio: The secret relationships of the Church with ESMA) (Buenos Aires: Sudamericana, 2005); and Martin Obregon, *Entre la cruz y la espada: La Iglesia Católica durante los primeros años del "Proceso"* (Between a rock and a hard place: The Catholic Church during the first year of "the Process") (Quilmes: National University of Quilmes, 2005).
7. Mariana Heredia, "La identificación del enemigo: La ideología liberal conservadora frente a los conflictos sociales y políticos de los años '70" (Indentification of the enemy: Liberal conservative ideology in the face of social and political conflicts of the 1970s), a paper presented at the 22nd Conference of the Latin American Sociology Association (ALAS), Concepción, Chile, 1999, unpublished, courtesy of the author.
8. Ibid., 12.
9. See chapter 2—in particular, the proposed typology of genocidal social practices.

10. See Carlos Figueroa Ibarra, "Cultura del Terror y Guerra Fría en Guatemala" (Culture of terror and cold war in Guatemala), in *Hasta que la muerte nos separe: Poder y prácticas sociales genocidas en América Latina* (Until death do us part: Power and social genocide practices in Latina America), ed. Daniel Feierstein and Guillermo Levy (La Plata: Ediciones al Margen, 2004).

11. José Luis D'Andrea Mohr, *Memoria debida* (Buenos Aires: Cocihue, 1999), 70. For the education policies of the dictatorship, see the work of Carolina Kaufman, ed., *Dictadura y Educación* (Madrid: Miño y Dávila, 2001).

12. Racism "contaminates" genocide because it is unnecessary for the destruction and remaking of social relations. Ethnic persecution increases the number of victims to be killed without any increase in the overall efficiency of the process. Of course, I use the term "contaminate" ironically.

13. For an analysis of the connections between genocidal social practices and the neoliberal economic model in Argentina, see Guillermo Levy's "Consideraciones acerca de la relación entre raza, política, economía y genocidio," in *Hasta que la muerte nos separe* (Until death do us part), ed. Feierstein and Levy. While these policies have been applied in other societies that did not necessarily undergo a genocidal process, note that Argentina was unique as regards the level of social integration achieved after Peronism. This society was more difficult to fracture than other more fragmented societies or societies where inequality had never been overcome.

14. Note that the link between the political and the criminal (mediated by ethnicity) was also present in Nazism in the persecution of "asocial" people, especially during the period from 1936 to 1938 and again toward the end of the war as the Nazi regime crumbled. This process is traced in depth by Robert Gellately, *The Gestapo and German Society: Enforcing Racial Policy, 1933–1945* (Oxford: Oxford University Press, 1990); and particularly in Philip W. Blood, *Hitler's Bandit Hunters: The SS and the Nazi Occupation of Europe* (Dulles, VA: DC Potomac Books, 2008).

15. Statements of Harguindeguy to French journalist Marie Monique Robin, cited in Horacio Verbitsky, "Torturas y desapariciones según Harguindeguy. Pecados y Delitos" (Torture and disappearances according to Harguindeguy: Sins and crimes), *Página/12*, 2 September 2003.

16. Ariel Armony, *La Argentina, los Estados Unidos y la cruzada anticomunista en América Central, 1977–1984* (Argentina, the United States and the anticommunist crusade in Latin America) (Quilmes: National University of Quilmes, 1999). Again, it is possible to trace the genealogies. In the case of the Nazis, Gellately stresses that the arrests that began in the late 1930s (when persecution became truly massive and then led to mass murder) were based on prior intelligence work consisting of tens of thousands of files about the political behavior of the German population. See Gellately, *The Gestapo and German Society*.

17. The history of these intelligence investigations in Argentina and their continuance after the genocide can be seen in one of the few files that were recovered about the functioning of the intelligence agencies. This is the DIPBA file (Intelligence Directorate of the Police of the Province of Buenos Aires), recovered by the Provincial Committee of Memory of the Province of Buenos Aires.

18. For an account of the Ezeiza massacre, see Horacio Verbitsky, *Ezeiza* (Buenos Aires: Planeta, 2002).

19. For the origins and activities of the Triple A, see Ignacio González Jansen, *La Triple A* (Buenos Aires: Contrapunto, 1986).

20. Fragment of Videla's first speech as de facto president, in María Seoane and Vicente Muleiro, *El Dictador: La historia secreta y pública de Jorge Rafael Videla* (The dictator: The secret and public history of Jorge Rafael Videla) (Buenos Aires: Sudamericana, 2001). I thank Gabriela Roffinelli for pointing out this quote.

21. This tolerance of governmental and/or quasi-governmental groups, however, is one of the elements that transformed criminality in Argentina. Once democracy was restored, these groups (and later ones), made up of common criminals, members of the security forces, and prominent members of the political apparatus, devoted their energies to fund-raising for local politicians and their political brokers—especially in the province of Buenos Aires. This action has led to a corrupt political system, in which social welfare services are traded for votes, and a corrupt police force, which systematically participates in organized crime. These new social relations are also a result of the disappearance of reciprocal relations and the legitimizing of an informer culture through genocide.

22. Teresa Meschiatti, interviewed as part of the course "Analysis of Genocidal Social Practices," Faculty of Social Sciences, University of Buenos Aires. Eric Johnson also notes the "selective" nature of Nazi terror implemented by the Gestapo. Johnson's research shows that that terror was never haphazard or indiscriminate. For Johnson's work, see *Nazi Terror* (New York: Basic Books, 2000).

23. Hernán López Echagüe, "Tucumán: El caso Bussi" (The case of Bussi), in *Revista Plural* 9 (1988), 56.

24. Juan Carlos del Cerro "Colores" used to point this out to various survivors of Argentine concentration camps and detention centers. See "Archivo de Testimonios de Sobrevivientes de Campos de Concentración en Argentina" (Testimonials of Argentine concentration camp survivors) Course on analysis of genocidal social practices and Association of Ex-Disappeared Detainees.

25. There were six death camps: Auschwitz-Birkenau (one of the three subcamps of Auschwitz), Treblinka, Belzec, Sobibor, Majdanek, and Chelmno. Because their sole function was to systematically eliminate people, they were different from the thousands of concentration camps, such as Dachau, Buchenwald, Ravensbruck, or Theresienstadt. The fundamental difference lay not in the number of people killed at each site, but in the way this annihilation was organized and the innovative use of "factories" producing "collective death."

26. For a discussion of political artifacts, see Langdon Winner, *The Social Shaping of Technology*, 2nd ed., ed. Donald A. MacKenzie and Judy Wajcman (London: Open University Press, 1999).

27. It is possible, as Guillermo Levy pointed out to me, to think of the Argentine case as part of a continentwide application of the National Security Doctrine—which would change this comparison somewhat, though not in its core linked to the differential role of the extermination camp.

28. If the political expression of these statements can be found in Ernesto Sabato's foreword to the CONADEP, their clearest cinematographic expression may be the film directed by Héctor Olivera, *La noche de los lápices* (The night of the pencils) (1986), in which victims appear as decontextualized youngsters—young people of the 1970s who speak and think like young people of the 1980s—who are only interested in trivial matters such as student tickets and are absolutely isolated and critical of those they describe as the "crazy Montoneros." This type of political perception cannot be found

in any school in the 1970s, and much less so in La Plata, where the link between social organizations and political movements was highly effective, even among students—a fact that determined the relatively high percentage of victims from this town. The expression of this same type of approach in educational textbooks is summarized in Inés Dussel, Silvia Finocchio, and Silvia Gojman, *Haciendo memoria en el país del Nunca Más* (Constructing memory in the country of Never Again) (Buenos Aires: EUDEBA, 1997), where, again, young people are ahistorically represented, as youths from the 1980s, with interests, passions and ways of relating from the 1980s that are transferred to the youths of the 1970s, as if that were an essential attribute of youth. A counterpoint to this mode of cultural analysis can be found in the aforementioned article by Cattaruzza who, not coincidentally, was a politicized young man during the 1970s, and for whom this lack of historical authenticity is presumably even more inconsistent with his own memories.

29. It should be noted, however, that for a new generation to ask questions or problematize existing hegemonic discourses, a persistent hard core of older militants was necessary. It was the members of human rights organizations, trade unionists, political, student, and social activists, intellectuals, and survivors of the concentration camps who continued to resist and discuss these matters, which generated discourses and representations that would provoke questions and criticisms among the new generation from 1996 onward.

30. The fact that this task is still necessary tells us no more than that. Also, without the clarity and political will to seize it, it cannot be captured by new ways—no less effective for being new—of structuring a new "symbolic enactment," both of the Argentine genocide and of the events of 2001.

31. Roberto Jacoby, "¿Se puede vencer el miedo?" (Can one overcome fear?), *Crisis*, nos. 47 and 48 (1986).

32. To Graciela Daleo I owe many of the reflections in this paragraph. She was also kind enough to let me have a transcription of the 1996 and 1997 seminars, which have extraordinary value. I am aware that Graciela's reflections are, in turn, the product of discussions among members of the Association of Ex-Disappeared Detainees, as she never forgets to point out to me. However, the chain of concepts—always collectively contributed—can always be traced further back. I have come to these conclusions through the word of Graciela Daleo. To Elsa Drucaroff, I am indebted as well, for having noted the various symbolic uses of the phrase "Never Again" and the ways in which it can be redefined.

33. I find it much more difficult to assess the case of Guatemala, which shares elements of both processes. I do not understand it clearly enough to decide whether it is more similar to the Southern Cone genocides or to those in Central America. The consequences of the genocide in Guatemala are comparable to those of the Southern Cone. The scale of social rebellion, however, and its military challenge to the social order make it more similar to the Central American cases. This ambiguity makes it difficult to analyze satisfactorily.

34. It is highly significant that Alfonsín's impunity laws had placed property rights above the right to life, establishing that theft (as opposed to murder, torture, illegal deprivation of liberty, or rape) should be excluded from both the Full Stop Law and the Law of Due Obedience.

35. Emile Durkheim, *The Rules of the Sociological Method*, trans. W. D. Halls (New York: Free Press, 1982 (1895]). See especially chap. 5, "Rules for the Explanation of Social Facts."

36. Elsa Drucaroff, "Por algo fue: Análisis del prólogo al Nunca Más de Ernesto Sábato" (There was a reason: Analysis of the prologue to Sábato's Never Again), *Tres Galgos* 3 (November 2002).
37. Michel Foucault, "Truth and Juridical Forms," in *Power: The Essential Works of Michel Foucault, 1954–1984*, vol. 3, ed. J. Faubion, trans. Robert Hurley et al. (New York: New Press, 2000 [1981]); also developed in Foucault's second lecture *Genealogía del racismo* (Montevideo: Altamira, 1993).

CHAPTER 9 CONCENTRATION CAMP LOGIC

1. Juan Gelman, "Químicas" (Chemistry), *Página/12*, 10 February 1996.
2. It was thought that this story—their "own" story—would delegitimize attempts to convict the perpetrators. The hegemonic discourse about the victims during the 1980s was that all were saints or angels. This discourse colored both the CONADEP Report and the Trial of the Juntas.
3. For this line, see the work of Miguel Khavisse and Eduardo Basualdo, including *Acerca de la Deuda Externa* (About the termination of debt) (Quilmes: National University of Quilmes, 2002), among many other works published by the Center of Argentine Workers and the Department of Economics at FLACSO. The link between these policies and the need for a genocidal process is shown very suggestively in Mirta Mántaras, *Genocidio en Argentina* (Buenos Aires: Cooperativa Chilavert, 2005). An earlier work that suggests the existence of a joint political and economic project can be found in Juan Villarreal, "Los hilos sociales del poder" (Social strings of power), in *Crisis de la dictadura argentina: Política económica y cambio social [1976–1983]* (Crisis of Argentina's dictatorship: Political economy and social change [1976–1983]), by Eduardo Jozami, Pedro Paz, and Juan Villarreal (Buenos Aires: Siglo XXI, 1985), 201–283.
4. Social facilitation studies the ways in which an individual's behavior is affected by the real, imagined, or implied presence of others.
5. In contrast, most major account holders were warned by the banks in advance to move their funds abroad or to safe-deposit boxes.
6. The bombing was an attack on the Asociación Mutual Israelita Argentina (AMIA) Jewish community center in Buenos Aires on 18 July 1994, in which 85 people were killed and over 100 others were injured.
7. The República Cromañón nightclub fire occurred in Buenos Aires on 30 December 2004 and killed 194 people. The tragedy symbolized corruption and incompetence in Argentina, since the club was given a permit despite a lack of basic safety measures like fire extinguishers.
8. Guillermo O'Donnell, "¿Y a mí qué mierda me importa? Notas sobre sociabilidad y política en Argentina y Brasil" (And why the fuck should I care? Notes on sociability and politics in Argentina and Brazil), in *Contrapuntos: Ensayos escogidos sobre autoritarismo y democratización* (Counterpoint: Selected essays on authoritarianism and democratization) (Buenos Aires: Paidós, 1997). While O'Donnell uses the term in another sense, there is undoubtedly a shift in the meaning of this expression as a result of genocide.
9. Transcription of the seminars held by the Association of Ex-Disappeared Detainees (AEDD) in 1996 and 1997 (hereafter SAEDD). I would like to thank Graciela Daleo for lending me these transcriptions.
10. Transcription of SAEDD.

11. This image is found in various testimonies, although the names were different in different concentration or extermination camps. In Auschwitz these people were known as *Muschelmänner* or Moslems (perhaps because they had gone into their shells like mussels but also because the SS looked on Arabs as fatalistic); in Majdanek they were called *Gamel* (bowls, because food was their only interest), in Dachau *Kretiner* (idiots), and in Stutthof *Krüppel* (cripples—because of their immobility). In Mauthausen, they were *Schwimmer*, kept afloat by playing dead, while in Buchenwald the same people were known as *müde Scheichs* (tired sheikhs—fatalistic Arabs again). At the women's camp of Ravensbruck, *Schmuckstücke* (jewels) was a euphemism for *Schmutzstücke* (filth). In all these cases, the images refer to the same social process: the loss of any capacity for self-determination. The "living dead" lost all control over their own lives. See Bruno Bettelheim, *Surviving and Other Essays* (New York: Knopf, 1979).

12. "An ideal type is formed by the one-sided *accentuation* of one or more points of view and by the synthesis of a great many diffuse, discrete, more or less present and occasionally absent *concrete individual* phenomena, which are arranged according to those one-sidedly emphasized viewpoints into a unified *analytical* construct. In its conceptual purity, this mental construct cannot be found empirically anywhere in reality." Max Weber, *The Methodology of the Social Sciences*, trans. and ed. Lutz Kaelber (New York: Free Press, 1949), 90.

13. Erving Goffman, *Asylums: Essays on the Social Situation of Mental Patients and Other Inmates* (New York: Anchor Books, 1961).

14. See Bruno Bettelheim, *The Informed Heart* (New York: Alfred A. Knopf, 1960); Pilar Calveiro, *Poder y desaparición: Los campos de concentración en Argentina* (Power and disappearance: The concentration camps in Argentina) (Buenos Aires: Colihue, 1998); Goffman, *Asylums*. For an analysis of "subjective demolition" in the concentration camps, see Sylvia Bermann, Lucila Edelman, Diana Kordon, et al., *Efectos psicosociales de la represión política: Sus secuelas en Alemania, Argentina y Uruguay* (Psychosocial effects of political repression: Its aftermath in Germany, Argentina and Uruguay) (Córdoba: Goethe Institut, 1994).

15. Viktor E. Frankl, *Man's Search for Meaning* (Boston: Beacon Press, [1959] 1992), 72.

16. Calveiro, *Poder y desaparición*.

17. Bettelheim, *Surviving and Other Essays*.

18. Street sweeps involved an ex-detainee accompanying a group of repressors in random searches for former activist-friends in cafes, train stations, border crossings, and so forth where political dissidents might be circulating.

19. Interview with Mario Villani, Project "Archive of testimonies from survivors of clandestine detention centers in Argentina," Chair of Analysis of Genocidal Social Practices, Faculty of Social Sciences, University of Buenos Aires, and Association of Ex-Disappeared Detainees (AEDD). This story was told earlier by Villani at the hearings of the trial against the military junta in 1985.

20. *Münchner Neueste Nachrichten* (The Munich latest news), 21 March 1933. Cited in http://en.wikipedia.org/wiki/Dachau_concentration_camp.

21. Gellately estimates that more than 100,000 prisoners passed through the Nazi concentration camps during 1933 and 1934, mostly political dissidents. Their average stay was between one and two weeks and not more than one thousand prisoners died. However, the experience profoundly shook German society and paved the way for Nazi totalitarian rule. See Robert Gellately, *The Gestapo and German Society: Enforcing Racial Policy, 1933–1945* (Oxford: Oxford University Press, 1990).

22. For a list of the main camps, see http://www.jewishvirtuallibrary.org/jsource/Holocaust/cclist.html.
23. For the impact of such practices in Chile, see Elias Padilla Ballesteros, *La memoria y el olvido: Detenidos desaparecidos en Chile* (Memory and forgetting: Disappeared detainees in Chile) (Santiago: Ediciones Orígenes, 1995).
24. The impact of genocidal social practices on the hardest hit and most socially excluded sectors of Argentina has been little explored. A preliminary study can be found in Eva Camelli and Verónica Daián, "El genocidio en las villas de Buenos Aires durante la última dictadura militar (a través del testimonio de los sobrevivientes)" (Genocide in the slums of Buenos Aires during the military dictatorship [through the testimony of survivors]), a paper presented at the First International Symposium on the Analysis of Genocide as a Social Practice, Buenos Aires, 2003, published in the CD of the symposium.
25. The criticism of this type of discourse is very well developed in León Rozitchner, *Las desventuras del sujeto político* (The sorrows of the political subject) (Buenos Aires: El Cielo por Asalto, 1996).
26. For the concept of "mortification," see Goffman, *Asylums*. I am indebted to Beatriz Granda for the concept of "confusion" and some of the ideas in this paragraph. An analysis of types of confusion can also be found in Sylvia Bermann, "Sociedad, psicología y tortura en América Latina" (Society, psychology, and torture in Latin America), published in Sylvia Bermann, Lucila Edelman, Diana Kordon, et al., *Efectos Psicosociales de la represion politica* (Cordoba: Goethe Institute, 1994), 11 to 29.
27. Erving Goffman, *Asylums* (New York: Anchor Books, 1961).
28. Michel Foucault, *The History of Sexuality* (Harmondsworth, UK: Penguin Books, 1979), 94–95.
29. Ibid.
30. On the role of the "rumors" in the experience of prisons during the last Argentine military dictatorship, see Emilio De Ipola, *La bemba: Acerca del rumor carcelario* (The lip: On prison rumors) (Buenos Aires: Siglo XXI, 2005).
31. Testimony of Jorge Paladino, SAEDD, 1996.
32. Ricardo Falcón, "La resistencia obrera a la dictadura militar (Una reescritura de un texto contemporáneo a los acontecimientos)" (The workers' resistance to the military dictatorship [a rewrite of a contemporary text to events]), in *A veinte años del golpe: Con memoria democrática* [Twenty years after the coup: With democratic memory], ed. Hugo Quiroga and César Tcach (Rosario: Homo Sapiens Ediciones, 1996), 123–142; and Pablo Pozzi, "Combatiendo al general: Resistencia obrera, dictadura y apertura democrática" (Fighting the general: Worker resistance and opening democratic dictatorship), *Revista Puentes*, no. 4 (2001).
33. By "walls" detainees meant hoods, bandages, etc. that prevented them from seeing. In contrast, "symbolic walls" prevent people from seeing other people or observing their physical environment even if they keep their eyes open. In both cases, the purpose of the "wall" is to place subjects in a situation where they can be seen but cannot see.

CHAPTER 10 IN CONCLUSION

1. Robert Cribb, "Genocide in the Non-Western World," in *Genocide: Cases, Comparisons, and Contemporary Debates*, ed. Steven Jensen (Copenhagen: Danish Center for Holocaust and Genocide Studies, 2003).

2. See Mario Margulis et al., *La segregación negada: Cultura y discriminación social* (Segregation denied: Culture and social discrimination) (Buenos Aires: Biblos, 1998).
3. An interesting reflection on the functioning of these processes with reference to the notion of "Arabs" and the way they are perceived in Argentina can be found in Hammurabi Noufouri, *Del Islam y los árabes: Acerca de la percepción argentina de lo propio y de lo ajeno* (Islam and the Arabs: About Argentine perceptions of self and others) (Buenos Aires: Cálamo, 2001).
4. Zygmunt Bauman, *Modernity and the Holocaust* (Ithaca, NY: Cornell University Press, 2001).
5. As Jaspers himself observed, "People do not like to hear of guilt, of the past; world history is not their concern. They simply do not want to suffer any more; they want to get out of this misery, to live but not to think. There is a feeling as though after such fearful suffering one had to be rewarded, as it were, or at least comforted, but not burdened with guilt on top of it all." Karl Jaspers, *The Question of German Guilt*, 2nd ed. (New York: Fordham University Press, 2001), 21.
6. The "intellectual and symbolic consequences" of this legal process, which I call "processes of transfer of guilt or responsibility," are discussed in chapters 7 and 8.
7. This type of "confusion" has, in my view, played a critical role in creating a culture of impunity extending to all kinds of behavior in Argentine society, not only to genocide.
8. By way of illustration, it is worth rereading Alejandra Correa's interviews with various leading figures from the world of culture in the first half of 2001. These appeared in *Revista Puentes*, no. 4. Center for Memory Studies, La Plata, July 2001. It is noteworthy that, unlike the concentration camp survivors, almost none of these celebrities admits to any moral guilt for not doing more than they actually did as journalists, academics, lawyers, and artists. No one feels that they should have given their lives to save others and most slip easily into the role of abstract victim without imagining that their omissions—however justified they may have been—helped to make genocide successful.
9. For a more complete version of Levinas's ideas on this subject, see his books *Totality and Infinity* (1969) and *Otherwise than Being: Or Beyond Essence* (1998).

INDEX

ABOUT THE AUTHOR

DR. DANIEL FEIERSTEIN is the director of the Center for Genocide Studies at the National University of Tres de Febrero, Argentina. He holds a Ph.D. in social sciences from the University of Buenos Aires, Argentina, where he founded and heads the Chair of Genocide.

He is currently president of the International Association of Genocide Scholars. While a United Nations consultant, he helped prepare Argentina's National Plan to Combat Discrimination (2004–2006) and the National Human Rights Plan (2007–2008).

His recent books include *Genocidio como práctica social: Entre el nazismo y la experiencia argentina* (Buenos Aires: FCE, 2007); *Terrorismo de estado y genocidio en América Latina* (Buenos Aires: Prometeo, 2009); *State Violence and Genocide in Latin America* (New York: Routledge, 2010); and *Memorias y representaciones: Sobre la elaboración del genocidio I* (Buenos Aires: FCE, 2012).

www.ingramcontent.com/pod-product-compliance
Lightning Source LLC
Chambersburg PA
CBHW021812270326
41932CB00007B/148
* 9 7 8 0 8 1 3 5 6 3 1 7 6 *